NEWS FROM
RAIN SHADOW COUNTRY

Tim Wheeler

Published by BookLocker.com, Inc., Bradenton, Florida.

Printed on acid-free paper.

BookLocker.com, Inc.
2017

First Edition

Cover art: Timothy Wheeler
Artwork throughout this book by Timothy Wheeler unless noted otherwise.

FORWARD

Once you read the first pages of this volume you will not be able to put it down! Tim Wheeler is the best story teller I know. Yes, he is a master wordsmith, journalist and artist. But much more than that, he is a partisan of ordinary people and their struggles and lives. He is not a bystander. Throughout his life from childhood to today, he has been in the thick of working class social change. He has dedicated his life to a better world and that makes his story telling extraordinary.

You will enjoy stories about the Wheeler family going back to Tim's great grandfather who served in the Union Army during the Civil War. You will laugh and cry with the remarkable tale of the Wheeler family establishing a farm in Sequim and their courage during the Red Scare in the 1950's.

Interspersed with experiences of family life on the farm, you will get a birds-eye view into countless struggles for equality and justice that Tim participated in with the Communist Party. He wrote these up for the *People's World,* a newspaper founded in 1921 as the *Daily Worker.*

Tim's journey takes us from the 1950's McCarthyism through the fightback against Donald Trump. We meet courageous artists and leaders as Paul Robeson and Pete Seeger. We hear from striking port workers and paper workers, Native Americans, immigrant workers facing deportation, peace and climate change marchers spanning Tim's fifty years as a journalist and editor.

This preface is being written days after Republican billionaire Donald Trump has been declared president-elect of the United States. Democrat Hillary Clinton won the popular vote majority, but Donald Trump prevailed in the Electoral College.

Trump's disgraceful political venture began in 2008 when he founded the racist "birther movement" in an attempt to prevent Barack Obama, the nation's first African American president, from serving in office. In his presidential campaign,

Trump fomented fear and division in the country with his attacks on Latino immigrants, women, Muslims and African Americans. He demagogically claimed that a vote for him was a vote for jobs and against the establishment. As soon as the election was declared for Trump, thousands of people came together in solidarity with their neighbors and friends against hate and fear.

A new chapter is now to be written in the struggle for democracy and equality in our country. The insights and vast experience of Tim Wheeler shared in this book will serve us well.

Tim, Joyce and their family made Washington State a bright spot in this year's election, with door belling, phone calling and organizing. Voters approved an increase in the state minimum wage, voted for repeal of Citizens United, and elected progressive community organizer Pramila Jayapal, who campaigned with Bernie Sanders, to represent Washington's 7th Congressional District in the U.S. House of Representatives.

"We must stay focused on the imperative need to continue building the 'all people's front' against the ultra-right. Mass action in the streets in an imperative!" says Tim looking forward.

Over the decades, Tim's strong working class struggle approach has provided wonderful leadership in his community, in the pages of the *People's World*, and in the Political Action Commission of the Communist Party where I have had the privilege to work with him side by side.

This book is a must read on how to live a life with a purpose. It is a guide for how to build the kind of unity that can move our country forward. It offers a powerful vision for a radical restructuring and expansion of democracy in our country necessary to put people and nature before profits.

—Joelle Fishman
Chair of the Connecticut Communist Party, a member of the Communist Party USA National Committee and Chair of the CPUSA Political Action Commission.

DEDICATION

I could not have done this labor of love without Joyce, my best friend, devoted wife and mother. She was, and is, our family breadwinner, bringing home the paycheck, the health care benefits, the defined pension. She was a skilled, dedicated classroom teacher, an active member of the Baltimore Teachers Union. She was a picket captain in the 1974 teachers strike, elected and reelected Treasurer of AFT Local 340. She is a fighter for trade union democracy, equality, and world peace. I dedicate this book to the love of my life, Joyce.

TABLE OF CONTENTS

Tim Wheeler

PREFACE

Prevailing winds blow northeast off the Pacific Ocean driving moisture laden clouds up across the summits of the Olympic Mountains. The clouds cool quickly and dump torrential rains on the western slopes of the Olympics, 144 inches annually, twelve feet. Douglas Fir, Hemlock, Cedar and Spruce, luxuriate, a temperate rain forest, winding mossy ways. Rivers pour out of the mountains fed by the heavy rain. And in the crystalline streams, salmon, steelhead, and trout abound. It is a paradise now protected by the Olympic National Park.

The clouds dissipate over the mountains and a blue hole opens on the prairie north of the Olympics, the delta of the Dungeness River, once the greatest steelhead river anywhere. Here the climate is so dry that a variety of cactus has evolved and the Sequim prairie is home to the Garry Oak, a gnarled, tough tree that grows well in dry, windblown semi-desert country.

This is the Olympic "rain shadow," a place so arid that pioneers had to build an irrigation system to carry water from the Dungeness River to water the land. Their efforts turned the pastures green and transformed the valley into rich farmland where more than 200 dairy farms sprang up. Every year, in the first week of May, the entire community of the Sequim-Dungeness Valley celebrates the "Irrigation Festival" with a parade through Sequim, a logging show, a "Pioneer Banquet." The festival pays homage to the S'Klallam Indians, the farmers, loggers, mill workers and others who toiled—and still do—to make this valley bloom.

My family arrived here in the summer of 1948. I was eight years old. I grew up here in the "rain shadow," under the "blue hole of Sequim." Here I learned to milk cows, drive a team of horses, properly build a hay load on our hay wagon. I learned some lessons that lasted me a lifetime. I moved away in the 1960s, married Joyce, had children. I served as a journalist

1

for half a century in the east living mostly in Baltimore, Maryland.

Yet my family still owns the farm. We lease it to the celebrated organic vegetable grower, Nash Huber who grows beets, Swiss chard, kale, cabbage, wheat, and other crops. When Joyce retired from the Baltimore school system we returned to the farm and have lived here since 2006. A little over a year ago, I decided to compile a book consisting of some of the 10,000 stories and commentaries I have written in the past half century. It has been a monumental task that involved tracking down and scanning hundreds of my articles from microfilm collections at Frostburg State University in Maryland, the Tamiment Library at NYU in New York City, and at the University of Washington library. I want to express my profound gratitude to all the librarians who helped me.

These scanned articles then had to be digitalized. My typist-editor, Leneé Cobb, of A Writer's Helper, undertook this enormous task for me. I owe her, too, a debt of gratitude.

As we added one story after another, along with my commentary on the articles, the book got longer and longer. Finally, I decided to divide it into two books: *News for the 99%: My Life, The Stories I Wrote*, and this book, *News From Rain Shadow Country*. For this book I selected stories I have written, most of them printed in the *People's World*, about my youth here in Clallam County and also stories about mass struggles in Washington State since we returned to the valley. I hope you will read both books and be inspired to join in the struggle to turn our country around.

My life has been one filled with much joy, being a part of the class struggle, sharing the trials and tribulations of the people fighting back against the exploitation imposed by the "billionaire class." I was part of a team of very talented writers, editors, printers, and rank and file distributors who produced the *Worker*, *Daily World*, and *People's World*. We not only wrote the articles and printed them; we also put the paper into the hands of "the 99%" who are not billionaires or millionaires.

We Move a 1929 House, Live in It
April 16, 2015

Joyce and I took a stroll in the summer of 2005 out across the alfalfa field of our farm just west of the Dungeness River near the little town of Sequim, Washington. We were inspecting the five acres parcel of the farm that my parents had given us. We gazed off across the magnificent farmland at the green foothills and the snow-capped Olympic Mountains in the distance.

Joyce asked a question. "Why do we come here just to take a look? Why don't we build something here, a place we can stay when we visit?"

I was remembering the sweltering heat of Baltimore. It had been our home since 1969, the city where we raised our three children, where they all lived today along with our grandchildren and great grandchildren. It was the town where we had cultivated a wide circle of friends, neighbors and comrades. Wasn't Baltimore our true home? Deliberately, we had left our five acres untouched knowing that if we built any kind of house here it would be like a magnet pulling us west.

For half a century I had been a reporter with a home base in New York City and Washington, D.C. commuting to the latter from Baltimore. Was I tempting myself to leave that home base in the east, turning my back on my duty as a reporter for the movements of the people?

Yet the lure of returning to the valley where I grew up was strong. And for half a century Joyce had put my priorities first, serving as the main breadwinner for ourselves and our children, living a continent away from where she wanted to live because like me, she placed the struggle ahead of her personal preferences.

That afternoon, we drove through the charming little village of Carlsborg, once a sawmill town, about three miles south of our farm. Joyce was admiring the sawmill workers' cottages that line the street when she saw an especially

3

handsome little house with a hand-lettered sign plastered to the door: "FOR SALE. MAKE AN OFFER. MUST BE MOVED."

"Stop," Joyce commanded.

So I pulled over.

We waded through the overgrown front yard. Joyce tried the door. It was open. We entered and walked through the little house. It had lofty ceilings; nearly nine feet high, beautifully proportioned front windows. It reeked of heating oil from an old oil heater in the living room. It had two tiny bedrooms, a cramped kitchen with a dining nook. It had no bathroom. Ablutions were accommodated in an outhouse in the back yard.

Maybe it was the lovely yellow rose blooming just outside the kitchen window or the romance of imagining Mrs. Bates and her sawmill worker family who once lived here before the sawmill closed down and the Milwaukee Railroad ended its steam-powered service. For whatever reason, Joyce fell in love with the house.

We spoke to the owner who operates a restaurant nearby who sold the house to us for $1,000. We arranged for Jeff Monroe, a renowned mover of immovable objects, to come and inspect the house. He told us he could move it for the munificent sum of $15,000. And so he did.

Our general contractor, Dan Burdick, inspected the house as it rested on cribs on the gravel bar at our place. The house had wooden shiplap boards for walls. Not a square inch of plaster anywhere in the house. The only foundation under the house had been logs. Powder-post beetles had gnawed their way up through the logs and had been devouring the house itself for decades since it was constructed in 1929.

Dan gave us the bad news: To prevent the house from dissolving in a pile of sawdust around us, he must pull off the shiplap and cut out the bottom foot of every stud around the entire perimeter of the house and sister-in replacement studs. He also replaced the plate the studs are nailed into. He installed brand new floors throughout the entire house.

Dan also built a new addition consisting of a bathroom, utility room and spacious new master bedroom.

Add on electricity, a new well, septic field, a road out to our place, an efficient wood stove to keep us warm and we had a delightful little jewel box to call our home. Oh paradise! We have arrived! I can take out my autoharp and sing a few hymns to the glory of rural life. I can set up my easel and paint a landscape or two. We moved to our home in 2006, leaving our children and grandchildren behind in the east.

Little did I know that the class struggle had followed me to Clallam County. In the years that followed, we were deeply engaged in all the struggles of the good people of Washington State, and the nation. I continued to write many articles for the *People's World*. I continue to this day to write for the *PW*.

Once a month, Joyce and I journey down to Seattle to attend our CP Club meeting.

I also participate twice monthly in meetings of the Communist Party Political Action Commission chaired with great spirit and wisdom by Joelle Fishman, chairperson of the Communist Party of Connecticut.

Joyce and I, my sister, Honeybee Wheeler Burns, my elder brother, Steve Vause and his wife Carlyn, have formed a tightknit family collective that oversees "New Farm," the fifty-five acres owned by our family. We are determined to preserve this lovely place as farmland forever. Nash Huber has leased the farm that produces bountiful crops of carrots, beets, kale, cabbage, and also wheat and buck wheat. At this writing we are in the midst of negotiating the sale of the development rights with the North Olympic Land Trust (NOLT) preserving this place as farmland forever.

Clallam County is a "bellwether" district that see-saws between Tea Party Republicans and moderate Democrats with only a handful of votes determining the winner. George W. Bush carried Clallam County, narrowly in 2000 and 2004. Barack Obama carried it narrowly in 2008 and 2012.

When a district is closely divided, every vote counts. Only a fool blind to reality could ignore the fact that all a candidate needs to win—if every vote is counted—is a majority of one.

We have invested many, many hours doorbelling for progressive and moderate Democrats. We also punched doorbells and spoke to scores of voters in the 2015 election on why it was important to elect Mark Ozias as Clallam County Commissioner. Ozias, director of the Sequim Food Bank, an active member of the Sierra Club, spoke out strongly for measures to reverse climate change and save our beautiful Olympic Peninsula. He won, defeating the incumbent Tea Party Republican decisively.

At the same time, we have been active in building the grassroots movement in support of Bernie Sanders candidacy for President. Later, we door-belled for Hillary Clinton.

The other project that has consumed so many hours of my time in the past year was writing—or more accurately, "compiling"—this book or rather, books. I want to bring together in two volumes, a representative collection of the articles I have written over the half century totaling about 10,000 news reports, feature articles, opinion pieces and even an occasional poem. Nearly all the stories featured in both books are reprinted from the pages of the *Worker, Daily World* and *People's World*. A few are reprinted from newspapers and newsletters here in Washington State and a few I wrote for this book to provide context and continuity.

Why am I writing these books? In 1991, the Soviet Union collapsed. The Berlin Wall came down. The USSR, the German Democratic Republic, and a half dozen other socialist nations disappeared. Cold Warriors exulted, proclaiming this catastrophe the "end of history." Marx, Engels, Lenin, and all the other founders of scientific socialism were refuted. Socialism was dead.

I offer some of the 10,000 articles I have written over half a century as a refutation of that "free market" triumphalism.

Read these stories and you will see that the class struggle is alive and well. Workers and their allies are organizing in a multi-faceted struggle. Hatred of what Machinist Union President, William Winpisinger called the "corporate rightwing phalanx" has never been so widespread as it is today. And look at the reality we face: The income gap between the millionaires and billionaires and the other 99% has never been so wide. The very survival of the planet and life on it is in question because the super-rich energy monopolies block every meaningful step to curb greenhouse gases, the engine of global warming.

Here is my first book. It begins in Washington D.C., far from the "rain shadow" of Clallam County where I grew up and came of age politically. I dwell on those early years of my life because I want to tell of my life in the best way I know, through the stories I wrote. I hope you also read my second book, *News for the 99%* about my years as Washington correspondent and editor of the *Daily World* and *People's World*.

[1]

IN THE BEGINNING

National Homeopathic Hospital

of WASHINGTON, D. C.

HOSPITAL BIRTH CERTIFICATE

This Certifies that _____

was born in National Homeopathic Hospital of Washington, D. C.

on the _____ day of _____ A.D. 19__

In Witness Whereof the said Hospital has caused this Certificate to be
signed by the duly authorized officer and its Corporate Seal to be hereunto affixed.

Doctor _____

Hospital
Number _____   _____
                                              Superintendent

Born in One Washington,
Move West to the Other

My mother gave birth to me on January 24, 1940 at Homeopathic Hospital in Washington, D.C. I know this is true because I have a handsome parchment-like birth certificate to prove it. I was too young to sign it but the hospital authorities dipped my feet in India ink and stamped the document with my footprints.

It was an inauspicious time to arrive on Planet Earth. The nation and the world had not even recovered from the Great Depression and already humanity was sliding toward World War II, a struggle to eradicate fascism that would cost more than fifty million lives. Maybe some of the trials and tribulations of the human race made its way through my mother's placenta walls, invading my consciousness "in utero."

For whatever reason, my earliest memory in my infancy was not of any experience while I was awake. It was a dream, a bad dream at that. A nightmare. I must have been lying asleep in my crib in our home in Brookmont, Maryland when this event engulfed me.

Empty space opened under me. I fell into a black void. My heart constricted in terror and I cried out. I fell forever and ever, tumbling in the jet-black night. I cried out again and again.

Then two strong hands slipped under me. I stopped falling. The hands lifted me. I felt something soft yet prickly pressed against my forehead and a low, deep, lullaby voice crooned words full of comfort even though I did not know their meaning.

My father laid me in a warm place. My head pressed into his bicep, my cheek cradled against the soft curly hair of his forearm. I smelled the warm body of my mother. I heard her voice murmuring and my father answering. I slipped back into a deep peaceful sleep.

That is my earliest memory. I was only a few months or a year old, living in our house along the C&O Canal just outside Washington, D.C.

Other moments followed: terror, then swift rescue. For my fourth birthday, my parents bought me a pair of shiny black rubber boots with a bright red star just below each knee. Later that spring we went on vacation to Woods Hole, Massachusetts. By then there were five of us, my parents, my older brother Steve, my infant sister, Susan Elizabeth, and me. We rode in the 1929 Silver Ghost Rolls Royce that my father had recently bought from Hans Henrick a friend who collected old cars.

I wore my black boots the whole way. When we arrived at Woods Hole, we checked into a rented cabin and went for a walk along the beach. There was a fresh spring breeze blowing and the bay was flecked with white caps. The surf was pounding. I dashed ahead, racing along the shoreline. I ran down into the surf just after a wave broke, playing tag with the ebbing water line.

I felt the sand slipping from beneath my feet. The undertow was pulling me out to sea. I turned, crying out in terror. And then I saw him racing across the sand, reaching down in one motion, pulling me once again from the cold abyss, my father, once more, the power that protected me.

My dad left home each morning heading for the trolley with a newspaper tucked under his arm. Sometimes my mother and I walked down to the trolley stop and waited with him for the Cabin John trolley; my folks chatting as we walked. He would board the trolley, turn and wave to us. Off the trolley rolled down the line toward his office.

I rode with him one day, my nose pressed to the window, watching the bluffs flash by, crossing a long bridge, entering Georgetown where the houses climbed up the steep canyon on the left hand side and the C&O Canal and the Potomac reached out broad and beautiful on the right. He was taking me to work with him, and all I remember was the barracks building on the Capitol Mall, the men and women, some of them in dress fatigues, the long gleaming corridors of the Office of Strategic Services (OSS,) and the cramped office where he worked.

When World War II erupted, my father became a section chief in the research division at OSS. Among his assignments was reporting to the Joint Chiefs of Staff on the casualties suffered by the Axis powers, especially the German Wehrmacht. He also did work on the famous OSS Strategic Bombing Survey, which concluded that German war production in most categories continued to rise despite the very extensive—and expensive— bombing in terms of lost pilots, crews, and aircraft.

Bombing was no substitute for confronting the Third Reich on the ground. It confirmed the correctness of the argument for a U.S. invasion of continental Europe, the opening of the "Second Front."

That was my father's brainpower at work in international affairs. Yet he was also a man of more immediate action. He was an active member of the United Public Workers, a union affiliated with the Congress of Industrial Organizations (CIO). He was so active that his fellow workers, whether at Treasury or OSS, elected him as their shop steward.

One morning, I decided to go visit him. It wouldn't be hard. Wait for the trolley and get on when it arrived. The conductor would lift me up and sit me down on a seat. The trolley driver would pull the lever up and down. "Taaaw-da, taaaw-da," the ratchet sounded. Off we would go, "Click la lin, wa-woooo wa-wooo."

Somehow, I managed to elude the watchful eyes of our maid, Juanita Branch. Maybe she was busy doing laundry. I left the house, walked down to the trolley stop, and sat on the bench waiting for the trolley to arrive. I waited for what seemed an eternity and in my impatience decided, "I'll walk."

I started out trudging along the middle of the tracks, walking and playing games with the ties to pass the time away. I soon passed the last of the houses in Brookmont and was walking beside the steep bluffs on the left. To my right, and far below me, the C&O Canal and the Potomac River lay shimmering in the morning mist.

I was walking across a trestle when I looked back and saw a big man sprinting toward me. It was Mr. Neil, our next door neighbor. He reached down, without a word, and pulled me up, without breaking his stride, and ran the rest of the way across the trestle. Seconds after he reached the other end of the trestle, the trolley sped past. He knelt in front of me, out of breath, mopping sweat from his brow. "Where on EARTH were you going, young man," he said, still trembling at his close call,

November 1945—I am wearing my U.S. Army helmet, ready to repel a Nazi invasion. My comrades are my sister Susan and our friends Jerry and Puddin'

14

and mine. Only later did I learn that Mr. Neil had saved my life.

He was the African American man who lived next door, the man with the warm smile and easy laugh. Our house in Brookmont was near an enclave of African American homes, down a little dirt lane, hidden behind trees, and standing beside a stream we called "The Branch" that flowed into the Potomac River. I remember still, their names: the Faulkner family, Mason family, Branch family and the Neil family next door.

That was the era of mean Jim Crow segregation. White children in Brookmont were forbidden to play with the children who lived in that enclave. Not us. They were our bosom buddies. Cornelia Faulkner, with jet-black curls and mahogany skin, was my first girlfriend. Dicky, her older brother, was my best friend. We hung out together constantly.

One day we walked up to the Hilltop Tavern. It was the middle of World War II and the tavern was crowded with GIs drinking beer. We sidled into the tavern. One of the GIs caught sight of me and grabbed me, pulling me up into his lap. "Give me a kiss on the cheek and I'll give you 50¢," the GI said to me. He pointed to a spot right on his left cheek. The GIs broke into laughter.

Dicky poked me and said, "Do it! Do it!"

So I did. A big cheer went up from the GIs.

And sure enough, the soldier reached in his pocket and pulled out a big, silvery, half dollar and put it in my hand. The GIs cheered and applauded again, already missing their own families, their own children. I'd never felt so rich. I bought Moon Pies for Dicky and me and still had change left over.

Another day I walked alone up the hill to the Army Map Service where mother worked. The sole of my shoe came loose as I walked and by the time I reached the gate of the Army Map Service, it was flapping loudly.

The sentry at the gate pushed back his helmet. "Hello, my friend. What can I do for you?"

I told him I had come to see my mother.

"Well, you'll be lucky if you don't fall down and hurt your knee." He took the rifle off his shoulder, leaned it against the sentry house, and sat down on a chair. He lifted me up on his lap and pulled off the shoe with the dangling sole. He pulled a jack knife from his pocket and cut the sole neatly off the shoe. He put the shoe back on my foot and pulled the shoestrings tight and made a knot. Then he called my mother who came hurrying out to get me.

How I had escaped the watchful eyes of Mrs. Branch, our maid from down the hill in the Black community, I will never know. I do know that my mother, ever the egalitarian, split her Army Map Service weekly paycheck, fifty-fifty with Mrs. Branch.

The memories of those wartime days flow together—the convoys of jeeps and army trucks loaded with GIs that trundled up and down Conduit Road—later renamed MacArthur Boulevard—and my father wearing his white Air Warden helmet and going out door-to-door to insure that everyone obeyed the black-out rules.

I remember my cousins, my African American friends, and I started bonfires. We danced in a big circle singing: "Hitler's house is burning down . . ."

We went to the theater one afternoon. News reports were standard fare in movie theaters in those days. On the screen flashed a news report showing tanks rolling fast through heavy snow and two armies coming together, racing toward each other across the snow. They met and embraced each other, dancing, and dancing, and dancing. It was the Red Army meeting up. They had encircled Hitler's army in the first major defeat of fascism outside the gates of Stalingrad. My parents and anti-fascists everywhere were cheering.

Weekends, we drove to Arlington to visit my aunt and uncle, Armistead and Marian Coleman, and my cousins, Beau and Winfield. Arm Coleman, an artist, and my mother, had both found jobs at the Army Map Service. Other weekends we drove out to the George Wheeler farm near Wolf Trap, Virginia. My uncle and aunt, George and Eleanor Wheeler, lived in a big old white farmhouse with my cousins, Frank, Toby, Nora, and Mary Jo.

The word never appeared in my vocabulary, then, but I was growing up surrounded by *"the movement."* My aunt Eleanor was a manager of the Co-Op Bookstore on DuPont Circle. We visited there often. Sometimes it was crowded with people buying books, newspapers, and magazines. It was a left-wing bookshop with a thriving clientele from among the many left and pro-socialist people in the District of Columbia, African American and white.

We were immersed in what then was a booming culture of leftwing literature, art, and music.

My parents never earned so much money as they did in those days. It is hard to imagine their living a "bare bones" existence through the Great Depression with hardly two nickels to rub together. But now they both had well-paying jobs.

We must have imagined there would be permanence in these living arrangements even amid the upheaval of war. But nothing in those days, or since, is forever. My parents mostly rode the trolley, conserving the precious gasoline coupons issued during the war; so in 1942 they drove across the nation to visit our extended family in the Pacific Northwest. We did the same again in 1946.

For us children, these cross-country trips were pure adventure. We did not hear the worried exchanges between our parents as the Cold War storm clouds gathered. Representative Martin Dies had been active with his non-stop redbaiting even as the left-led coalition reached out and built a broad movement against the fascist danger in the world.

The ink was not even dry on the articles of surrender of Hitler, Mussolini, and Tojo when the axe fell on my parents and millions of other left-wingers' who were fighting against fascism and for peace, equality, and economic justice. When we made that round-trip journey in 1946, the return to Washington D.C. was only for the purpose of closing down, selling the house, saying goodbye to Washington, D.C. and moving west to Washington State.

[2]

GROWING UP IN
THE OLYMPIC RAIN SHADOW:
Memories of My Youth

The Flagbearer

Published in the *Worker* on December 11, 1966

I come to carry flags
My people took the west with
Fish-hook, pitchfork, and rolling
Wheel. Dynamite we set—
Blasted a bed through granite peaks
To hold the ribbons of steel.
And we became the shingleweavers of America
Saying: Only I shall build the roof
Above my head and below this, my sky.
I have hewn myself with ax roughly out
Of virgin wood.
Long as spruce and deep as Douglas fir,
The sinews of my arms are ready.
Bring your ax and come with me.

We Buy the Old Bell Hill Farm
and Milk Cows for a Living

My father drove the old 1930 Lincoln off the ferry at Port Ludlow and we wound our way through deep evergreen forests for many twisting miles with breaks now and then showing tall snowcapped mountain peaks on our left. On our right, through the occasional openings, sunlight gleamed on the Strait of Juan de Fuca to the north.

For the youngsters in the car, this was an adventure, the search for a farm with many lush, green acres, with cattle and horses and other livestock, somewhere in the state of Washington. Already, we had driven across Stevens Pass to Wenatchee and north into the Methow Valley to visit farms on the eastern slopes of the Cascade Mountains. All of us marveled at the beauty of the farms we visited.

Yet this project was very different for our parents. They were Cold War refugees, fleeing the vicious war already unleashed by the House Un-American Activities Committee and by their local incarnation, the Canwell Committee. It didn't matter how remote or isolated the community that we settled in. These vultures would come after us, forcing my father to travel to Seattle, Tacoma, San Francisco and even to

Washington D.C. to appear as an "uncooperative" witness in their witch-hunt hearings.

When father lost his job with the federal government and the blacklist closed off all chance of a job in the academic world, an old friend from college days, Dick Watt, got him a job with Watt Electric, a furnace company in Seattle. My father excelled at the job. He joined the International Brotherhood of Electrical Workers (IBEW). He took top honors in the apprenticeship program, just as he had won a "First" at Oxford University as a Rhodes Scholar.

But a downturn in the economy wiped out the job and he was laid off. Obeying the wisdom of that old folk song, *Acres of Clams*, my folks "made up their mind to try farming, the only pursuit that is sure."

Yet I can only imagine the mixed feelings of hope and dread that filled them as we drove up on the north Olympic Peninsula that day.

We came around a bay and up the long narrow highway between the trees. We emerged from the dark gloom into brilliant open sunlight. Overhead was an azure sky, a great circle of blue with the snowy mountains to the south. We were in the "rain shadow" of the Olympic Mountains.

We pulled off onto a gravel viewpoint. A sign proclaimed, "Sequim, Where Water is Wealth. Pop. 880." My brother Steve, my little sister Susan and I clambered out of the car and ran over to look out across the peaceful valley.

Dad came behind. We all stood, silently taking in the scene spread out before us. Herds of milking cows browsed. In the distance, a farmer drove a team pulling a mowing machine that cut swaths of green through a lush hayfield. Other field workers with pitchforks were stacking shocks of hay in long windrows. Irrigation ditches traced like silvery threads across the valley with, here and there, long wooden flumes constructed so that the water could flow to the higher ground beyond.

In the near foreground was the little town of Sequim, mostly one-story cottages, one long main street and one traffic-light. The tracks of the Chicago, Milwaukee, Saint Paul and Pacific Rail Road lay in the distance.

This was to be our new home. Here we would put down roots, struggling like the other farmers in the valley to wrest enough income from the land to stay in business.

We drove on into town and stopped on Washington Avenue where Peter Black, the real estate agent, had his office. He retrieved his car and led us up Bell Hill to the Steve Tripp place.

A tall farmhouse stood near the top of the hill bordered on the east by an old windbreak of lilacs. A fine, gnarled Gravenstein apple tree stood nearby, its boughs heavy with white blossoms. It was spring and the lilacs were in bloom. Once painted white, the siding was now peeling and weatherworn.

It had a commanding view of the Sequim valley. Its grandeur might be expected for a dwelling called "Bell House." It had been built by the pioneer homesteader in the valley, John Bell, a Scotsman who had crossed the Strait of Juan de Fuca in 1858 from Vancouver Island and laid claim to more than a hundred acres in the Sequim valley.

Tripp led us across the old orchard with moss-covered apple and cherry trees. An irrigation ditch carried clear, crystal cold water across the orchard. Tripp showed us the handsome old barn and the recently poured concrete milk stalls with wooden stanchions, long enough to hold twenty-five cows.

In a big bull pen behind the barn, Chimacum, the irritable near-sighted Holstein bull, was pawing the ground. We soon discovered that Chimacum made his escape often, from the broken down fence meant to keep him in, an emergency that required the adults, or near-adults, to grab pitchforks and round him up and get him back into the bull pen.

We bought the farm with my mother's $25,000 inheritance. For that munificent sum, we got fifty-three acres of marginal farmland, much of it too steep to cultivate. We got twenty-five cows, the barn, the milk house, the tool shed, and a faulty pump.

We also got a flock of chickens and a pair of greedy, noisy pigs.

There was no tractor. Instead, Tripp had a team of draft horses, Bonnie and Daisy. Bonnie was a big, sleek bay. Daisy, a gray, was a bit smaller but also with big sorrowful eyes.

Tripp also furnished harnesses and a collection of horse-drawn implements: a John Deere mower, a buck rake, a four-wheel hay wagon, a single-share plow, spring-tooth harrow and a stone boat.

Of course, we also got the Bell House, one of the most stately homes in Clallam County, and Trixie, a lovely collie trained to run down into the bottom pastures and round up the herd for milking. She slept in the crawl space under the house.

In choosing the Dungeness Valley as our home, my folks rejected the farms on the east side of the Cascades. They weighed many options, pro and con. One of the factors was clear-sighted and political. We needed to be nearer to our very extensive and progressive-minded family. And western Washington was more congenial politically overall. Even though Clallam County was politically conservative, it still had a strong working class and an active labor movement, especially among the loggers whose radical roots went back to the Industrial Workers of the World.

Port Angeles, the county seat of Clallam County and the biggest city, was a paper mill town. The city had been founded by utopian socialists in 1889, the Puget Sound

Cooperative Colony, a movement that left many deep roots in the community. We were to forge strong friendships with the heirs to that movement.

I was young enough to be charmed by the irrigation ditches that ran across our farm. I floated toy boats down the ditches and waded in the icy, glacial waters until my toes hurt.

Soon it became a job entrusted to my elder brother Steve and me to walk up through the woods of Bell Hill to the Highland Ditch to clear our head-gate and keep the waters drawn from the Dungeness River flowing swiftly down to irrigate our fields.

Flood irrigation of our farm was a task I loathed, walking with a shovel along the ditches that snaked around the many knolls scattered across our farm. I would cut open a sluiceway in the ditch and let the waters run down across the parched earth.

Years later, like our neighbors all across the valley, we bought a system of aluminum irrigation pipes with sprinklers that delivered the water far more efficiently to every square foot of our land. We had to move the pipes forty feet twice a day, a job that was even more strenuous than the flood irrigation. As the farm operation expanded, just to keep financially afloat, we were soon renting the neighboring farm of Mrs. Miller whose husband, a steamfitter by trade, had died when the steam pipe he was fixing at the Sequim saw mill burst and scalded him to death.

Mr. Miller had been a part time "stump farmer" and watered his acres with a system of old steel irrigation pipes. So we used those steel pipes to continue irrigating his acres. At one time, we were changing two sets of irrigation pipes twice each day and drawing a hefty amount of water from the Dungeness River to water our land.

My mother's sister, Janet Helms, named our farm: "Far Pastures." She was a witty, droll woman who understood well the perils of even the most well-conceived endeavors and how vulnerable we all are to the illusion that the pastures just beyond our own reach are, indeed, the greenest.

Bonnie & Daisy: The Team That Pulled Until They Couldn't

I was too young and too small to harness our draft horses, Bonnie and Daisy, as they stood in their stalls in the back of our old barn. In the earlier years, my father or my elder brother, Steve, would help put the big collars around the horse's necks, lift the harness from the peg in the wall and swing it over their sleek backs.

I would then scramble under the behemoths, pulling the hames into position, tightening the belts and straightening the tugs that we later hooked to the doubletree on whatever implement we were using.

I was likewise too short to pitch hay from the ground. So my assignment during the haying season was to drive the wagon from the barn, down the long road to the hayfields in the lower forty.

I drove the team around the hayfield from one shock to the next as my father, brother, my cousins and other workers pitched the hay up to me. I used a pitchfork to keep the load wide and flat, wading back and forth from front to rear of the wagon, mashing down the loose hay with my feet to keep it well-packed.

More than once, I did not pack the hay down carefully or I allowed the load to narrow toward the top. As the wagon trundled across the field, one of the wheels would bump down suddenly into a ditch. The load shifted and hay would slide off the side of the wagon onto the ground—a small but irritating disaster. I became skilled at building good, square, well-packed loads.

When the wagon arrived at the barn, my job, once again, was up in the mow spreading out the hay delivered to us by a grapple-hook and a complicated system of cables. The loose hay rose steadily toward the rafters of the barn, the fragrance of the dried clover and alfalfa perfuming the mow. Swallows built their nests in the rafters of the barn. Our haymow rose so high I could peer over the edge of the swallow nests and see the fledglings waiting for their parents to return, their beaks filled with mosquitoes. They swooped and soared around their suddenly dangerously exposed nests. Yet somehow, the swallows thrived, despite the ever-menacing cats that dwelled in our barnyard.

Bonnie and Daisy were a great team, gentle, easy to handle, and intelligent enough to anticipate where we needed to go next. One day, a year or so after we had become farmers, the team was pulling a load of hay up Bell Hill to the barn. Daisy was not pulling her share.

Bonnie was snorting, her nostrils extended as she struggled to pull the load up the steep hill mostly by herself. Her flanks were covered with sweat and my heart filled with pity for her. It got worse and worse with every load we delivered to the barn that afternoon. It was even worse the next day and I found myself whipping Daisy and shouting at her to pull harder to relieve the burden poor Bonnie was carrying.

The next morning we awoke and found Daisy down, lying on her side in the orchard, blood-flecked foam pouring from around her nostrils and mouth. She was in convulsions. We telephoned the veterinarian, Dr. Stevens, who came immediately.

The vet diagnosed her ailment as a brain tumor. She had to be put down. It was a sad job my father carried out with the only firearm we had in the house, an old bolt-action single-shot .22 rifle. I will never forget the sharp crack from that rifle that put Daisy out of her misery.

We were in the middle of the haying season. We could not be denied the need of traction power. My father visited Mrs. Miller, a quarter mile down the road and asked her if her late husband's Ford Ferguson tractor was for sale. It was.

So out of the tragedy, we gained a new machine that revolutionized our work. We had to make modifications, cutting off the tongue of the hay wagon, substituting a far shorter tongue suitable to be pulled by a tractor. It was a new beginning for us but also signaled the end of an era. My folks sold Bonnie to Mr. Calkins, a farmer in Happy Valley.

In the days that followed Daisy's death, I recalled the whippings I had inflicted on her, the angry curses, all in the name of sympathy for Bonnie. I vowed to myself never again to be cruel to another living being, inflicting pain and suffering while I was ignorant of the truth.

We Learn to Farm and Find Solace in Books

An excerpt from this story appeared in the *People's World* November 18, 2016

Looked at from one perspective, it is good that the Wheeler family was immersed in learning how to be dairy farmers in the late 1940s and early 1950s. We were so absorbed in the intricacies of dairy farming that we barely had time to absorb the political insanity unleashed on us—and the rest of the world—by Senator Joe

McCarthy and the other Cold War bullies in Washington D.C. and in our own Washington State.

We didn't even have a radio—of course, no television—and did not subscribe to a newspaper. We were targets for Cold War isolation but part of it was that we isolated ourselves. For months, we had no family friends. We made up for it with dawn to dark toil on our steep, rocky fifty-three acre farm on the slopes of Bell Hill. Evenings were filled with games and reading, much of it aloud. We played "Authors" many evenings after we milked the cows.

Our mother read children's books aloud to us every evening, *Honk The Moose,* and later *The Adventures of Huckleberry Finn.* Books by James Willard Schultz were a favorite, *Lone Bull's Mistake, With the Indians in the Rockies* and *Quest of the Fishdog Skin.* Frank T. Bullen's *Cruise of the Cachalot* was another yarn that gripped us. We also loved *Trailmakers of the Middle Border* by Hamlin Garlin, with his vivid description of the struggle of sodbusters on the great American prairie. I listened as in a dream to the sound of my mother's voice as she read aloud these fabulous adventure stories. The fire in the wood stove warmed us against the chill winds off the Strait of Juan de Fuca.

We read widely. One two-volume book was *The Road to Life* by a Soviet author, Makarenko. We listened intently as mother read of how Makarenko struggled to win over the orphaned street urchins of the infant Soviet Union, rescuing them from hopelessness, despair, and a life of crime, the evil fruit of counter-revolutionary civil war and famine.

Later, I read John Reed's *Ten Days that Shook the World.* I understood much of what John Reed wrote. Yet I was barely in my teens and I remember my deep confusion about the "Cadets," visualizing them as young men in uniforms like the cadets at West Point marching around Petrograd with rifles on their shoulders. In fact, "Cadet" was John Reed's shorthand for "Constitutional Democrats."

We children enrolled in the Sequim Consolidated Schools exactly one mile from our farm. Every weekday morning, we finished up the morning chores, washed the barnyard manure from our forearms, got dressed, and walked down the hill through the town of Sequim and on out to the school on the prairie.

My third grade teacher was a tall, handsome woman named Mrs. Lotzgezell. She was married into one of the pioneer families of the Dungeness valley. We got on famously, especially after I mentioned in her class my admiration for the silent films of Charlie Chaplin. A twinkle appeared in Mrs. Lotzgezell's large blue eyes. "I appeared in several Charlie Chaplin movies," she said. I could see how she would have caught Chaplin's eye.

Soon after, Mrs. Lotzgezell told the class she wanted us to memorize a poem by William Wordsworth that begins, "I wandered lonely as a cloud that floats on high o'er vale and hill."

I went home that afternoon angry at being forced to memorize such a silly ditty. In high dudgeon, I poured out my scorn to my father. "Why that's a great assignment," my father replied. "It's a wonderful poem and we want you to memorize it right away."

I was taken aback. Yet I was under my father's influence so completely that I worked hard to memorize the poem. Many years later, a professor in my freshmen English literature class at Amherst College used that poem as an example of the deceptive simplicity of Wordsworth's poetry, using what seems a child-like experience to express the romantic poets' concept of the human imagination: "But most when on my couch I lie in solemn or in pensive mood/ They flash upon the inward eye that is the bliss of solitude/And then my heart with pleasure fills and dances with the daffodils."

My maternal grandmother, Marion Robinson Lukes, sold off or gave away most of her possessions that had filled her handsome house on Queen Anne Hill with the sweeping view of downtown Seattle and Mount Rainier. She was moving to Los Angeles to be near my uncle, Joe Lukes, and his wife Charlotte. Among the possessions she gave us was an RCA table model radio. We became regular listeners of CBC broadcasts from Vancouver, B.C. and programs like *Jake and the Kid*.

We also took out a subscription to the *National Guardian* around this time, and later the *People's World*, both leftwing weekly publications. It brought an end to our self-imposed news embargo.

I was in awe of my father's vast intellect. Yet in many ways, it was my mother who exerted the deepest influence on me. I must have been twelve or thirteen when she handed me a slim volume. "You might find this interesting," she said quietly. It was the *Communist Manifesto*. As soon as I read the opening lines, I was gripped by the *Manifesto* and read it from cover to cover that evening. Already, I was caught up in the ruthless dynamism of capitalist production on our family farm, conscious of forces in the larger economy beyond our control and the relentless struggle of workers, including rural workers, against the giant corporations and the rich. The pamphlet rang true to me.

All of us children thrived at the school, winning the highest grades, making many friends. Living less than a mile from Sequim, we befriended the sons and daughters of the town-dwellers. Among them were the Duncan children, the Joslins, the Midkiff brothers, Cecil Sullivan, a member of the S'Klallam tribe, all of whom visited us often on our hillside farm. We children also spent the night with the families of our newly bonded friends, sometimes attending movies at the Dresden Theater at 12¢ per ticket.

We were drawn to some of the farmers, especially the Robins family who operated a dairy farm much like ours nestled between the railroad tracks and the Sequim town line less than a mile away from us. One of Steve's best friends was Ralph Robins. Don "Shorty" Robins was one of my bosom buddies. In my sophomore year in high school, Shorty Robins and I hitchhiked into Port Angeles one Sunday to see the matinee of Hollywood's version of Leo Tolstoy's *War and Peace*.

I immediately checked *War and Peace* out of the library and read it avidly from start to finish. For months, I walked around in a swoon, imagining myself as a shaved down version of Pierre Bazukhov. If Henry Fonda could pass for the gentle, illegitimate, giant, why not me? I fell deeply in love with Natasha Rostov played with such beguiling charm by Audrey Hepburn.

The Robins family had emigrated to Sequim from Alabama and exuded much of the hospitality we associate with the south. We formed an informal, ad hoc partnership during haying season to share equipment one family had but the other didn't. Both families provided manpower to get the hay cut, raked, shocked, loaded and into the hay mow before it got rained on.

Mr. Robins was a rail-thin, quiet-spoken man. Maybe he was homesick for Alabama. Maybe he suffered from hay fever or some other allergy. His pale blue eyes were always watering. It looked like he was crying. Maybe he was crying.

Mrs. Robins, another gentle soul, put ample, down-home dinners on her table in the old fading farmhouse where the family lived. When the Wheelers and the Robins were haying together we sat at her table and wolfed down succulent ham, sweet potatoes, greens and corn-bread. That and her mouth-watering fruit pies.

Bell Creek flowed down a canyon at the western boundary of our place and on down through the Robins' farm. Mr. Robins had dug out a big irrigation pond and that is where all of us—the Robins, the Wheelers, and all the rest of the children in the town of Sequim—went swimming to cool off during the heat of the summer and especially during the lunch breaks when we were putting up the hay.

The Cold War isolation—as well as the self-imposed isolation—was beginning to break down. We were drawn step-by-step into the social and political life of the community on the North Olympic Peninsula. It was a conservative community yet even here democracy had struck deep roots among the people, a spirit that looked with skepticism on the attempts by the McCarthyite Cold Warriors to demonize my father and mother and people like them.

Mother Courage of Clallam County

People's World June 23, 2014

One late autumn afternoon, I believe in 1949, Clallam County Sheriff, Mutt Breece, arrived in his big blue Pontiac. He knocked at the door and my father answered. Breece was bringing a summons. My dad read the summons silently and handed it to mother standing beside him. I could see an expression of anger and alarm spread across Mama's face as she read the document. Breece was a big, florid faced man but he didn't look comfortable in carrying out this particular assignment.

A new word entered my vocabulary that day: subpoena. Daddy was ordered to appear before a Grand Jury in Washington, D.C. to answer the charges of an FBI stool pigeon that he was one of the hundreds of communists who had infiltrated our government in the nation's capital. Indeed, these communists, according to the self-appointed guardians of national security, had "wormed their way" into every facet of American life from Hollywood to the local factories, not to speak of logging operations right in Clallam County.

Daddy was to endure many of these forced separations, summoned to appear seven times before witch hunt hearings in Washington D.C., San Francisco, Seattle and Tacoma in the years that followed. In fact, he had been blacklisted and that was the reason we were then eking out an existence on a dairy farm in Sequim, Washington. But none of those later subpoenas hangs in my memory more ominously than that first summons to Washington D.C.

He would cross the country on the train, being absent for more than a week, to appear before the tribunal. He would refuse to testify no matter what questions the inquisitors asked. He was represented in that hearing by wonderful progressive attorneys Joe Forer and David Rein, both of whom we were to get to know years later when I was assigned to Washington D.C. by the *Daily World*, later the *People's World*.

Father left behind my mother, then nursing our newborn, brother, Nat. My little sister Marion was still in diapers. There was my elder brother, Steve and my little sister Susan, then seven, and me. Mama had twenty-five cows to milk twice daily, keeping the herd fed, the barn cleaned. How did my mother, so small of stature, of such genteel birth, with five to care for, manage such an impossible task by herself?

Part of the answer was Steve, my elder brother. He was in his teens and took on responsibilities far beyond his years. To add to his misery the first time our father was summoned, Steve had come down with flu, suffering terrible stomach cramps, fever, dizziness. Yet without complaining, he donned his boots, jacket, milking cap and gloves and went out to do the milking. Then nine years old, I went with him.

My grandfather, Bapa, also known as Francis Marion Wheeler, in his eighties, came up from Bainbridge Island to help milk the cows. He was an old man, already suffering from dementia. But he was lucid enough to help us stave off collapse.

An ice storm gripped the valley and the power went out. Our house, and more important, the barn and milk house, were without power. It meant no lights and no milking machines. Steve and Bapa made an executive decision.

We wouldn't try to milk the cows dry. Just strip milk them enough to relieve the pressure on their udders. "Maybe the power will be back on tomorrow morning so we can milk the cows properly," Bapa said.

No one argued. Bapa, Steve, and I hand-stripped the cows by kerosene lantern light that frigid night. Sure enough, the next morning, PUD managed to restore power and we milked the cows as they should be milked.

My father's summons to appear at a hearing in Washington D.C. was front-page news. Before he left, the *Sequim Press* asked him if he wanted space to answer the charges and granted him an entire page to tell his side of the story.

He wrote an eloquent defense. I remember only one student spoke to me about the issue. Jerry McNamara, whose father worked for the U.S. Postal Service, came up to me before our class began one morning. "I heard about your father's troubles," he said. "I'm very sorry."

We celebrated when Daddy returned. No one was more relieved than Mama. One evening after the barn chores were completed, after we had eaten dinner, my mother suffered a break down. She had been holding herself together, grimly. Now she could give vent to her feelings and she did. She fell into bed weeping uncontrollably. We all gathered in the bedroom with her, trying to console her. I burst into tears. "Don't cry Mama. Please don't cry."

So what did Mama do as tears streamed down her cheeks and mine? She started to laugh. Yes! She burst into laughter, seeing in our situation something absurd, so ludicrous what could you do but laugh about it. Then Daddy started to laugh. And Steve, Susan, little Honey Bee in her diapers. And I too began to laugh even as I wiped away the tears. We all had a great laugh together.

Years later, Mama told me, "When your father was subpoenaed and went away, I didn't know if he would come back." Those were the days when the Rosenbergs were on death row. The nation was caught in the grip of fear and hate. One evening, we sat around our dining room table writing postcards to President Eisenhower urging clemency for the Rosenbergs. I remember the evening when the news came that the Rosenbergs had been executed. Mama's dark, sorrowful, eyes filled with tears. She was not immune to the fear. I saw her hands tremble when she rolled a cigarette. Yet she stood her ground. She stayed by Daddy's side. She did not flinch. She was Mother Courage.

Great Forks Fire of 1951

One hot, dry, September, in 1951, a forest fire broke out in the West End of Clallam County. It had been an exceptionally arid summer and all the forests were like tinder. The loggers of the region had come in and worked to extinguish a wild fire that erupted in the Calawah river valley. They thought they had won the fight but the fire was smoldering in the brush despite their best efforts. A wind arose and brought the fire back to life. The wind drove the flames across the treetops toward the logging town of Forks. The heroism of the working people of Forks saved the town from certain incineration. They refused orders to evacuate and stayed behind to kill the flames that erupted on their rooftops.

The sun arose in the morning amid a glory of red and orange across the valley and the Strait of Juan de Fuca. At noon, in our valley seventy miles east, the sky was still a fiery red, the sun an orange disc, as it arced upward and westward in a perpetual sunset. We were miles from the flames of Forks but the air was still laden with the smoke of that inferno that seemed to set heaven itself on fire. I always associate those fearsome days, the depth of the Cold War, with the "Great Forks Fire," the sunset at mid-day.

I Hear Paul Robeson Sing, My World Begins to Change

I inherited a pure singing voice and a love of solo and choral singing. I never learned to read music but I have a good ear and can harmonize. Later, a college classmate gave me an autoharp and I learned to accompany myself.

Yet in the early years, I was self-conscious about my natural talent until Miss Maltman, the music teacher, finally drew me out. I spent many hours singing in a popular high school quartet and practicing with other gifted singers at the home of Don Kirner whose mother played the piano well to accompany us.

My favorite was Paul Robeson and I often listened on our old windup Victrola to my parent's 78-RPM recordings of Robeson singing spirituals and popular compositions such as Earl Robinson's *Ballad for Americans*.

One day in the spring of 1952, my mother read aloud an ad in the *National Guardian*. Robeson would be singing at the Peace Arch on the U.S.-Canadian Border May 18 at the invitation of the Mine, Mill and Smelter Workers Union. Two days later, Robeson would sing in Seattle in a concert sponsored by the National Negro Labor Council. I was twelve-years-old, too young to go to Seattle by myself. Also, we were too poor to afford the Greyhound ticket and admission to the concert.

Still I wouldn't stop pleading with mother to let me go. Finally, she relented.

"Alright, you and Steve can hitch-hike down to Seattle. It will be on a school day so you will have to get an excuse from your teachers to leave early to make it there in time."

I was elated. Yet it was short-lived because I had to ask my sixth grade teacher, Mr. Joe Pettelle, for permission to leave school at noon. "Why are you going to Seattle," Pettelle demanded.

I was tongue-tied. If I told him the truth, maybe he would refuse permission. I girded myself. I could not avoid telling him the truth.

"We're going down to hear Paul Robeson sing at a concert," I blurted.

He nodded. "Lucky you! I wish I could go with you."

It was not the last time I was to learn that Mr. Pettelle and other faculty members in Sequim were progressive-minded. Later that year, Mr. Pettelle asked me who I was supporting for President in that election year. I told him we were supporting the Progressive Party candidates, Vincent Hallinan, and Charlotta Bass. "So am I," he replied.

So the great adventure began that May afternoon in 1952. At noon, Steve and I left school and walked to the east outskirts of town where we began hitchhiking. I remember a long trip with several stretches of walking along Old Olympic Highway toward the ferry at Shine and on to the Kingston-Edmunds ferry.

We arrived in Seattle and found our way to the concert at the Civic Arena. I remember little of the concert itself. But during the intermission, my aunt, Margaret Jean Schudakopf, hurried up and embraced Steve and me. She reached out and pinched the sleeve of a man standing nearby. It was Bill Pennock, executive director of the Washington Pension Union, a slim, lively man wearing gold-rimmed spectacles.

Margaret Jean introduced us to Pennock as residents of Sequim. His eyes lit up. "You're from Sequim? Why we're having the Pension Union state picnic in Sequim in three weeks. It starts at 10a.m. at the Sequim Bay State Park. You must come and bring your parents, your entire family," he said.

That Saturday, we loaded the entire family into the car and trundled down the highway to Sequim Bay State Park. Soon after we arrived, a handsome woman with curly, golden hair and bright blue eyes came up to the picnic table where we were sitting.

"Hello, I'm Vivian Gaboury. Bill Pennock tells me you are the Wheelers. I want to welcome you."

It was like opening a floodgate. My mom and dad were soon immersed in conversation with Vivian Gaboury who had come over with her husband, Harvey, and their children, Gail, David, and Adele. Her eldest son, Fred, a logger, was working that day. We were surrounded by friends, including neighbors living on the remote North Olympic Peninsula.

That picnic was a turning point in my family's life. From being politically isolated, we were suddenly drawn into a circle of people active on a daily basis in every struggle that mattered for the working class of the region.

Within days, Vivian Gaboury had recruited my parents into the Communist Party of Clallam County. And within a month or so, the monthly meetings of the Party were being held in the big, spacious living room of our house. At first, the doors were kept closed. There was fear that the FBI might pick up the children on their way home from school and grill us on what plot was being hatched in our living room.

Soon, the doors were opened and the children were invited in. We sat on the oriental rugs in the living room listening to Vivian, her son Fred Gaboury, a logger and an active member of the International Woodworkers of America, and other Party comrades planning the fightback against the witch-hunt, the defense of union organizing rights, the struggle for peace and against racism.

I remember vividly that one mobilization was against the Taft-Hartley trial of Karly Larsen, a leader of the International Woodworkers of America in the Pacific Northwest. The aim of Weyerhaeuser, Crown Zellerbach, and the other timber interests was to drive Communists and other left-wingers out of the logging industry. Militant fightback by the IWA, led by class struggle left-wingers, had won the highest wages in the region for loggers.

The club decided to distribute in Port Angeles a leaflet exposing Larsen's trial in Seattle. We gathered at Fred and Betty Gaboury's home in Port Angeles that Saturday morning. Fred took charge, dividing us into teams to cover the neighborhood of the mill town. Fred and my dad made up one team. I was assigned to work with Fred's younger brother David.

David and I walked door-to-door dropping the leaflets on front porches. I had dropped a leaflet and was walking away when the front door opened and a man stepped out. He bent over and picked up the leaflet. He scanned it quickly and then called out in a gruff voice, "Hey, kid. Come back here. I want to talk to you."

I shouted at him, "Read it. Maybe it will do you some good."

Then David and I ran.

We resumed leafleting in the next block, far out of earshot of the gruff-spoken man who wanted to talk to me. I wonder now what he would have said to me. I assumed he would be hostile and maybe he would have been. But not necessarily. I should have gone back to talk to him. I might have discovered a friend and ally.

We had distributed the last of our leaflets and walked back to Fred and Betty's house. Betty made hot chocolate for us and we waited for the others to return. An hour after everyone else had come home, Fred and my father arrived.

Fred was all excited. "A cop stopped us and ordered us into his cruiser," Fred reported. "I was about to get in when Don told the cop, 'I'm not getting in unless you arrest me. And if you arrest me, I want to know the charges.'"

Fred broke into a hearty laugh. "That cop was flabbergasted. He didn't know what to do. He called in on his radio: 'Chief, this guy won't get into the squad car unless I arrest him and if I arrest him, he wants to know the charges.' The cop and his chief went on like that, back and forth for about five minutes. Finally, I hear the chief shout at the cop angrily, 'Just let them go.' So that's what happened, He let us go! And here we are."

Today, it may seem like a small incident. But in America in 1952 in a remote sawmill and paper mill town, my dad's stand against authoritarian police meant a great deal. Our leafleting did not prevent the timber barons and their yes men in the judicial system from running Karly Larsen out of the International Woodworkers of America, But it was a harbinger of the fightback that was to follow decades later as the left and progressive workers united and fought to restore the labor movement and its fighting spirit.

Karly Larson was not the only martyr in that fight. A few months after Larson was on trial, so was Bill Pennock, the slim, lively, bespectacled young man who fought tirelessly for the rights of senior citizens to a secure retirement. He was so beloved he was elected repeatedly to the Washington State Legislature from Seattle. Like many other Communist Party members, Pennock was elected on the Democratic Party ticket.

He was on trial, pilloried by the mass media. He died one night of an overdose of sleeping pills. His family said it was an accident, not suicide. Someday a monument will be built honoring William Pennock who never quit fighting for the rights of the poor and downtrodden.

Robeson: "That Sight and That Song . . ."
(Written days after Robeson died)
Daily World February 5, 1976

We drove in the Gaboury's green pre-war Plymouth towards Blaine, Washington, on that bright day in August 1953, riding the ferry from Port Townsend to Keystone on Whidbey Island, north across Deception Pass and then north to the Canadian border.

As we approached Blaine, the highway became clogged with cars and chartered buses and we inched our way toward the Peace Arch that straddles the U.S-Canada border. A human river was flowing north.

When we reached the Peace Arch, an awesome sight came into view. Flowing south from the Canadian side to meet us was a river of buses and cars and people on foot even larger than our own. The two streams flowed together to form a multitude on the grassy slopes of the natural amphitheater that surrounded the Peace Arch.

Vivian and Harvey Gaboury and all of us children were sitting on blankets high up on the rim of the bowl along with thousands of other U.S. and Canadian families waiting on the grass.

An air of quickening excitement and expectation grew as the minutes passed away. We looked down on the towering white marble arch set against the brilliant emerald green grass with a flatbed truck parked just on the U.S. side of the border. The agitation of the teeming crowd was most acute right near the flatbed truck with the microphone. And attracted like all children toward excitement, I left Vivian and Harvey and pushed down the hill toward the truck.

Then suddenly a roar went up from the crowd. All around me, women and men stood up, obstructing my view. I slipped and twisted my way through until I was so near I could look directly up to the bed of the truck. There standing behind the microphone was a tall African American man. I recognized him instantly as Paul Robeson.

Beside me in the crowd was a Black man with a little boy on his shoulders. "Paul, hey Paul," the little child shouted in a peanut whistle voice so loud and insistent he could be heard even above the deafening tumult of the cheering crowd.

Robeson heard the child shouting and looked down quizzically into the crowd. He spotted the little boy. His eyes were shining and he was smiling with pleasure. He reached down and grasped the child's hand.

The crowd responded with laughter and renewed applause.

A leader of the Mine, Mill, and Smelter Workers Union introduced Robeson and again a roar of applause greeted his words. Then the crowd fell silent as Robeson stepped forward to the microphone. His majestic voice rolled over the amphitheater. I was so near I could see the beads of sweat form on his forehead. "Go down, Moses, way down in Egypt land. Tell old pharaoh, let my people go."

I turned and looked back up the slope at that listening multitude. That sight and that song changed my life forever. Never before had I seen with my own eyes so many people who shared my vision of the future. I understood then that my ideas were not those of a discredited, even despised, minority. They were ideas shared by tens of thousands if not millions, ideas as broad and deep as the mainstream of a mighty river.

It was only in later years that I learned the full meaning of Robeson's Peace Arch concerts, which I had heard at the tender age of thirteen. It was one of those turning points in history when the working people of this continent—Canadian and American, Black, Latino, Native American Indian and white—gathered 40,000 strong to say "No" to McCarthyism.

They came to defy the State Department's attempt to silence Robeson in withholding his passport.

The people fell into an uncanny quietness when Robeson began to sing that day at the Peace Arch as if through his voice they could hear themselves singing.

After Robeson, the Voices of Earl Robinson, Pete Seeger Ring Out in Clallam County

The Robeson concerts were only the beginning of the music in our lives. Vivian was so enthused by the Peace Arch concert that she urged a follow-up. The famed songwriter, Earl Robinson, who had composed *Ballad for Americans* and other popular musicals with songs like *The House I Live In* had retired to nearby Poulsbo on the Kitsap Peninsula.

In those days, before the floating bridge was built, it was a ferry ride and a long drive through the woods from Sequim. We invited Robinson to come and perform. He accepted.

Robinson performed *Sandhog*, his most recent musical solo on my mother's piano in our living room. He played the piano masterfully and sang all the various parts of this "folk opera" in his sweet Irish tenor voice. *Sandhog* had opened in the Phoenix Theater in New York City in December 1954. It closed in February 1955, another victim of the Cold War despite its obvious appeal to the residents of a city who rely on the Holland and Lincoln tunnels for transport in and out of their city. The opera was in three acts and told the story of Irish American tunnel diggers digging the tunnels under the Hudson River.

Robinson sat at the piano and sang the Irish love song he had penned for the opera, "Katie o-o-o-o! Katie o-o-o, you're the breath of the heather air!" I was entranced by the beauty of the music and the poignancy of his lyrics.

A few months later, my younger sister, Susan Elizabeth, just then entering her teenage years, heard a recording of "The Weavers." She was smitten by Pete Seeger, in love with the tall, clear-voiced banjo-picker. Later Susan wrote that her classmates were falling in love with Elvis Presley. "I was in love with Pete."

She wrote a fan letter to Seeger. A few weeks later, to her joy, and our amazement, Pete answered. If she organized a concert for him, he would come and perform. That letter galvanized Susan and the rest of us into action. I suppose it was 1957 that Seeger came and performed in the Port Angeles High School Auditorium to a crowd of about forty people. As always, Pete enlisted everyone in the audience to sing with him. I sat in a front row and harmonized. He thanked me afterward with helping make the concert a great success.

I was away at college when Pete returned the following spring bringing with him the legendary blues singer, Sonny Terrie, to perform once again in Port Angeles. My younger sister, Marion (Honeybee,) was felled by the flu and could not attend that concert. So Pete came to our home and sang to her.

I can't say that Pete fell in love with Susan, a girl young enough to be his daughter. But they formed a lifelong friendship during the depths of the Cold War when Pete faced a vicious blacklist that banned him, like Paul Robeson, from stages and broadcast venues all across the nation.

Decades later, Pete Seeger sent out an offer to those who had supported him during those bleak years. To repay people who had taken a heroic stand against the blacklist, he would perform gratis, with all proceeds going to any worthy cause his supporters chose.

Susan, then living in Portland, Oregon, was among those who received this message from Pete. Because she was deeply engaged in mass struggles in Portland, Susan knew that the Oregon farm workers' union, Pineiros y Campesinos Unidos, was struggling to raise money to buy or build a union hall in Portland. Susan contacted the union and then called Pete. A month or so later, Pete Seeger performed in Portland to a standing room crowd. Nearly $40,000 was raised for the farm workers union.

Susan never promoted herself in that cause. In fact, I first heard of it at Susan's memorial in Portland after she died prematurely of cancer. A leader of Pineiros y Campesinos Unidos with tears in his eyes told the story to the crowd of mourners. Her death was a heavy blow to me. Pete could not come to the memorial at the Quaker House in Portland but he sent a letter read aloud to the mourners that he would never forget the young girl who organized concerts for him, breaking the Cold War curtain of silence.

Maybe & May: Life and Death on a Family Farm

Dairy farmers in Clallam County sold their bull calves to the local mink farmer who fed them to his mink. Like the ill-fated husbands of black widow spiders, those bull calves were a testament to the disadvantage of being born male.

One day the mink farmer came in his truck to pick up one of our newborn bull calves. When my dad looked into the back of the pickup, he spotted a little Jersey heifer among the bulls. "What's she doing in there?" my father asked.

"Well, one of your neighbors put her in. He didn't want her."

"I'll trade you straight across—my bull calf for that heifer."

The mink farmer chuckled. "Alright, maybe she will turn out to be a prize winner."

The mink farmer unloaded the heifer from the pickup.

Daddy turned the little heifer over to my sisters, Susan and Honeybee, whose job was to care for the calves, feeding them, cleaning out their stalls. We had a mixed herd, Jerseys, Guernseys, Brown Swiss, and Holstein. Honeybee and Susan would mix up the formula in a bucket fitted with an artificial teat. The heifers suckled the fake teat greedily.

We never knew whether it was a deficiency in the formula or some other explanation. Scours was endemic and the majority of the calves sickened and died. They were like pets to my sisters and they were devastated.

Susan and Honeybee named the calves. They chose a name for the Jersey heifer that reflected the "iffy" circumstances of her arrival on our farm: "Maybe." As in, maybe she will make it to milk-producing age. But then again, maybe she wouldn't.

A few years later, the answer was in. In 1967, the Dairy Herd Improvement Association (DHIA) proclaimed "Maybe" the Butterfat Queen of Clallam County. Over six lactations, she produced 37,000 pounds of milk—over eighteen tons. At 8.1 percent fat, she produced over a ton of butterfat, enough to supply the entire town of Sequim with all the ice cream we could eat.

Her photograph is on the front cover of the DHIA's 1967 Annual Report, a dark, beautiful Jersey cow with a very large udder. Her parentage, if known at all, is a secret held by the mink man.

The happy ending of Maybe's story brings back a memory of another cow, May—a similar name. Her story is very different.

One of my jobs in those early years was to walk out to the pastures and bring in the herd for morning milking. "Keep your eyes peeled for May," my father told me one morning. "She's going to freshen any time now and she's a prime candidate for milk fever."

Milk fever is a catastrophic calcium deficiency in cows just when they drop their calf. Heavy producers are at greatest risk. All the calcium rushes into the milk they are producing. It can cause a sudden neurological collapse. The cow falls, goes into convulsions, drifts into a coma and can be dead in an hour or so.

One of veterinary science's greatest breakthroughs is calcium glutamate. A bottle of the drug delivered intravenously through a needle and tube in the cow's neck will bring her back from a deep coma almost instantaneously.

I walked out along Miller Road with the sun just breaking, Trixie running on ahead. It seemed the start of a perfect day in Clallam County. When I got to the second pasture, I looked down and saw in the semi-darkness, a shape that made my heart go cold. It was May, among the tullies, down on her side, her newborn calf bawling at her side.

I clambered through the barbed wire fence and raced down the hill to where May was lying. Her head was flat on the ground. Her breathing was labored.

I turned and ran up the hill at top speed. My mother telephoned Dr. Stevens who came immediately. We drew a bucket of hot water in the milk house and floated the bottle of calcium glutamate in it. I rode with the vet in his Ford wagon back out along Miller Road to the second pasture. We hurried down the long hill to the bottom of the pasture where May was lying. We put the nose clamp in her nostrils and ran the rope across her back and pulled her head around. Both of us pushed mightily to bring her up to a cow's normal lying position. Finally, she rolled up on her knees.

Doctor Stevens searched for the vein in her neck, scrubbed it with disinfectant, and ran the needle in. He held the bottle up and we waited while the calcium glutamate flowed in and took effect. She began to shiver, always the first sign that the calcium glutamate was taking effect.

Sure enough, within minutes, she tried to stand and minutes later succeeded. Then she turned her attention to the calf bawling loudly a few feet away. She began licking off the afterbirth. A few minutes later, the calf tottered over and started bumping her udder to make her colostrum come down.

Dr. Stevens poured out the water from the bucket. "Keep an eye on her. She doesn't look quite right to me," he said. "Give me a call later this morning to let me know how she's doing."

We walked back up the hill. I helped my dad with the milking but after about fifteen minutes he stopped me. "You better go back out and check on May."

When I arrived, I discovered the worst. May was down again. The calf was bawling. I hurried over behind May, digging my knee into her ribs. "Get up, May. Get up."

She barely responded. I tried again and again.

Then I was running up the hill toward the house once more. My mother called and Dr. Stevens came, administering another dose of calcium glutamate. He left, hurrying on to the next emergency. May hardly responded this time.

She lay on her side for hours. Her breathing grew lighter and lighter. I had other chores to perform, not least, carrying May's newborn up to the barn. I left May among the tullies.

I put the calf in the calf stalls and walked back over to the milking parlor where Daddy was finishing up the morning milking. I read the question on my father's face. "May isn't going to make it," I said.

The look in his eyes said it all: defeat. May was one of our top producers. She was a family pet. Later that day, we walked down to the bottom pasture. May was dead.

My Coldest Winter
People's Weekly World (abridged) January 8, 2000

I walked in the darkness to bring down the cows that cold January morning in 1950, a few days before my tenth birthday. Usually, the cows were beneath the cedar boughs chewing their cuds. But this morning, they were milling around restlessly. When I opened the gate, they headed for the barn without prodding. Bonnie and Daisy, our workhorses, were pacing in their corral and snorting nervously. I stood still. I could feel it, too. A dense, cold, humidity in the air, an urgency of something big and menacing rolling near.

The cows filed into their stanchions. "It feels like snow," my father said. "A storm is coming on." As the sky grew lighter in the east, this air of expectancy deepened. I walked to the end of the milking barn and looked out. The clouds over the Strait of Juan de Fuca had turned black.

After milking, my brother Steve and I washed, changed into our school clothes and walked with our little sister Susan down the hill through town to school on the north side of Sequim. The first flakes of snow were falling and by the time we reached the school, it was coming down fast. We attended classes in the venerable Sequim schoolhouse, a tall clapboard building with a belfry and lofty, small-paned windows that looked out on the Olympic Mountains. That morning, I joined my classmates huddling near the steam radiators that clanked and hissed as they poured out the heat. The snow was falling so thick we could not see as far as the old gymnasium across the playground.

School Days 58-59

Neva Wheeler. Photo courtesy of her daughter, Bonnie Wheeler Halberg.

My teacher was Neva Wheeler, not related to my family, but a kindred spirit in other ways. Her husband was a dairy farmer like my father. She was a handsome, prematurely graying woman with a deep voice. She had a rumbling laugh and she laughed often at the shambling ways of children.

She called the class to order. We labored through arithmetic and had just taken out our reading textbooks when Mrs. Haller, the principal, appeared at the door. She conferred in a whisper with Mrs. Wheeler who then turned to us.

"School is closing early because of the storm," she said. "Put your desks in order now." By rows, we went to the cloakroom to retrieve our coats, caps, mittens, and galoshes.

For the majority of pupils, the early dismissal was cause for celebration. Sequim had a consolidated school district with the farm children riding school buses from their homes to school. The town children walked and so did we since our farm was only a mile away, in the foothills of the Olympics.

We had enrolled in the Sequim schools in the autumn of 1948 and thrived. We were enthusiastic students and outspoken in our political views. We defended the innocence of the Rosenbergs and opposed the oncoming Korean War.

We were Cold War refugees forced into farming by the anti-communist black-listers. My dad was subpoenaed repeatedly to appear as an unfriendly witness before witch-hunt committees in Washington D.C.

I got into an angry exchange with a fellow student when he claimed with a sneer that the S'Klallam Indians were "rich," proven, he said, by their preference for big luxury cars. A visit to the S'Klallam's impoverished village, Jamestown, would expose this absurdity. The Indians were among the poorest people in the county. Every inch of land had been stolen from them. They finally scraped together $500 to buy back a few acres of the county that bore their name. It was a narrow strip of beach property on the Strait of Juan de Fuca, far from the Dungeness River and its teeming salmon that had sustained them.

I told this student, "If they are rich and own fancy cars, why does their chief, Jake Hall, walk everywhere he goes in the valley?" The kid was stumped. And it was true. Jacob Hall, Chief Whitefeather, was a familiar sight to everyone in the valley, his bent form striding along Clallam County roads with a gunnysack over his shoulder. He was a handsome, dignified man, a hunchback, who often came to deliver lectures to the schoolchildren on his people's exile in their own land. My father often gave him rides.

Within minutes of our dismissal, the classroom emptied, the children climbed into buses and they pulled away into the storm. Somehow, I missed my brother and sister. I zipped my jacket, pulled my cap down over my ears and stepped into the snow. It was already four inches deep and getting deeper. I walked south past the Clyde Rhodefer Memorial Library. I waded into the library door on the chance that Steve and Susan had stopped there. The door was locked.

I was always a dawdler. "Tim, you're as slow as molasses in January," my father would say. I know about molasses in January. It was my chore to draw buckets of molasses from the fifty-gallon drum lying on a wooden frame in our grain room and pour it on the hay in the manger. It was cold as ice and sticky. That's how slow I was walking through the storm.

I just made it into the comforting warmth of the Sequim Drug Store. The place was nearly empty and I ordered a cup of hot cocoa at the soda fountain. I wrapped my frozen hands around the steaming cup and felt the ache as my fingers thawed. The wind screeched in the highest octaves and banged the drug store sign. Clouds of snow whirled up the deserted street. I dreaded the walk home.

I heard a familiar voice speaking with the pharmacist. A minute later my teacher, Mrs. Wheeler, hurried past. She caught sight of me. "Tim, what are you doing here? You must get right home! This storm is getting worse! Why didn't you go straight home when classes were dismissed?"

She shook her head in disbelief, turned and hurried out. I saw her step into her car and drive off into the tempest. I knew where her farm was, far north on the Dungeness River at least seven miles away. She had good reason to be in a hurry.

I took the last sip of cocoa, slid from the stool, zipped my jacket, and stepped out into the snow. When I turned the corner at the bank, half a block away, a blast of wind nearly bowled me over. I leaned into it and struggled to put one foot after another.

A chill I had never felt before traveled up from my fingertips and toes. My ears were frozen. The wind whipped particles of ice into my face, blinding me, stinging my cheeks and nose. After twenty minutes of plodding south, I had walked less than halfway to the old abandoned Milwaukee Road passenger station. Even when I reached the tracks, I would have two hills to climb and a valley between.

I was so far from home, the pain in my fingers and toes so unbearable. I slowed to a standstill. A feeling of self-pity flooded over me. I will die right here!

I don't know how long I stood there with the storm howling. Headlights lit the swirling snow and I heard the sound of a motor. Then came the familiar voice shouting to me, "Tim! Tim Wheeler! Come, come!"

I couldn't move. Someone's arms were around me, pushing me into the front seat of a car. A minute later, my fourth grade teacher was there beside me. The car heater was on full blast. It brought excruciating pain to my frozen fingers. I was shivering uncontrollably. Tears rolled down my freezing cheeks. "Poor boy," she said, "Why did I leave you in that drug store! I should have known!"

She drove through the blizzard, past the railroad station, up the hill past our neighbor's farmhouse, down past the snowy bottom pastures of our farm. The hill grew steeper and I could feel the car fishtailing. Mrs. Wheeler kept a steady foot on the accelerator. Slowly it inched to the crest of the hill. She turned into our driveway and stopped. "I'm not going to try to get up your driveway," she said, "I'd get stuck. You can make it from here. Have your mother put your hands into cool water. It will relieve the pain."

My mother, bent against the wind, hurried down the driveway towards us. She had been watching anxiously at the window for me and rushed out when she saw the headlights. Mrs. Wheeler rolled down the window. My mother put both her hands in and grasped Neva Wheeler's hands. "Thank you!" she said. "I was so worried. You must come in. It is dangerous."

Neva Wheeler would not stay. She had a family of her own and a herd of cows to tend across the valley. But I saw her return my mother's handclasp, the sympathy of two farm women in a cold and unforgiving time. She turned the car around and headed back down into the maelstrom.

The warmth of the woodstove hit me when I came into the house. My father was there, dressed for the storm, on his way to look for me. Steve and Susan had caught a ride home with a neighbor who happened to pass by. It was only a little past 1 p.m. My ordeal had lasted only two hours. For me, it was an ice age.

That storm was fifty years ago this month. It is hard to remember now, in this new century of promise and hope, that fear stalked our country as cold-hearted as that January blizzard. "The FBI knew exactly what our situation was," my father told me a few days ago. "They knew that taking me away from the farm for a week or ten days could break us. I might crack under the pressure and start naming names."

In the years that followed, our family won the respect and affection of many people in the valley. We became active members of the Communist Party of Clallam County, an organized force in defending my father and other victims of repression. A few years ago, Clallam County dedicated the Mary Lukes Wheeler Park, a cedar grove on the banks of the Dungeness River, on land donated by my family.

The cold warriors underestimated the courage of my mother and father. They also underestimated people like Neva Wheeler, a woman who took seriously the principle that school teachers are "in loco parentis."

At the end of that school year, Mrs. Wheeler handed out report cards. I opened mine. Opposite Social Studies she had written, "Shows special ability."

Mary Brown
Sequim's Perennial Postmaster

SEQUIM—An item in the *Port Angeles Evening News* reports that as of 1968, Mary Brown had served as Postmaster of Sequim for thirty-two years having been appointed to the post on November 16, 1936.

How many more years she served in that position I do not know. Perhaps she reached forty years in that post before retiring.

It made her one of the most visible people in our little town, presiding over the cramped Post Office next door to Sequim Drugs on Washington Avenue. She drove to the Post

Office from her charming cottage in downtown Sequim every day in an Isetta, a tiny little Italian single cylinder vehicle.

Doubtless she was appointed postmaster as a reward for her outspoken advocacy of President Franklin Roosevelt's reelection in 1936. The *Evening News* of November 7, 1936 reports that Mrs. Brown, at that time serving as Sequim City Clerk, had made bets with thirty or more of her Republican friends that Roosevelt would win.

Too cash-strapped to cover their bets in currency, these Republicans, most of them farmers, wagered their cabbage, carrots, beets, potatoes, milk and cream, and a smoked ham shank or two betting on Republican, Alf Landon. If she could collect her winnings, Mrs. Brown would provide a wholesome diet for herself and her children, that winter, the *Evening News* reported.

Often, she posted notices in the local media like this one in the June 10, 1965 *Evening News*: "Will the party who dropped the live rat in our street mail box last week come forth, claim his property, pay the cost of upkeep and also the fee for the cardiograph it necessitated for the postmaster."

I knew Mary Brown in my childhood and youth. She was a tall, handsome, woman with shrewd, intelligent eyes. She was a native of County Cork, Ireland, and conversed with a droll, witty, Irish accent. She was turning gray when I knew her but there was a tinge in her hair that suggested that as a young woman she had been a flaming redhead with a fiery temper to go with it.

Either my brothers, sisters or I went to the Post Office every afternoon on our way home from school to pick up our mail in one of the little postal boxes with the combination locks in the lobby. There would be Mrs. Brown or one of the clerks to hand us packages too big to fit in our mail box.

We had moved here in 1948 after buying the Steve Tripp farm up on Bell Hill. My father had been blacklisted, a victim of Joe McCarthy repression. Unable to find work elsewhere, my folks decided to try farming.

They didn't subscribe to many periodicals but among them was *China Reconstructs*, a publication that covered—and celebrated—the victory of the Chinese communists in 1949. The magazine was on the Attorney General's list of "subversive" literature. My Mom or Dad were required to go into Sequim and sign a waiver that they wanted to receive this seditious publication in our home.

Mary Brown made no secret of her outrage that she was required to enforce this federal Cold War censorship. Even though she was committed to the democratic rights of free speech and privacy, Mary Brown and the others in the Post Office surely observed unusual mail coming from our home and addressed to it. There were the post cards addressed to President Eisenhower that my entire family filled out one evening as we sat around the dining room table. Those post cards pleaded for clemency for Ethel and Julius Rosenberg, the similar post cards asking that Willy McGee not be executed. There was the *National Guardian* and the *People's World* both leftwing newsweeklys opposed to the Korean War and upholding union rights. They came in the mail wrapped against prying eyes but some were ripped open, spilling the truth for all to see.

In the years that followed, Mrs. Brown befriended my parents. She came to dinner at our home. She was a "mover and shaker" in a group called the World Affairs Discussion Group (WADG) that met at the Clyde Rhodefor Library. WADG was closely linked to the U.S. State Department and sponsored a series called *Great Decisions*. One of the topics was "Should the U.S. Open Trade with Red China?"

Mary Brown invited my parents to participate in the WADG. She knew my father was a Rhodes Scholar, an economist who had served in the Treasury Department, who wrote speeches on monetary affairs for New York Senator Robert Wagner. He had served as a researcher for the Office of Strategic Services (OSS) during World War II.

I was there at the discussion that evening, listening as prominent Cold War elements in the community raved against any form of recognition of the People's Republic of China.

"Well," said my father quietly, "You certainly don't have Senator Magnuson on your side on this issue. He says—and this is his word—that it is 'stupid' for the U.S. to refuse to recognize China, acting as if 700 million people don't exist. We here in the Pacific Northwest need trade with China. They are a great market for our apples."

The rightwing elements turned ashen white at this flagrant heresy. But Mary Brown's eyes twinkled.

She made a trip home to visit the family she left in County Cork in 1959. She was felled by illness and stayed two weeks in Ireland. Then she traveled to Poland and on to Czechoslovakia where, she visited my uncle and aunt, George and Eleanor Wheeler, who had settled in Prague. Then she traveled on to the Soviet Union where she visited for a week. When she returned home to Sequim she came to dinner to report on her trip and especially her visit with the Prague Wheelers.

Later, Mary Brown flew to Boston to attend the graduation of her granddaughter, Kimba Wood, from Harvard Law School. Wood is now a highly respected U.S. Federal Judge for the District Court of New York State. President Bill Clinton nominated her in 1993 to serve as his Attorney General. She stepped down in the "Nannygate" affair when her child care employee was found to be an undocumented immigrant.

Mary Brown was the living embodiment of the "fighting Irish," a "never give up, never give in" spirit of independence and progressivism. No wonder the business community of Sequim elected her as the first woman President of the Sequim Chamber of Commerce. They were Democrats, Republicans, and independents who knew a quality candidate when they saw one and voted for her.

Mary Brown visits us for dinner. Don Wheeler carves the roast, on left, Marion and Susan Wheeler, on right, Mary Brown and Nat Wheeler photo by Mary Lukes Wheeler.

Four Crazy Teens Nearly Make It to the Lighthouse

Published in the *Ditchwalker*

SEQUIM—We all need a spiritual destination for at least one pilgrimage in our lifetime. It might be Canterbury, St. Peters, Mecca, the Mormon Tabernacle.

The Dungeness Lighthouse was my spiritual destination. Often I rode my bicycle down and sat on a driftwood log on the beach gazing out across Dungeness Bay at the lighthouse. Since 1857 its Fresnel light has been warning sailors away from the treacherous shores of the Strait of Juan de Fuca. It is a symbol of wisdom and enlightenment in Clallam County.

One Friday afternoon in the spring of 1956, my school chum, Chuck Lewis, and I were retrieving books from our lockers in the hallway of Sequim High School.

"Hey, Tim," Chuck said, "want to go out to the lighthouse Sunday?"

"I don't think there would be time enough, Chuck. I have to milk the cows morning and evening."

"So do I," Chuck replied. "That's why I came up with an idea: We'll use my dad's tractor. We can hook up our two-wheel wagon. You and Don Kirner and Larry Grant can ride in the wagon. We can drive out and back in four hours in time for the evening milking."

I milked the cows in high excitement that Sunday morning. I rode my bike over to the Lewis farm. Don and Larry were already there. We climbed aboard.

All went well. We arrived at the bluff and rolled down the dirt road to sea level. The Coast Guard, keepers of the lighthouse in those days, had cut through the driftwood logs so they could drive back and forth in their jeep with supplies for the lighthouse. We trundled through that opening onto the shore of the spit facing the Strait.

The tide was out and the beach was wide and sandy. We turned east and tooled along. We passed sweating hikers and felt a little superior at our leisurely mode of transportation. A lovely breeze cooled my brow and I lay back with sun shining on my face. "This is really living!" I said to myself.

Two of the driftwood logs projected more or less straight out from the jumbled line of driftwood and Chuck had to turn down toward the waterline to get around the end of those logs. Otherwise, it was full speed ahead, nearer and nearer to the lighthouse in the distance.

We heard a "beep-beep" behind us. I turned. There was the Coast Guard jeep gaining on us. Three Guardsmen were in the jeep packed with groceries. They pulled up beside us. "Good afternoon," the Guardsmen in the passenger seat greeted us.

"I hope you guys brought sleeping bags. The tide is coming in. In an hour it is going to be high tide. No beach. No tractors."

Our jaws dropped. We were less than 100 yards from the base of the lighthouse. Without a word Chuck turned the tractor around.

He headed back toward the base of the spit at full throttle.

The tide was coming in fast. Within a mile, the waves were rolling in and breaking on the right wheels of the tractor, front and rear.

There ahead of us was the first of the two logs pointing north down the beach, the surf breaking over the top of the log. Chuck waited for a wave to break. Then as the sea water retreated, he raced ahead, turning down toward the end of the log. But another wave crashed over the wheels. The tractor engine coughed, sputtered, nearly died. Then it coughed again and roared back to life. Chuck made it around that log.

Half a mile further down the beach was the second log. By now, the tide was so far in that the end of the log was under water. Chuck brought the tractor to a stop and turned to us.

"I'm going to gun the tractor and try to roll over the log. Hold on!"

We raced toward that log at top speed. The front wheels of the tractor bounced over the log. The rear wheels slammed into the log. The tractor went airborne. And the wagon also went airborne and so did we. We came crashing down onto the bed of the wagon.

We had made it, bruised in body and soul. Yet the surf was still rolling higher and we had a mile more to go. By the time we reached the base of the spit, the water was a foot high on the right side of the tractor. We all had our hearts in our mouths.

We had made a narrow escape. If that engine had died, seawater would have engulfed the tractor. It would have joined a long line of shipwrecks on the Dungeness Spit.

The axle of the wagon was so badly bent that we limped back to the Lewis farm at half speed. Chuck arrived just in time for evening milking. Poor Chuck had to deal, as well, with the fury of his father at this crazed teen-age adventure.

I rode my bike home, arriving late but safe, for the evening milking.

That was the closest I ever got to the Dungeness Lighthouse. Fifty-six years later, it is still flashing its light at me, beckoning me to try again.

Honor at Sequim High
People's World Online December 1, 2015

SEQUIM—I was a very big frog in a small pond at Sequim High School in 1958. I was on the "honor roll" and a member of the National Honor Society with high though not perfect grades.

I won a Hallmark Gold Medal for my watercolor still life painted in Mrs. Dorcas Taylor's art class. That watercolor was displayed in the window of Frederick & Nelson department store in Seattle along with many other lovely pieces of art by other young artists.

I was a "Thespian" and played leading roles in the two plays we put on in those years, *Our Hearts Were Young and Gay* and *The Night of January 16.*

In the latter play I was "Flint," the prosecutor assigned to convict and send to prison the young woman accused of murdering her lover—played in our production by my classmate Linda Matriotti. The audience served as the jury. I was as flinty and nasty as they come. But the jury acquitted Miss Karen Andre played so bewitchingly by Linda.

I also played center and defensive linebacker on the Sequim Wolves football team that lost more than it won.

I was such a big man on campus I decided to run for Student Council Treasurer although more than once I added two and two and came up with five.

My greatest enthusiast---actually my de facto campaign manager---was my younger sister, Susan, who conceived my campaign slogan: "Dave Beck can Go to Heck."

Dave Beck was the notoriously corrupt President of the Teamsters union, in the Pacific Northwest, ultimately removed from office. We made home-made lapel badges with that slogan and many in school were wearing them.

I won in a landslide.

I went to the Principal's office and asked the secretary, Mrs. Logan, if I could inspect the books. She was astonished.

AWARD PICTURE — Doreen Taylor, Sequim art teacher and Tim Wheeler have a second look at her award winning watercolor.

Sequim Art Student's Watercolor Picture Wins Award in State Wide Competition

By ESTHER WEBSTER
Student awards in athletics and other fields are frequent. We seldom hear of an award in the arts . . . particularly in the fine arts.

own painting. Her pictures have won recognition in many parts of the state.
Beginning May 7 the work of Mrs. Taylor's Sequim High School students will be displayed at the KONP gallery.

"You actually want to do the bookkeeping?"

"That's what the student body elected me to do," I replied.

"You are the first Student Council treasurer who has ever proposed to keep the books. I always do that," Mrs. Logan said. "I'll show you how to do it."

She took a big ledger book off the shelf behind her. I sat down at a table and she sat beside me. Step by step she told my how to make entries, add and subtract sub-totals and then add up the grand totals.

I was able to perform this task with the help of the office adding machine. On this wondrous device, two and two always came out four. The Sequim High School student body treasury had a munificent balance of a few hundred dollars occasionally swelling to a thousand dollars depending on how many bake sales and car washes we organized.

With many hours of toil, I was able to make the books balance.

Then one day, I opened the books and scanned over the columns and received the shock of my life. A check had been written to buy new football uniforms and the amount subtracted from the total without consulting me or the Student Council.

I then opened the check book. Sure enough, there was the check stub proving that several hundred dollars had been spent to buy football uniforms.

"Mrs. Logan," I said. "Look at this debit from our account. Who did that? On whose authority?"

Mrs. Logan went deathly pale and stood as if frozen to the spot where she was standing, unable to speak.

Leonard Beil was the principal and he happened to be in his office. I knocked on the door. He invited me in.

I took the ledger book and check book in and showed him the unauthorized expenditure.

"Do you know who did this?"

"I did," he replied.

"You had no right. It is not your money," I blurted. "That money could not be spent without it being discussed and approved by the Student Council and by me."

Mr. Beil turned beet red. He defended himself as best he could, citing the shabby condition of the teams' uniforms—something I knew from first-hand experience since I suited up in one of those sorry uniforms myself.

Somehow, the issue was resolved without it becoming a scandal.

A few days later, I was removed from the National Honor Society. For what? Defending the fiscal integrity of the books I was assigned to balance?

Nor was I the only member of my family to suffer retribution for crimes not committed.

My sister, Susan Elizabeth, had perfect grades and was on her way to be valedictorian of her class in 1960. But when it came Susan's turn, the rules were changed. The valedictorian would be chosen on the basis not only of the highest grade point average but also on the basis of extra-curricular activities.

We all knew the meaning of this dirty trick. The powers-that-be feared what Susan might say in her valedictory address. She was not only a brilliant student, she was a staunch progressive.

I can hear Susan delivering her valedictory now: That it is the task of our generation to ban nuclear testing and nuclear weapons; that we must work to end the Cold War and uphold peaceful coexistence. That we must end segregation and uphold race and gender equality; that workers must enjoy union organizing rights and living wages. That every human being must be assured quality cradle-to-grave health care. That all youth must be guaranteed quality education, jobs, a decent future.

I hear her calling for socialism as humanity's singing tomorrow.

For the ruling powers of Sequim High, these were ideas the people must never hear.

Susan and Her Mare, Trumpet

When I returned home from my first year in college in the spring of 1959, everything seemed changed here in the Sequim-Dungeness Valley. My sister Susan seemed to sum it up.

She was still just a young girl when I left for Amherst. When I came home, she was a vivacious, poised young woman—like a butterfly emerging from its cocoon. Susan received straight "As" at Sequim High School and had a reputation as a quiet, studious, no-nonsense person. But when she rode horseback she was transformed, filled with high spirits, wit, and joy. You might mistake her quiet, studious, ways for timidity. She was as bold as the horse she rode.

I stepped out on the front porch of our house—the old Bell house up on Bell Hill—one morning a day or so after I had returned. I heard the faint drumbeat of a horse's hooves far to

the east up Miller Road. I stared into the morning light. I could see the horse galloping along the road toward me. It was Susan riding bareback on her mare, Trumpet. Susan rode up into the front yard. Trumpet's nostrils were flared. Her eyes flashed with a wild, barely controlled fire. She snorted and pranced as they sidled up into our front yard.

Trumpet, a bay, was renowned as the fastest horse in Clallam County. She was a Quarter-horse. Everything about her was bred for sudden, explosive speed, her slim ankles, her tapered legs, her massive shoulders and haunches, the handsome, finally chiseled features of her head and face. She never walked. It was always a sidewise prance. A rider had to keep the reins pulled back tight or she was gone with the wind.

Susan slid from Trumpet. "Good morning," she said.

"She is magnificent. Do you take her for a ride every morning?" I asked.

"As often as I can. I can't ride as often as I would like during the school year."

"Do you mind if I take her for a spin?"

"Not at all. Be my guest."

She handed me the reins and I led Trumpet over to the split rail fence, stepped up on a rail and swung my leg over the mare's back.

I turned her back out toward Miller Road and touched her sides with my heels.

In an instant, Trumpet's hindquarters went down and I felt the mighty muscles of her body churning. She shot forward, already at a dead-run. My heart was in my mouth. There was no saddle, no horn, nothing to hold on to. All I had was the reins and her mane to keep me attached to this speeding equine missile.

She was racing full-throttle due east, spewing gravel in all directions and I believed seeking with every sinew of her being to spew me as well from her back. She was streaking along the top of our forty acres divided into three pastures and at the bottom a large field of hay. All the pasture gates were closed except the gate to the far pasture. I knew it was open....and so did Trumpet.

There was a battle of wits going on between Trumpet and me. I was trying to anticipate what she would do. I thought to myself: When she gets to that open gate of the far pasture, she is going to turn left at a dead run.

That is exactly what she did. Without slowing, she swerved left though the open gate. I managed, somehow, not to be thrown, clinging with as much pressure as I could exert with my knees, clinging with my right hand to her mane.

Now she was racing down the far pasture. At the bottom of the pasture, the ground fell steeply away, not a cliff, but close enough. If she were to run over that drop-off, she was certain to fall, break a leg, roll and kill me!

What could I do to stop her? In desperation, I dropped the right rein, grasped the left rein with both hands and pulled with all my might. Her head swung around against my knee. She came to a stop.

I slid off, quaking in sheer terror. My knees trembled like jelly. But I was also enraged. I cursed her, jerking the reins down over and over, surely inflicting pain on her tender mouth.

That was my closest brush with death. I led her up to Miller Road and back down toward the house. Susan had watched this drama and was hurrying out to rescue me. A few minutes later, Susan took Trumpet by the reins, found a rail fence and mounted her.

It was as if nothing had happened. Trumpet pranced away up the road. Susan touched her heels to Trumpet's sides and Trumpet broke into a canter and then into an easy gallop. The horse and rider were like one.

I shook my head. "That mare is a feminist," I said to myself. "She will not accept any man riding on her back. No wonder Susan and Trumpet are so eye-to-eye."

About a year later, Susan decided to have Trumpet bred. She arranged for the owner of an Appaloosa stallion to bring his horse and leave it in the corral with Trumpet. She came in heat. When the poor little Appaloosa tried to do his duty, Trumpet went wild, her hooves flying in all directions. When the Appaloosa tried to approach her from the rear, Trumpet hammered his chest with both her hind hooves. The air was filled with his shrieks of pain. And Trumpet too was screeching out her protests. I listened to this loud outcry against the injustice of procreation. My heart filled with pity for the young stallion. "I feel your pain," I said out loud.

Yet somehow, he completed his mission. Trumpet was bred and at the end of her gestation, she gave birth to a lovely little Appaloosa colt with the sprinkling of white markings on his rump like bright, shining stars. Susan named him "Brandywine" and he was known thereafter as "Brandy."

And while Trumpet may have held the male gender of all species in contempt, she made an exception of Brandy. She was a loving mother and he grew into a handsome horse that any Nez Perce would have recognized and admired.

75 Hour Bus Ride to Freedom
People's Weekly World August 23, 2003

SEQUIM, WASHINGTON—Wayne Ostlund, a member of the International Association of Machinists (IAM), was one of tens of thousands of trade union members who traveled to Washington, D.C., for the August 28, 1963 March on Washington for Jobs and Freedom.

He may have traveled the greatest distance. Ostlund then was a diesel locomotive mechanic at the Milwaukee Railroad roundhouse in Port Angeles, Washington. He was one of two delegates sent by an ad hoc committee on the Olympic Peninsula initiated by the Communist Party of Clallam County. The other delegate was Marion Melissa Wheeler, a sophomore at Sequim High School.

Wayne Ostlund, photo courtesy of his family.

The committee crisscrossed the county raising more than $600 in contributions from loggers, mill workers, farmers, teachers and a librarian to cover the costs of sending them to the demonstration.

Ostlund traveled by airplane, arriving two days early. He was assigned to assemble signs and other chores to get ready for the march.

Wheeler joined thirty-nine others on a chartered Greyhound bus in Portland, Oregon, for the seventy-five-hour cross country marathon to the nation's capital. It was exhausting but she remembers with special fondness how the NAACP in Cheyenne, Wyoming, organized a soul food feast for the busload of weary travelers.

The residents of the capital provided each of them a bed. They marched the next day, listened to King's immortal "I have a dream" speech and boarded the bus for the grueling seventy-five-hour ride home.

Both delegates still live in this idyllic valley in the rain shadow of the Olympic Mountains. In a joint interview at

Ostlund's home on Lost Mountain Road, they told the World the march changed their lives forever.

"It was one of the most impressive experiences of my life," Ostlund told the *World*. "To see the dedication and spirit of so many people was quite amazing. I can still remember clearly Dr. King's speech. Certainly it was the defining moment of the demonstration."

He pointed out that the media leaves out King's thunderous indictment of the racist oppressors with their "promissory note" marked "insufficient funds" and his sharp rebuttal of gradualism in the struggle for equality. Ostlund said his union was quite inactive at that time. But he remembers his discussions with African American trade unionists as they marched together. It impressed upon him the imperative need for a strong alliance of organized labor and people of color as the bedrock of progressive change in America.

Marion Melissa Wheeler (Honeybee) from an original pencil sketch by Seattle artist, Cecelia Corr

In August 1993, Ostlund traveled again to Washington for the 30th anniversary of the march when once again the labor movement and civil rights movement filled the streets of the capital to demand jobs and freedom. Wheeler, who now goes by her married name, Burns, added, "The march was a watershed event for me. It was so uplifting to see 250,000 people marching who thought the way I did." Both expressed the view that the demonstration proved it was possible to win a majority to support our view that segregation is wrong and must be ended.

After she returned home and the new school year began, her principal said to her one day, "Marion, I can't understand why you would want to go to that march. You're not Black." She replied, "If you don't understand why I went, there's probably nothing I can say that would explain it to you, but I wanted to be a part of history." Asked what he sees as the most urgent task for today, Ostlund replied, "The essential thing now is to organize an effective movement to get Bush and his crowd out of the White House. We need to remove that whole element of American capitalism that wants to dominate the world. The election in 2004 is about as urgent as an election can be."

Burns interjected, "Take his attack on affirmative action. Everyone has gained because of affirmative action but he attacks it as reverse discrimination. Who made the greatest gains under affirmative action? Women."

Said Ostlund, "They use racism to hold everyone back. It's always been true. Their strategy is divide and conquer."

Bush was riding high in the polls but now he is trending down, he added. He cited the growing opposition to both Bush's economic policies and his pre-emptive war on Iraq. "Unless they can pull a rabbit out of the hat, I think Bush is in trouble," he said. "Their biggest rabbit trick would be another war."

Yet even here in this farthest northwest corner of the "lower 48" the antiwar movement is surging. "We had 350 people turn out for a demonstration against war on Iraq last February," said Ostlund. "That's pretty good for Port Angeles."

Topping the Tallest Tree

One day in 1953 Fred Gaboury invited me to come to work with him so I could witness first hand his skill in rigging a spar tree high in the foothills of the Olympic Mountains in the West End of Clallam County.

I eagerly accepted. I was only thirteen at the time but Fred may have seen in me a future choker-setter, faller, or even a topper like him. Fred had rugged good looks. He had broad shoulders, snapping blue eyes and wavy golden hair. Movie star handsome, he should have been a heartthrob. Yet his speech was a steady stream of unprintable four-letter words.

Somehow, Fred didn't remind me of Gary Cooper after I had heard him utter a stream of profanity.

The night before the long trip out to the West End of Clallam County, I spent the night at Fred and Betty Gaboury's house. Fred woke me up at 4:30 a.m. and fed me a breakfast of flapjacks soaked in butter and syrup. In his haste, he burned the flapjacks, badly. Fred was always in a hurry.

In the pitch dark, we boarded the Weyerhaeuser crew bus in Port Angeles along with fifteen or twenty other loggers. They came on to the bus quietly, still groggy in the morning chill. They were dressed in their tin hats, flannel shirts and jeans chopped off just below the knees. The jeans were held up by wide, brightly colored galluses. They wore high caulk boots bristling with spikes from the soles and heels to give them extra footing in the slippery underbrush on the deadly mountainsides.

The crew bus roared out at breakneck speed, twisting along Highway 101 around Lake Crescent. About twenty miles west of the lake, we made a left turn onto a gravel road that soon turned into a dirt track that wound its way up the mountainside. The crew bus pitched wildly as it toiled its way up the muddy track. The crew snored peacefully.

Soon we pulled into a staging area that had been cleared in the deep forest. We were so high on the mountain we could look out to the east. Dawn was breaking over the Strait of Juan de Fuca. Mount Baker gleamed like a pink strawberry sundae in the morning sun. The San Juan Islands lay darkly in the glittering waters of the Salish Sea.

Sitting in the staging area was an old "donkey" engine with a heavy steel cable for pulling the logs off the mountainside.

Standing alone beside the donkey was a Douglas fir nearly 200 feet high. It would serve as the spar tree once Fred had climbed and rigged it. He strapped the spikes onto the inside ankles of his boots, whipped the steel-core lifeline around the tree and secured it to the belt around his middle. He also secured a rope to his belt

Then he pushed his tin hat back from his brow and began to walk his way up the tree, stopping every few steps to whip the lifeline higher on the tree trunk. When he reached the first branch, he pulled up a chain saw. Hanging in midair, he pulled on the starter cord until the saw sputtered into life. He cut off the branch above him, swinging around out of the way, as the thick branch broke away and plunged to the ground.

Higher and higher he climbed, cutting off the limbs as he worked his way up to the tree top. When he was 170-feet up, he cut off the top of the tree. He worked the chain saw around the trunk so it would break cleanly and not split the top of the tree. That was a mishap that could ruin the spar tree and also kill the rigger.

Fred dropped his rope and the crew below tied on a big iron ring. He pulled the ring up and worked it down like a collar around the top of the spar tree. With a wrench, he tightened the ring so it clamped to the trunk of the tree. Next, the ground crew hoisted the giant mainline block, an enormous pulley, up to Fred. He attached that pulley and threaded the mainline cable through it. He also attached the four guy lines to keep the spar tree from swaying.

While he toiled high in the air, the ground crew was also hard at work. The "fallers" were out on the slopes with chainsaws cutting down the trees. The catskinner, a cigarette dangling casually from his lips, was roaring back and forth with his D-9 crawler tractor smoothing out the staging area that the loggers called a "yard." Once he got stuck four feet deep in a pool of quicksand. The giant Cat couldn't move. He jumped off the tractor, unhitched a cable from the huge winch at the back of the Cat, and wound the cable around a nearby stump about six feet in diameter. He jumped back on the Cat and engaged the winch. With a big sucking sound, the winch pulled that Cat, all twenty tons of it, out of the mire.

By now, Fred had completed his task and descended with breathtaking speed to the yard. The donkey belched and roared, the mainline cable snaking the logs off the steep slopes and dragging them into the yard. A loader was picking up the logs, one by one, and loading them on the back of the first of several log trucks idling in the yard.

Years later, I watched Fred Gaboury win first prize in the high climbing contest during the logging show at the Sequim Irrigation Festival. He left the other contestants in the dust, racing up the 100-foot tree, his spurs flashing, the steel-core lifeline slapping as he raced up the spar tree and then slid back down. For those who remember, Fred joined the staff of the *People's World* in New York City when I was editor in the 1990s. He chose "Hy Climber" as his byline and he served as our most able labor editor. I will always remember him with his Paul Bunyan hands pounding away on his desktop computer with fingers so thick he struggled to hit the right keys.

All of us loved Fred for his hard driving, if too profane, approach to the class struggle. He was out of the office interviewing workers on their picket lines. He got to know top leaders like AFL-CIO President John Sweeney and AFSCME leaders Gerald McEntee and Bill Lucy. He was on a first

Fred Gaboury on right. Photo courtesy of *People's World*

name basis with all these leaders. They respected Fred, knowing he had "paid his dues."

Fred's display of courage and skill that day gave me a special appreciation of workers in basic industry. They need a fighting union—and a political party—of their own to defend their interests toiling in the nation's most dangerous industries.

The fight to save workers' lives is not limited to on-the-job safety. Fred's mother, Vivian Gaboury, with a lot of help from her husband, her son, and the Communist Party of Clallam County worked tirelessly from one end of the county to the other lining up the IWA, the ILWU, the Teamsters, the

Grange, and a score more mass organizations to demand construction of a full-service hospital in Port Angeles. It is now called the Olympic Medical Center. Before construction of that hospital, plenty of loggers and millworkers died because no emergency medical care was available for them. OMC opened in 1951.

Wayne Ostlund, a locomotive mechanic, a member of the International Association of Machinists, who worked out of the Milwaukee Saint Paul roundhouse in Port Angeles put it succinctly: "They might just as well call it the 'Vivian Gaboury Memorial Hospital.' If it hadn't been for Vivian there wouldn't have been a hospital in Port Angeles."

There is no plaque on the hospital honoring her or any other labor movement activist paying tribute to labor's role in its construction.

Fred Booth's Mighty Kick
Read aloud at Rainshadow Café May 24, 2012

Of all the dairymen who toiled to make ends meet on the Sequim prairie in the 1950's, none worked harder than Fred Booth. He and his wife owned a little farm on the outskirts of Sequim with a herd of twenty-five registered Jersey cows. The Booths defied the laws of capitalism by refusing to get bigger. They never had more and never had fewer than twenty-five cows even as their neighbors either went broke or expanded. The bigger farmers gobbled up the land and dairy herds of their neighbors in a big-fish-eat-the-little fish race to survive.

It meant that Fred had to work at jobs off his farm to bring in the income necessary to stay afloat. He worked as one of the school bus drivers for the Sequim consolidated schools, finishing the morning milking in time to clean up and head into town, only a stone's throw away, to drive the bus around the valley picking up the school children waiting by the side of the road. He repeated the process in reverse every afternoon, dropping off the last kid and racing back in time to milk the cows in the evening.

Fred also did custom work for his neighbors with his Ford tractor mower and baler. We hired him several times to mow and bale our hay. I remember him as a rail-thin man, a rather grouchy, irascible type.

The apple of Fred Booth's eye was his lovely sleek brown Jersey cows with their enormous doe-like eyes. His herd was among the most fabulously productive in the valley, many of the cows winning top honors with the Dairy Herd Improvement Association. The DHIA honored Fred with a banquet at the McLeay Grange Hall in 1988. He died that same year at age 74. For decades, the Booth dairy herd browsing peacefully on the lush clover in his irrigated pastures north of Sequim was a living icon of the valley.

Fred was up and began milking his cows before sunrise. One morning, he brought the cows into his milking parlor, stanchioned them, and began preparing for the milking. Something in the grain room spooked the cows who lunged back against the stanchions. It happened over and over. Fred cursed under his breath. Probably some stray cat, he muttered to himself.

But the disturbance ended and Fred went on with the milking, completing the task on schedule. Yet that evening it happened again. And the next morning for a third time. Evening milking came. Once again, the stray cat spooked the cows, with some of them slamming back against the stanchions to escape whatever was frightening them.

The next morning, he was just preparing to put the milking machine on Flossie when she lunged back, knocking the milking machine into the gutter.

By now, Fred was seething with rage. Silently, he retrieved the milking machine and set it down out of the way. He tiptoed around the end of the stanchions and opened the door into the grain room. He would not turn on the grain room light. It would alert the damnable intruder, giving it time to escape.

Fred crept down the line in front of the stanchioned cows. All of them had stopped chewing their cuds and were watching with their huge eyes, their ears all pointed forward, to see what would happen next. Fred peered into the darkness. Sure enough, there was a set of glowing eyes, staring back at him. He moved up quickly and swung his leg forward, fetching the accursed cat a rattling good kick. He could feel the feline ribs collapse from the force of his kick. A feeling of well-being spread through Fred. Revenge at last!

The problem was it was not a feline. It was a skunk. It turned its hind end, lifted its tail and sprayed Fred from the top of his striped dairyman's cap to the point of his rubber boots. Then the skunk lumbered off into the darkness leaving Fred standing there, dripping.

Fred retreated to the house. But his aroma preceded him. His wife was awake when he got to the front door and would not let him in. She handed him a change of clothes and told him to take a bath in the milk house.

The glacial waters from the milk house hose removed only the top layer of the perfume leaving him freezing cold and still redolent.

Two hours later, at 7:45 a.m., Fred was at the wheel of his yellow school bus. He would drive up to a group of children, stop and open the bus doors. The children would recoil at the blast of perfumed air and more than one exclaimed, "Pee-you!"

"Get on the bus, sit down, and shut up," Fred would snap.

The story went like wildfire through the ranks of all the children in the school and of course every child took the story home. It became part of the folklore of the Sequim-Dungeness Valley. Mention the name Fred Booth to anyone who grew up in Sequim and he or she will remember the day of Fred Booth's mighty kick.

I think about Fred Booth every time I drive north on Sequim-Dungeness Way and pass the modest little two story red ranch house just outside town where he and his wife lived. The house is abandoned now, the paint peeling. The barn is still standing but it is sagging. In due time, it will collapse. A for sale sign is posted on the rusting barbed wire fence. Long gone is the herd of Jerseys with the huge soulful eyes that Fred Booth milked twice a day for as long as he lived. A way of life is gone from the valley.

Remembering a Town Wiped from the Map
People's World June 2, 2006

<u>Book Review:</u> *Orchards of Eden: White Bluffs on the Columbia*, 1907-1943, By Nancy Mendenhall. Far Eastern Press, Seattle. 469 pages. paperback. $23.95

Nancy Mendenhall photo courtesy of Nancy Mendenhall

Nancy Mendenhall's story begins in 1907 with the decision of her grandparents (and mine) to flee Tacoma's smog to start a fruit farm irrigated with water pumped from the Columbia River in eastern Washington.

Frank M. Wheeler was a union bricklayer and his wife, Jeanie, was a schoolteacher. Frank had picked up a land speculator brochure offering cheap land. Soon the young couple moved into a tent house on their five acre farm near the little town of White Bluffs on the Hanford Reach of the Columbia. It was to be their home for thirty-six years. Mendenhall likens the enterprise to a mirage, always shimmering just out of reach across the desert.

Frank Wheeler was forced to travel to construction sites as far as New York City, toiling for meager wages, living in boarding houses and sending home most of what he earned. Jeanie worked in fruit packing sheds. "Mater commonly packed 100 boxes in a ten hour day, or 11,300 apples, for a wage of $7," writes her eldest son, George Shaw Wheeler. Then she went home to cook for her six children and tend her own orchard. This off-farm income kept the farm afloat.

Mendenhall, who resides in Nome, Alaska, based her book on family correspondence and interviews with the Wheeler children and grandchildren, as well as her own memories of summers amid those fruit laden boughs in White Bluffs.

The book is illustrated with many pages of archival photos.

She writes sympathetically of the people's struggle to build a viable and civilized rural community. Political toleration seems to have guided the project. The Wheelers were socialists, subscribers to the "Appeal to Reason." Jeanie became a member of the Board of Elections of White Bluffs representing the Socialist Party.

A tiny but energetic woman, she and her mother, Jane Shaw, helped establish the Parent Teacher Association, the Well Baby Clinic, and the public library in the town. How they found the time after their dawn-to-dark toil is a mystery. They were also stalwarts in their church.

This grassroots dynamism made it difficult to isolate the Wheeler family even during the World War I "Red Scare." Socialist leader, Eugene Victor Debs, was imprisoned for his anti-war stand and Attorney General Mitchell Palmer launched a nationwide witch-hunt. In Washington State IWW members were lynched in the infamous Centralia massacre.

Yet the Wheelers, outspoken war opponents, seemed to escape relatively unscathed. They were anti-racists, opposing the infamous Oriental Exclusion Act and befriending the Wanapum Indians who came through White Bluffs each spring on their way to Yakima from their village on the east bank of the river. Frank Wheeler often presented them with boxes of succulent apples and peaches

The F.M. Wheeler family at White Bluffs, Washington photo courtesy of Wheeler family

when they returned home in the fall.

Members of the Grange, they fought for programs that benefited rural America such as full parity prices for farm commodities. Whether Republican, Democrat, or Socialist, every farmer in the valley was caught by what Mendenhall calls the "three-headed beast," the railroads, power companies, and "market" that had the small producers at their mercy. They set smudge pots to ward off late frosts and sprayed arsenic to kill the coddling moths and other infestations.

The book describes vividly an era when being an outspoken socialist or communist was accepted by neighbors and co-workers as "normal," a spirit of democracy that seems to be regaining ground in our crisis wracked country.

Mendenhall writes that Wheeler family members were drawn deeper into the struggles against mass unemployment and poverty and the rising menace of fascism during the Great Depression. Some joined the Communist Party and Young Communist League.

Mendenhall ends her book in 1943 with the mass eviction of the farm families from White Bluffs and Hanford to make way for the Hanford Nuclear Reservation where plutonium was enriched for the bomb that destroyed Nagasaki.

Mendenhall writes that the eviction notices arrived like a bolt from the blue just as the war was pushing farm prices higher and a mild spring had promised bumper crops. Since the Manhattan Project was top secret, no one had a clue as to why their land was being confiscated. Families were given sixty days to clear out. The U.S. Army sent Army trucks to carry family belongings to wherever the evictees were moving, one truckload per family. A tragic high point, or low point, of Mendenhall's book was Bapa, as we called our grandfather, forced to ride on top of the loaded truck across frigid Snoqualmie pass to western Washington because there was no room in the cab for him. The orchards and homes of the settlers were bulldozed, their "Eden" on the Columbia transformed into a factory of nuclear death that is now the nation's most lethal radioactive waste zone.

Bapa mourned the loss of his beloved orchards for the rest of his life. But Nana, my grandma, lived to 104 and was honored as a "pioneer" during a special session of the Washington State legislature which she attended.

This book dramatizes a great American tragedy. Millions of men and women toiled in rural America and succeeded in realizing their dreams of a productive, rewarding life for themselves and their children only to be ruined by the iron law of capitalist profits. In my grandparent's case, their dream went up, literally, in a mushroom cloud.

Tim - thank you for your beautiful story about Nancy Mendenhall keep on Stay well old Pete

Beacon NY 12508

Note from Pete Seeger to Tim Wheeler

[3]

COLLEGE DAYS

Swinging Birches in Amherst

Johnson Chapel at Amherst College. Photo courtesy of photographer, Qin Zhi Lau.

I never would have made it through Amherst College without the help of Classics Professor, John Moore, who taught a humanities course I excelled in. I was flunking the required calculus and physics course and teetered on the brink of flunking out altogether. But when I went into Professor Moore's classroom, I was in my element. Dr. Moore sat with his legs crossed on top of a battered old desk in front of us and led us through the wonders of Plato's Symposium, Thucydides' Peloponnesian Wars, Tolstoy's War & Peace, and other masterpieces of world literature. He was like Socrates and his method was Socratic. We were expected to speak and I did.

A host of stories swirled around Moore. He had been a cryptographer during World War II and had broken several codes of the Nazis. It was considered a brilliant breakthrough that helped the Allies defeat Hitler. But the pressure had been so great he had suffered a breakdown, a stroke of some sort, so he walked in an awkward, ungainly stride. There was nothing awkward or ungainly about his mind or his teaching. What I remember most is his humanity, his kindness, his sensitivity to a youth pining for home 3,000 miles away. That was me.

It was a men's college in those days and I missed the companionship of women in my classrooms. My folks were dirt poor dairy farmers. I never could have afforded Amherst College without the full scholarship they awarded me. Back in those bad old days, that totaled the munificent sum of $1,850 for tuition, room and board. Yet there were still expenses: books, spending money, clothes, and travel from Amherst back to our farm on the Olympic Peninsula.

The remoteness of my home was a cause for hilarity in my freshmen English Class. Professor Cameron began the first day by going around the room asking each of us where we came from. One after another my classmates announced "Boston" "New York City" "Philadelphia" "Chicago." He called on me and I replied, "Sequim." There was a stir and a few giggles. "Sequim," said Professor Cameron. "Where is Sequim?"

"It's midway between Pysht and Blyn," I replied.

Amherst was a picturesque college town built around the town common with quaint shops like A.J. Hastings, a bookstore where I went with my chums to buy maple candies and Hava-Tampa cigars after a hard afternoon of homework.

In October, Amherst and the Pelham Hills to the north were flaming red, orange and yellow with autumn foliage. Amherst had been the home to one of America's greatest poets, Emily Dickenson. I often walked by the Dickenson House and admired its simple charm. I became a lifelong lover of her poetry.

The poetic tradition was continued by Robert Frost who often traveled down from New Hampshire's North Country to recite his poetry at the Lord Jeff Inn. A highpoint of my years at Amherst College was going to hear Frost in front of the fireplace in the library of that handsome old inn.

He recited *Birches*, one of his early poems, during one of those sessions.

Afterwards, my fellow freshmen and I were sharing our impressions of Frost and admiring his poetry. "I wonder if it works, if the birches actually do bend down if you climb them, hold on tight, and launch yourself out into space," said one friend.

"Let's go try and see if it works," said another.

So the next day, a dozen of us put on our hiking shoes. We walked along the railroad tracks that ran through Amherst. It was a frosty day in early winter. The leaves had fallen. We crossed the tracks and walked into the woods searching for birch trees. Sure enough, within a half mile or so of campus, we came upon a grove of birch trees. One of us shimmied his way up one of the trees.

Try as he might, he couldn't get the birch to cooperate. It remained standing, straight as an arrow, pointed toward heaven. I tried one and also failed. But then one of our classmates noticed one of the birch trees further down a path, already beginning to bend, its roots buried in mud. He waded through to the base of this tree and wrapped his legs around the trunk and pulled himself up. He got eight feet up the birch and it toppled over. We all gave a cheer. The "Bard of the North Country" had been vindicated. We looked around us and there were the trees Frost had written about, white and gray bark, some standing straight, others leaning to left and right across the line of straighter, darker trees. I said Frost's closing sentence of that lovely poem, "One could do worse than be a swinger of birches!"

Singing in the Shower
People's World (Online) March 29, 2016

The acoustics in the communal shower of Stearns Dormitory on the Amherst College campus were superb, like singing in the chapel of an Italian monastery.

One morning in the spring of 1959 I was standing with hot water jetting on my body and singing "Ave Maria," hitting every high heavenly note that Bach and Gounod had written into that sublime song. The notes bounced off the tiles and resounded out the window to the sidewalk below.

I heard a voice outside the shower. "Hello, hello. Excuse me. Do you always sing so high?" He stuck his head around the corner. "I'm sorry to intrude. I was passing by and heard you singing. Is that your normal range?"

"Yes. It is how I sing," I replied.

He was an upper classman, an African American guy. I recognized him as the assistant to the director of the Amherst College Glee Club.

"We need voices like yours in the Johnson Chapel Choir and in the Glee Club too. Would you be interested?"

By now I had turned off the shower and was dripping in all my stark nakedness.

"Yes. I would. Both."

That is how I became a member of the Chapel Choir. In those days, chapel attendance was required. Religious chapel was twice each week and the alternate days a secular program was offered for those brief, as I recall, half hour observances.

I arrived in the wee hours of the morning and stood with the other members of the choir behind the pulpit and sang: "Praise God from whom all blessings flow/Praise Him all creatures here below/Praise Him above, ye heavenly host/Praise Father Son and Holy Ghost. Aaaaamen."

Concert honoring Pete Seeger at Agnew Unitarian-Universalist Fellowship. From left, Tom Schindler, Steve Koehler, and Tim Wheeler. Photo courtesy Steve Vause.

For performing this sunrise service, I satisfied my chapel requirement and was paid sixty cents each morning I showed up. It was modest compensation but I was a dirt poor scholarship student and every penny helped.

Soon I was also recruited into the Amherst College Glee Club. We practiced regularly and even though I could not read music, I memorized my part and sang with lust and much joy in performances both in Amherst and elsewhere in New England. Since Amherst was a men's college, we teamed up with the choir of Pembroke College, an all-women's college in Providence, Rhode Island for some of our most memorable performances.

The town of Amherst was celebrating its bicentennial in 1959. The great composer, Randall Thompson, was commissioned to put music to a collection of Robert Frost's poems to celebrate this event. The result was "Frostiana." We practiced singing these lovely songs for weeks and Randall

Thompson came to Amherst and led us in the premier performance of this great, original work.

My best friend at Amherst, Alec Stewart, a physics major from Ellensburg, Washington, heard me sing in the Chapel Choir. I visited him often in his room in Morrow Dormitory.

"Tim," he said one day. "You have a great voice. Would you like to have my autoharp? It was given to me when I was in high school. I never use it. It's yours if you want it." He pulled from his closet a music instrument case and handed it to me. I opened it. Inside was a shiny black instrument, an Oscar Schmidt autoharp. I was over the moon! I accepted Alec's gift.

I pressed the button for the G-Major chord and strummed my finger across the strings. A heavenly harmony filled the room. A musical instrument that virtually played itself. It was a miracle.

I started teaching myself chord progressions immediately and soon I was singing the folk songs I had grown up singing a Capella. Once in my senior year in High School, I even harmonized when Pete Seeger was singing and playing his banjo at a concert in Port Angeles, Washington. Pete thanked me after the concert for "helping out" in the performance. He became a close friend of the Wheeler family.

I've been singing and strumming my autoharp, especially at family reunions where my father, my wife Joyce, our children, Morgan, Nick, and Susan and many cousins sang loud enough to lift the roof off even the open sky.

Yet never have I sung with so much joy as that day in the shower at Amherst College when I stood in all my naked glory, hitting every high note, as free and innocent as Adam before his expulsion from the garden.

Hitchhiking in Alzada

Back in the day, Amherst College was a fraternity college, the impressive fraternity houses spread out around town. The college circumvented the nasty reality of fraternity snobbery by having a policy of "100% rush." Everyone was admitted to a fraternity. I refused when one of the frat houses invited me to join. A delegation of these fraternity brothers came to meet with me to plead that I reconsider. They seemed genuinely disappointed when I turned them down.

I joined the anti-fraternity fraternity, about 100 independents, many of them foreign exchange students. We tended to sit together in the basement dining room of Valentine Hall. There was Tom Bailey, a tall upper classman from Philadelphia, a math major, a gentle Quaker. Tom tried to tutor me in calculus and failed. He too was an independent and we became friends.

There was the gifted poet, Murat Nemetnejat, from Turkey, who also became a bosom buddy. He was Jewish and spoke English with a strong Turkish accent. He loved the great Irish poet, W.B. Yeats and wandered around campus reciting out loud Sailing to Byzantium. "That is no country for old men/The young in one another's arms. . . ."

When spring vacation arrived in April of 1959, it drove the frigid cold of winter from town. Amherst burst forth in a riot of flowering trees, blooming lilacs, daffodils and tulips. We reeled like inebriates across the blossoming campus.

Young Ho Lee, an exchange student from South Korea, and I were both marooned on campus, unable to fly home for spring vacation. On the spur of the moment, we decided to hitchhike down to Washington D.C. We made it to New York City. I can't remember where we stayed, maybe with my friend Danny Watt and his family on Tremont Avenue in the Bronx. Young and I went to the United Nations. The General Assembly was meeting and we sat in the visitors section listening to UN delegates debate a resolution to condemn racist oppression in South Africa.

The representative from the apartheid regime poured out a litany of self-pity, the hardship sanctions would impose on the affluent white minority. Young sitting beside me, muttered under his breath, "Poor, poor, South Africa. . . . Pity poor South Africa!"

We made it down to Washington D.C. without trouble. The cherry trees were in bloom. The entire region was bathed in the warm breezes of spring. The streets teemed with students like us and many thousands of tourists who strolled the Capitol Mall late into the night. I telephoned my parents close friends, Oscar and Edna Gass. Gass was an economic consultant with a thriving consulting business in D.C.

Like my father, Gass was a graduate of Reed College. Both were brilliant scholars who had won Rhodes Scholarships to Oxford in the 1930s. Oscar greeted me warmly on the phone and invited Young and me to stay with them at their home. The next day, Young and I hitchhiked back to Amherst.

Perhaps it was that magical, springtime escape from Amherst in 1959 that induced me to undertake an even more ambitious adventure one year later, my sophomore year at Amherst. I was falling deeper and deeper into the quagmire of homesickness. As the spring thaw arrived in Amherst that March, I regaled my fellow westerners, Alec Stewart of Ellensburg, Washington, and Hal Smith of Missoula, Montana, with what a great adventure it would be to hitchhike home to Sequim during spring vacation.

Like me, Hal was too poor to afford to fly or take the train home. So he was enthusiastic about my plan and asked if he could come with me. I was delighted. Hal was a "Deans List" student, a brilliant concert pianist, thin as a rail.

We walked over to Northhampton Road on a perfect spring afternoon just after the last of our classes. Like the year before, Amherst was perfumed with the fragrance of lilacs. Each of us had a knapsack with a change of clothing, a razor, toothbrush, and other toiletries for our 3,000 mile odyssey. We stuck our thumbs out. A car pulled over. It was an Air Force enlisted man headed from Westover Air Force Base near Amherst to the Strategic Air Command headquarters just west of Omaha, a total of 1,368 miles! He was driving straight through, all night, stopping only to gas up, for bathroom breaks and meals.

Hal and I settled in and went to sleep, snoring contentedly all night long while our Air Force friend chauffeured us one third of the way home. We thought we had died and gone to heaven.

But as we drove west, the weather turned ugly. The sun was rising as we sped across Iowa. We were driving through a blizzard with blinding snow that reduced visibility to fifty yards. We reached Omaha. The Air Force friend dropped us off at a truck stop on U.S. Highway 30—the Lincoln Highway—at about 7:30 in the morning. We put on every shirt, sweater, jacket, and wool topcoat we had. We pulled wool stocking caps down over our ears. We were wearing gloves and had warm socks inside our hiking boots. But as we stood on the shoulder of the road hour after hour we froze to the bone. The blizzard was still howling so almost no cars were heading west. We stood for about three hours. Finally I spotted a yellow school bus approaching. The driver pulled over. The doors opened.

Hal and I, stiff as boards, managed to pull ourselves aboard. The heater was on full blast.

"I'm on my way to Denver," the driver said. "Where you guys headed?"

We told him our insane travel plans, Hal to Missoula, me to Sequim, Washington.

He shook his head in disbelief. "I thought the Denver School District was crazy to send me back to pick up this new bus in Goshen, Indiana. You're welcome to ride with me until I turn south to Denver. Then you'll be on your own again."

We were so cold and exhausted that we stretched out on the narrow seats of that school bus and fell into a deep sleep as the bus trundled across Nebraska. Yet it seemed no time at all when the driver pulled off at another truck stop and announced he was turning south to Denver. The blizzard had ended. But as the clouds were swept away, the temperature plunged to below zero.

We tramped into the café and started asking people if they would give us a ride. Soon I came on a young man sipping coffee and reading a newspaper. "Pardon me, sir. Are you driving west?"

"Yes I am?"

"Where you headed?"

"Portland."

"Could you give us a ride?"

"Sure. How far you going?"

I told him our travel plans.

"Well, you're welcome to ride with me to Portland. But I must warn you. It's a very small car."

We gratefully accepted his offer.

When we got out into the parking lot, we could see what he meant. It was a tiny rear engine French-built Renault.

We piled in and he took us west on the Lincoln Highway. A problem soon arose. The wheel-base of the car was about three inches narrower than American cars and trucks. The highway was like a railroad track in the sense that the wheels of many cars and trucks had carved out two deep ruts in the snow and ice. The Renault slip-slid from side to side crazily because the wheels were not wide enough to fit down into the grooves.

So we slip-slid our way west bouncing back and forth and up and down 100 miles to Cheyenne, Wyoming. Hal had made up his mind he would get out in Cheyenne and hitchhike north into Montana and west to his home in Missoula.

At the last minute, I made a brash decision. There was no way I could abandon Hal to the elements in the frigid, snow bound, high plains of Wyoming. I got out of the Renault with Hal. We thanked the driver. We went into yet another café.

After fifteen minutes of begging and pleading, we found a guy who was headed due north to Belle Fourche, South Dakota on the northern edge of the Black Hills. It was after midnight and we slept as our driver drove the twisting 312 miles arriving on the outskirts of Belle Fourche about 6:30 in the morning.

We climbed out and once again stuck our thumbs out. We were at a fork in the road and we saw a car come up to a stop sign a couple of dozen yards away. We ran waving and shouting to the driver. In the car were four young Native American Indian men. I pleaded our case one more time. We were frigidly cold, exhausted, starved. Would they please give us a ride.

The Indian youths, probably Lakota Sioux, had bemused looks on their faces. No doubt by now, Hal and I presented quite a spectacle of human misery, down-and-out vagabonds frozen, starving, in need of shaves, a bath and a bed to sleep in.

"I'm not headed north to Miles City," the driver told me. "We're ranch hands. We work at a ranch outside Alzada. You're welcome to ride with us, but Alzada is nowhere. You sure you want to come with us?"

It didn't take more than an instant for Hal and me to say yes.

We piled into the car. And off the driver zoomed at top speed, heading thirty-seven miles northwest to Alzada. We told our tale of woe to the other passengers in the car who shook their heads and laughed at our Quixotic misadventure. One of them offered us a beer to warm up our innards. We declined on grounds we were too exhausted and would fall asleep by the roadside if we imbibed any alcoholic beverage. Again they chuckled sympathetically as they quaffed another beer.

We crossed first into Wyoming and then into Montana and soon pulled into Alzada. It consisted of a combined general store, service station, and post office. Across the road was an abandoned motel. Hal and I stepped from the car, thanked the driver, and resumed our hitchhiking.

Here, in this Godforsaken place, there was one blessing. It began to warm up dramatically, so warm that I took off my overcoat and unzipped my jacket. Blossoms on the fruit trees were swelling. Meadowlarks were singing.

Yet there was also a curse in Alzada. Not a single car passed us headed west in three hours of hitchhiking. At noon I told Hal, "You stay on this side of the road. Keep hitchhiking west. I'm going across the road and hitchhike east. The first car or truck that stops, either direction, we take it."

So I did. We had been waiting for hours when a big cattle truck rumbled down a gravel road and turned into the gas station. A lanky man wearing blue jeans, a sheepskin coat, cowboy boots and a ten-gallon hat stepped from the driver side of the truck and started to gas up. I hurried across the road and approached him, looking even more forlorn than ever, the stubble on my chin looking like a shaggy, ill-kempt beard, my eyes bloodshot, my clothes looking grimy and tattered. I doubtless smelled like one of the steers the cowboy manhandled.

"Good afternoon, sir," I said. "By any chance are you headed back into Belle Fourche? Could my friend and I please hitch a ride with you?"

The man pushed the ten-gallon hat back from his brow and sized me up critically. "OK," he said.

We piled into the cab of that truck and he drove us back to Belle Fourche. He was a man of few words. That "OK" was the sum total of our conversation.

He dropped us at the Greyhound Bus Depot. With our precious few dollars, we bought tickets for Miles City, Montana. We rode in luxury the 137 miles to Miles City. The bus was one of those ancient, decrepit turtle-backed buses. Only six rows of seats were reserved for passengers. The back of the bus was sectioned off for mail, parcel post, and other miscellaneous cargo.

We were exultant when we arrived in Miles City. Now we were back on the newly-built Interstate-94, main east-west route to Missoula and Seattle. Once again in Miles City we stuck our thumbs out. Evening was falling and yes, spring was finally in the air. A two-door black Ford rumbled up and pulled off on the shoulder of the highway. Again it was a youthful Native American Indian man. We learned in the next few minutes that he was a member of the Blackfeet Tribe.

He waved for us to climb in. His Ford, he bragged, was equipped with a full-bore supercharged V-8, like one of those half-wild mustangs that will explode into a dead run when you touch their sides with your heels. His Ford was so hot he could barely keep the rear wheels from peeling as he pulled out onto the Interstate.

He had the accelerator pressed to the floorboard. Soon we were making up for lost time, erasing all the hours we had spent going nowhere in Alzada. I glanced at the speedometer and we were roaring along at over 100 miles per hour.

We were traveling parallel to the tracks of the Northern Pacific. I looked far up ahead and saw that the Interstate rose up and twisted southward across the railroad tracks and came down on the other side.

Hal and I were sitting in white-knuckle terror as the car bore down on this overpass. Surely, I thought to myself, he will slow down as he approaches this overpass.

Not at all. He pushed down harder on the gas and I heard the tires screaming, the gravitational forces on my body at two or three "Gs" as the car careened to the top of the overpass and came down like a guided missile on the south side. I had just experienced the wildest roller coaster ride west of the Mississippi.

We made the 137 miles to Billings in no time at all.

Hal and I stepped from the Ford, our knees quaking like jelly. We thanked him. We decided that we had satisfied our craving for hitchhiking. We considered hopping a Northern Pacific freight train, riding the rails home. We even went to the Northern Pacific marshalling yard, found the office where the yard crew was staying warm. We asked some of the old-timers sitting drinking coffee when the next freight train was scheduled to come through Billings and could they give us any tips on the best way of climbing on board?

They studied us, shaking their heads, telling us we would be ill-advised to try jumping aboard a freight train. "Think of it," said one. "The train rises up into the high Rockies from here. You'd be completely exposed to the cold. You could actually freeze to death."

That was it. We decided to take their advice. We went to the passenger depot and used our last dollars to purchase tickets to Missoula and Seattle. Luckily, the west bound North Coast Limited passenger train was scheduled to arrive in Billings in two hours. We boarded the train. I found in the lounge of the men's room a seat long enough that I could stretch out. I blessed my parents for designing me five-feet six-inches tall, short enough I could stretch out and sleep. Poor Hal, about a foot taller, had to sleep sitting up.

I was just drifting off to sleep when someone shook my shoulder. It was the conductor punching tickets. He examined me closely and asked me where I was from. I told him as briefly as I could the whole story. He chuckled. "Oh to be young again," he said. He pulled out his wallet, removed two dollar bills and handed them to me. "You and your friend should go to the dining car right now and get yourself a hamburger."

After that dinner we slept soundly until we arrived in Missoula in the early hours of the morning. I gave Hal a hug as he stepped down to the platform.

The train rolled west. It slowed to a stop in Ellensburg, Washington a few hours later. There was Alec Stewart waiting. He had flown home from Amherst for spring vacation. He jumped aboard with a picnic basket overflowing with fried chicken, potato salad, cookies, and other goodies. It turns out that Hal had telephoned ahead to let Alec and his parents know I would be arriving. At the bottom was an envelope with a card welcoming me home to Washington. Tucked inside was a ten dollar bill—just enough to pay the Greyhound bus fare from Seattle to Sequim.

I arrived in Sequim in the afternoon. I trudged up the road to our house on Bell Hill and up the driveway to our handsome frame house. I turned and looked out over the valley, across the Strait of Juan de Fuca to the San Juan Islands and Vancouver Island, British Columbia. Almost heaven. Then I turned and opened the door. For some reason, I still don't know why, my mother was at the top of a step ladder sweeping down cobwebs. She had no idea I was coming. "Hello, Mama," I said. She almost fell off the ladder.

That journey taught me a hard lesson: Never try to hitchhike north-south anywhere in the Rocky Mountain high plains. Heading west, following the path of manifest destiny, bowing to Horace Greeley's admonition, "Go west young man." That was fine. But north or south? Forget about it. Just remember Alzada, Montana, a place you can hitchhike both directions at once for half a day and still not get out of town.

(Tim Wheeler graduated from Amherst College in 1964)

Benjamin J. Davis, Jr. Returns to Amherst College. . . . and Jarvis Tyner Visits Too

Benjamin O. Davis (FBI mug shot)

We should have filled Johnson Chapel with Amherst College students and faculty to welcome one of Amherst College's greatest graduates, the African American, Benjamin J. Davis Jr., who earned his bachelor's degree from Amherst in 1929.

I believe Davis spoke at his alma mater in the autumn of 1959, beginning of my sophomore year at Amherst.

As I recall, Davis, did not speak in Johnson Chapel at all. It was a small crowd in the Octagon, a handsome octagonal building assigned to the music department and used by musicians to practice.

Amherst biology professor, Tom Yost, hosted Davis's visit. Yost introduced Davis as a hero of the struggle against racism and for democracy.

I remember almost nothing about Davis' speech. But I met him later at a reception at Professor Yost's home. Davis was a tall, genial, modest, man with a ready wit who seemed more interested in listening to the people around him than in talking about his eventful, celebrated life.

His return to Amherst was historic in the first place because Benjamin Davis was an African American who graduated with high honors from Amherst. He had been the president of the Debate Club at Amherst, a talented musician who played first violin in the Amherst orchestra and also sang in the Amherst Glee Club. He went on to win a degree from Harvard Law School in 1932.

Not many Black people graduated from places like Amherst College in the 1920s even though the institution had a reputation for standing up against racist oppression. In 1834, Amherst President, Heman Humphrey, ordered the Anti-Slavery Society of Amherst College to disband. The students refused.

The Reverend Henry Ward Beecher, one of the most celebrated Abolitionists, graduated from Amherst in 1834. Beecher's statue still stands on the Amherst campus right near the Octagon where Benjamin Davis spoke.

After he graduated from Harvard, Davis had returned to Atlanta to practice law. Angelo Herndon, a young African American, an organizer of the Unemployed Councils, was arrested in Atlanta on charges of "insurrection" for organizing an integrated march of Black and white unemployed workers demanding relief. Herndon, a member of the Communist Party USA (CPUSA), was facing execution if convicted of the crime.

In those deep, dark days of the Great Depression, the CPUSA's main slogans were "Organize or Starve" and "Black and White Unite! Same Class, Same Fight."

The descendants of the slave owners who controlled Georgia in those days trembled at the specter of Black workers and white workers uniting against their common enemy. It would have been a death knell for the entire system of segregation.

The International Labor Defense, an organization initiated by the CPUSA that also played a major role in saving the lives of the "Scottsboro Boys," seven young African American men framed up in Alabama on rape charges, approached Davis and asked him to represent Angelo Herndon. Davis agreed.

The case went all the way to the U.S. Supreme Court which overturned his conviction, a hugely important victory for human rights in the Jim Crow south and across the nation.

In the middle of this struggle, young Benjamin Davis joined the Communist Party USA.

Indeed, when he came back to speak to us that evening in 1960, Benjamin J. Davis Jr. had recently been released from a four year prison sentence, railroaded to jail for his communist beliefs and his membership in the CPUSA.

He had been convicted under the infamous Smith Act, falsely accused of "conspiring to teach and advocate the overthrow of the United States Government by force and violence." He served his sentence at Terre-Haute Federal Penitentiary. One of his fellow prisoners was Henry Winston who later served as National Chairman of the CPUSA. Winston had complained of crushing headaches and pleaded with prison authorities to treat him. They ignored his pleas and Winston went permanently blind. When Winston was released from prison, he said, "They robbed me of my sight but not my vision."

As I listened to Ben Davis, a gentle, soft-spoken man, I marveled that the Cold Warriors could have whipped up such a climate of hysteria they could ramrod a man like this to prison. This was a man so beloved by the people of Harlem they had elected him and reelected him to represent them on the City Council of New York City. Yet FBI Director, J. Edgar Hoover and other witchhunters had connived to expel him from the City Council after he was convicted. The New York City Council should apologize!

Who, I asked myself, posed the real danger to our Constitution and Bill of Rights? Not Benjamin J. Davis, Jr. He fought his whole life to defend and uphold our Constitution, to enlarge it to protect the civil rights and civil liberties of masses of people who were systematically denied their rights, like Angelo Herndon whose crime was working to unite Black and white to fight back against mass starvation.

Davis stood like a rock against the racists, the warmongers, the corporate profiteers. Like his close friend, Paul Robeson, Davis was a "Great Forerunner." His courage set the stage for another great African American from Atlanta, the Reverend Martin Luther King, Jr.

Ben Davis told us calmly, as befits an attorney, about the flagrant injustice perpetrated upon him by those who put him in jail, so vindictive, with such scant respect for freedom of speech, they seized the manuscript of his memoirs before he was released from prison. Those papers were not released until after Ben Davis died in 1964 of lung cancer. They were published posthumously under the title "Communist Councilman from Harlem."

Meeting Ben Davis was a high point of my years at Amherst College. I joined his Party and dedicated my life to writing for the Worker, a newspaper he once served as Editor.

Someday the criminal justice system in the United States will be transformed, led by women and men who understand who the real conspirators are—the real menace to democracy. Those who have committed crimes against the people, who have violated rights protected by our Constitution, will be tried and put in jail for a long time. They are members of what Vermont Senator Bernie Sanders calls "the billionaire class" who use racism and anti-communism to keep the people divided.

Jarvis Tyner

And someday, a statue will be erected in Harlem—and perhaps on the lovely campus of Amherst College too—honoring a real hero, Benjamin J. Davis, Jr.

Ben Davis was not the only African American Communist Party leader to visit Amherst College while Joyce and I were there. In the early spring of 1964, Jarvis Tyner arrived on a bus from New York City. He had been assigned to make a tour of New England to recruit youth to attend the founding convention of the W.E.B. DuBois Clubs of America in San Francisco that summer. He had telephoned me to ask if we could organize a meeting of students to hear his appeal. Joyce and I were deeply immersed in an organization called "Synthesis," a progressive youth discussion and action group consisting of students at Amherst College, the University of Massachusetts, Smith College and Mount Holyoke.

They were pacifists, equal rights activists, Marxists. We organized several vigils against the nuclear arms race at Westover Air Force Base, and in support of pending civil rights legislation in the U.S. Congress including the Civil Rights Act, and the upcoming Voting Rights Act.

President John F. Kennedy had come to Amherst College in the fall of 1963 and we organized a civil rights and peace vigil along the path he was scheduled to walk to get to the gymnasium where he was to speak. It was only a few weeks before he was assassinated.

I promised Jarvis we would telephone all our student contacts in the four-college area. Jarvis stepped off the bus. He was a tall, lanky, strikingly handsome youth, a union furniture worker and Teamster truck driver from Philadelphia. He was a dapper man, dressed in slacks, a sports jacket without even a sweater, and loafers. It snowed the night before and the temperature plunged to near zero. It was obvious that Jarvis might literally freeze to death. He was staying at the home of Party comrades on the outskirts of Amherst. He was also in touch with Professor Yost who had hosted Ben Davis.

Jarvis had a list of other Amherst faculty members to visit in hopes of raising funds to help pay for the DuBois Clubs founding convention. At the top of that list was American Studies Professor, Leo Marx. I had classes to attend so I was not free to escort Jarvis around the campus. So he found his own way to the office of Dr. Marx who welcomed him. Jarvis' teeth were chattering so loudly he could hardly explain why the time is right to establish a progressive youth organization. Marx pulled out his wallet, opened it and took out a twenty dollar bill. "Young man, your cause is a worthy one, a youth organization named for one of our country's greatest scholars and freedom fighters. I don't want you to freeze before you complete the assignment. Please take this and go to a haberdasher and get yourself a winter coat."

Dr. Marx, Yost, and other faculty members in town doubtless gave Jarvis more money to help organize the DuBois

Clubs, but that is one donation neither Jarvis nor I ever forgot.

When Jarvis showed up at our little off-campus apartment at Tyler Place, he was wearing a parka warm enough to organize in Antarctica. The next morning, a Saturday, our small living room was packed with about thirty students from all four campuses to hear Jarvis argue that it is high time we established a multiracial, multi-ethnic, working class youth organization guided by Marxism and the teachings of DuBois to fight for democracy, to stand up against racism, war, assassin's hatred, and to win socialism in America. He got much applause.

Joyce and I were unable to attend the DuBois Clubs founding convention but we joined the organization when we got to Portland, Oregon, and were active in the DuBois Clubs when we moved to New York City. It was the start of our lifelong friendship with Jarvis Tyner, an eloquent speaker, a fighter against oppression, a man filled with humanism and a profound love for the working people of the world.

They Shall Not Pass: Fighting fascism in 1930s Britain

People's World, November 18, 2016

Don Wheeler

When I was growing up back in the 1950s, my father would regale us with stories of his exploits as a Rhodes Scholar at Oxford University in the 1930s. Soon after he arrived in Oxford in 1936, the British Union of Fascists (BUF) announced that Sir Oswald Mosley, fuehrer of the BUF, would come to speak at a rally in Oxford. He would be accompanied by more than 100 of his Blackshirt thugs.

My dad said that Oxford's anti-fascist students, many of them members of the Communist Party of Britain, decided to give Moseley a "warm welcome." Reinforced by a couple of hundred workers from the MG auto plant in Oxford, they packed the meeting hall the night Moseley arrived. The Blackshirts were lined up along walls of the meeting hall glowering menacingly at the Oxford students, MG workers and others who crowded the hall. Moseley began to speak, spewing out a torrent of racist, anti-Semitic hate, gushing his eternal love of Hitler and Mussolini and promising the crowd that fascism would purify Great Britain by eliminating Jews, Gypsies, Bolsheviks, and other non-Aryans.

"The Battle of Cable Street"—a mural in London's East End depicts another anti-Mosley demonstration from 1936. | Trades Union Congress

The MG workers and the Oxford students began to heckle and boo. The chief of the Blackshirt thugs took the microphone from Moseley and snarled, "The next person who disrupts this meeting will be expelled forthwith." The crowd fell silent. Sir Oswald stepped back up to the microphone. The instant he opened his mouth, from the back of the hall, in a falsetto voice one of the students squeaked loudly, "Forthwith."

The Blackshirt thugs attempted to charge into the crowd to grab him. That was the signal. All the Oxford students and MG workers stood, picked up their folding chairs, folded them flat and hurled them at the advancing Nazis. "We mowed them down with those chairs," my dad exclaimed, laughing till tears streamed down his cheeks. The fascists beat a hasty retreat, Sir Oswald in his limousine, his goons in military-style army trucks. But the anti-fascists had planned another surprise for the Nazi invaders. They had poured sugar in the gas tanks of all the BUF vehicles. A couple of miles outside Oxford, they all came to a halt, the engines gummed up.

My father was a brilliant student who won a "First" in a graduate program called "Modern Greats" at Oxford. He transferred to the Sorbonne in Paris in 1937 and was recruited to serve as a courier travelling into the south of France with cash, visas, and other documents to help volunteers with the Abraham Lincoln Brigade get across the Pyrenees into Spain to fight the Franco fascists.

He was a dedicated anti-fascist organizer in England and France back in the 1930s. My mom and dad remained staunch anti-fascists their entire life. It takes different tactics in the United States today to fight the neo-Nazis. I do not recommend that we hurl folded chairs at David Duke, the KKK, and other members of Donald Trump's lynch mob. But we need to give them a "warm welcome" and then drive them out of town!

I Remember Ted Kennedy

I was a senior at Amherst College in the spring of 1964 when I boarded a chartered bus filled with a crowd of Amherst college students, my wife Joyce and our son Morgan, then less than six-months-old, for a trip to Washington, D.C., to lobby for passage of the Civil Rights Act of 1964. When the bus arrived in the nation's capital, all of us went to a hearing room in the Russell Senate Office Building.

We were greeted there by a young

Ted Kennedy speaking at Capitol Hill rally photo courtesy of Terrie Albano

freshman senator from Massachusetts named Edward M. Kennedy—better known as Ted. He welcomed us and offered some strong comments in favor of passage without crippling amendments of this landmark bill to end the shameful legacy of racist segregation. He was getting really wound up when Morgan started fretting. Joyce and I tried without success to quiet Morgan and finally I took him and started for the door.

"Don't leave. Come on back and sit down," Kennedy said. "A baby crying isn't going to hurt any of us. Someday he's going to be a Young Democrat." The crowd laughed and applauded and I sat down. And as I remember, Morgan stopped crying. I never forgot that incident. Ever since, I've had a warm spot in my heart for Ted Kennedy.

That feeling persisted even after I became the Washington correspondent for the Daily World. Kennedy sponsored S.1, a highly repressive piece of Cold War legislation that critics charged could open the door for Joe McCarthy-style witch-hunts. I wrote scathing articles quoting Frank Wilkinson, founder of the National Committee to Abolish HUAC. Thanks in part to their efforts, S.1, and its offspring, "son of S.1" died. But that stain on Kennedy's record was far outweighed by his many pro-labor, pro-worker, pro-people stands on a wide range of issues.

During most of the years I covered Washington, Kennedy was a lion, a powerful stump speaker who would come out of the Capitol building to address AFL-CIO rallies, blasting the union busting policies of President Reagan and later George W. Bush. Workers loved Kennedy's gravel-voiced, thundering orations against corporate America and the rich (notwithstanding the fact that he himself was a millionaire many times over). He loved to pump up the crowd with lines like. "Are you ready to fight? Let me hear you." The crowd would roar!

Health care was his defining issue. He was badly injured in the crash of a small plane near Northampton, Mass. (It happened while we were living a few miles away in Amherst. Kennedy recuperated at the Northampton Hospital where

Morgan had gone for surgery as an infant a few months earlier).

Kennedy suffered the rest of his life from chronic back pains and maybe that pain was a constant reminder of the urgent need for reform. I remember a conference on health care sometime in the mid-1970s sponsored by the AFL-CIO and other advocates of health care reform. A woman who lacked health insurance brought a computer printout of her hospital bill to the conference. A friend held one end while the woman unrolled the bill that stretched across the front of the ballroom, up one side, across the back, down the other side, all the way around the vast room. A gasp went through the crowd and while she unrolled that graphic emblem of financial ruin, Senator Kennedy delivered an angry stemwinder blasting the insurance companies for their profit greed. He demanded that Congress enact comprehensive, universal, health care for all.

Kennedy kept hammering away at that demand until he died. A fitting memorial for Edward (Ted) M. Kennedy would be enactment of comprehensive, universal health care for all, government financed, that protects every child, woman, and man in America. It should be called the "Kennedy Act."

I am Found "Morally Unfit"

I took a leave-of-absence from Amherst College at the end of my junior year in 1961 and headed home to our dairy farm in Sequim, Washington.

It was a stressful time on the farm because we were dramatically expanding operations to produce enough milk—and income—to support two families instead of one.

My cousin, Dave Helms and his wife Marilyn had gone into partnership with my parents. We were rapidly expanding from the herd of twenty-five cows we milked twice daily when we first went into farming in 1948 to over 100 cows when I arrived back home.

My parents and the Helms family had purchased the Ward farm, 140 acres along the west bank of the Dungeness River about two miles up from the river's mouth. William Ward had laid claim to this magnificent piece of virgin soil in 1858, cleared the cedar forest, planted it to white clover and started milking cows. He planted an orchard of apple, pear, plum, and cherry trees that still produce a cornucopia of fresh fruit today.

We were in the midst of moving our operation from the old Bell farm up on Bell Hill to the Ward farm about eight miles across the valley when I arrived home. It was an ordeal that took months to complete.

As soon as I dropped out of Amherst, my draft status changed. I lost my student deferment and was reclassified as "1-A," eligible to be summoned to military duty any time Uncle Sam deemed the time was right.

One day the letter from the draft board arrived: "Greetings!"

I was ordered to report to the military induction center near the waterfront in downtown Seattle.

The morning I left to answer this call, I embraced my mother. There was no war underway at that moment but the United States was making loud, persistent warlike noises toward Cuba. Already the Cold Warriors were pouring out a torrent of anti-communist propaganda that the world was like dominoes ready at any moment to topple in a chain reaction of communist expansionism. The very continued existence of the U.S.A. was threatened by a vast, global, communist conspiracy. So I could feel my mother's body trembling when I embraced her and she had tears in her eyes.

Daddy drove me down to the Greyhound Station. He too embraced me. I rode the bus to Seattle and made my way to the induction center. It was teeming with young men like myself. It all went smoothly. I filled out forms, went through a physical exam, waited in long lines.

Then late in the morning, two men in civilian clothes approached me. One of them stuck out his hand and said, "Good morning, Mr. Wheeler. My name is Louis Bourgeois."

My eyebrows went up. Bourgeois? Surely he was kidding. However, I was too polite to say this out loud.

They ushered me into an inner office and closed the door. "We need to ask you a few questions about your affiliations and your political activities," Bourgeois began.

Politely, I answered that my affiliations and my political activities were my own business.

"Well, the Department of Defense does not see it that way. Your affiliations place you in a different draft classification. They make your participation in the armed forces inconsistent with the national security of the United States. You are morally unfit to serve."

There was a bit more of an exchange with these two agents of U.S. military intelligence. Then they excused me and told me I could leave.

I went back to the Greyhound Depot with my head swimming with mixed emotions. I would not be compelled to fight and die in some jungle half way around the world. Surely that was a plus.

But the essence of the matter was that I was on a blacklist. It meant that the Cold Warriors were still keeping many doors locked, that I was in a category "No dissidents need apply . . . and we won't draft you either."

I rode home to Sequim and hiked up the hill to our farm. When I told my parents the story, my mother's eyes narrowed in anger. "Morally unfit!" she thundered. "Those scoundrels! They are the ones who are morally unfit! We can't let them get away with this!"

My mother had a real temper. When her dander was up, watch out! She telephoned the American Civil Liberties Union in Seattle. They agreed to represent me, pro bono, in a challenge to my new "morally unfit" draft status. The irony of this situation was extreme. Here I was fighting to get into the U.S. military even as we argued vehemently against the policies of U.S. global domination and hegemony, in a word, imperialism.

I met with the ACLU lawyer in Seattle. By now I was taking courses at the University of Washington. Whenever I visited Seattle, I stayed at a big, ramshackle frame house that was being rented by a crowd of UW students, all of them leftwingers—members of the Youth Club of the Communist Party of Washington State. The tenants also included pacifists, civil rights activists, members of the Student Peace Union and other peace and justice activists. There was a brilliant concert pianist named Jan who moved his baby grand into the living room and serenaded us at all hours practicing his scales and arpeggios. There was an aspiring novelist who admired some of my offerings in a course in creative writing I took at the university.

It was called the Roosevelt Street Commune and doubtless it was one of the affiliations that earned me my moral misfit draft status.

The young ACLU attorney met with me there and we planned my appeal. The U.S. Army scheduled a hearing at Fort Lawton in the Magnolia Heights neighborhood of Seattle.

We arrived at the fort that morning a few weeks later. The hearing was conducted in a large, handsome hearing room designed for court martials and other military tribunals.

A panel of high ranking military officers was hearing my appeal. The U.S. Army had sent up from the Presidio in San Francisco, a smartly uniformed officer of the Judge Adjutant General to serve as prosecutor.

He was resplendent in his perfectly pressed jacket emblazoned with a medallion on his chest, the crease in his chinos as sharp as a razor edge, his dress oxfords polished until they gleamed.

The high point of the hearing was when this lawyer put me on the witness stand for cross-examination:

"Will you obey any order given you by your commanding officer without question?" he demanded.

"I would obey any command that in my opinion was legal," I replied. "But I would not obey an order that was in my opinion contrary to U.S. law or international law."

"What do you mean? Can you give me an example of an order you think is contrary to the law?"

"Well, if I was ordered to open fire on people in the United States who were demonstrating or protesting, I would consider that an illegal order."

But this JAG lawyer was no fool. He came back with a follow-up question.

"Suppose you were ordered to defend Negro students as they attempted to enter a segregated school. Suppose those students were attacked by white supremacists. Suppose your officer ordered you to open fire to save those students lives. What would you do?"

"Yes. I can see circumstances in which I would open fire to save innocent lives. Each situation would require me to make a judgement about the legality and the morality of an order given to me."

Nuremburg was not mentioned in that hearing. But what I testified, in essence, is that I was bound, as is every officer, every soldier, to obey the Nuremburg Principle. I could not appeal that I was only "obeying orders," that someone higher up the chain of command was responsible if that order proved to be illegal.

No, I too would be guilty if it was proven I obeyed an illegal order.

I looked over at the panel of military officers of every branch of the armed forces, their chests encrusted with medals and battle ribbons. They were all looking at me with very grim expressions on their faces. Clearly, they did not like the way I was answering the questions.

The hearing ended. My attorney told me I would be informed of the verdict by mail.

A few weeks later, I received a letter. My appeal had been rejected. I was still "morally unfit" to serve in the U.S. armed forces. Grudgingly, my mother decided against appealing that verdict.

That change in my draft status was in many ways a turning point in my life.

Tim Wheeler

The Green Geyser of Dungeness

Right on schedule at 10:30 every morning, the Darigold tanker arrived outside our milk house. That was back in 1962 down on our dairy farm along the west bank of the Dungeness River.

The driver attached the hose to the valve of our stainless steel Dari-Kool tank and pumped 300 gallons of pure white Grade-A-milk into the tanker.

One ton of milk every day. That's what our herd of 100 cows were producing.

We prided ourselves on champion producers like "Tizzy," a Jersey admitted to the 4,000 Pounds Butterfat Club in 1965 by the Dairy Herd Improvement Association. She produced 69,680 pounds of milk and 4,089 pounds of butterfat. That's more than two tons of very rich vanilla ice cream.

Our milking parlor was a New Zealand herringbone that enabled one person to milk ten cows at a time.

There was only one hitch to this bucolic scenario. What goes in as grass at the front end came out at the back-end as a pungent by-product: cow manure.

All the concrete slabs around the loafing sheds were graded so that the oceans of liquid manure could be scraped into an 80,000 gallon below-ground manure tank at the back of the milking parlor.

I still remember the salesman coming to sell my dad on the wonders of the manure pump to be installed at the bottom of that enormous tank.

"This pump is so powerful, it will cut up and pump _anything_," the salesman gushed.

My dad scratched his ear and asked skeptically, "How about baler twine? We have miles of it when we break open hay bales."

"No problem," replied the salesman smoothly. "You can just toss that baler twin onto the slab. This pump will cut your baler twine like a knife through soft butter!"

We were sold! The acre of concrete was poured around the loafing sheds. The pump was installed. The 500-gallon manure wagon was hitched to the tractor and pulled up under the spout to receive its load of liquid manure. The pump was so powerful it filled that manure tank in about two minutes. We then drove the tractor out to the fields, opened the spigot on the tank as we rolled along and watched the pungent stuff gush out the rear onto the pastures.

Magnifique!

Yet a few days later, we discovered a sad truth. We would push the button on the electric motor. It would hum ominously. But the pump would not rotate. It was clogged, totally bound up. The villain was baler twine. The pump was indeed mighty but not mighty enough to cut up that infernal hemp.

There we were! An 80,000 gallon manure tank filling up! Close to overflowing.

Dad, ever inventive, discovered that the pump froze up only when the electric motor was turned on. If you could run it continuously, the pump did indeed chop up the twine.

We brought in a load of aluminum irrigation pipes. We laid out the pipes into the fields. We attached an elbow to the irrigation pipe, held in place by a latch, and slid the other end neatly over the end of the standpipe from the manure pump.

We turned on the pump. Sure enough, it ran smoothly, with manure pumped up out of the tank, flowing out the pipe and forming a vast smelly lake far out in our pastures.

I was attending the University of Washington part time in those days and had formed many friendships. One weekend they came to visit, Walter, his girlfriend, Joyce, and an exchange student from Kenya named Muga Ndenga. Muga spoke perfect "King's English" with a gentle, courteous, accent.

I took them on a Cook's Tour, showing off every magnificent gadget in our New Zealand milking system. The Crown Jewel was the manure tank and the ingenious pump. I was anxious to impress my friends but none more than the beguiling lass, Joyce. I suggested that they stand back to get the full effect.

"Now watch this!" I said with a grand flourish. I pushed the electric button.

The latch disengaged. The elbow lifted off.

A geyser of manure rose majestically forty feet into the air. The green torrent came crashing down, covering me from head to toe in pure, Grade-A liquid cow shit.

Muga was beside himself, jumping from one foot to the other and exclaiming in the purest King's English, "What a pity! What a pity! What a pity!"

I plodded to the house, my feet squishing with every step. My father was drinking his afternoon coffee. I stepped into the kitchen, cow shit dristling from the tip of my nose. My dad looked up. An expression of shock spread over his face at this ghost, this monster from the black lagoon looming over him.

"Damned *fool!*" he bellowed. "Look at yourself! You're a *disgrace!*"

Somehow, in the hour that followed, I managed to get out of my drenched work clothes and clean myself up. I could overhear my father still ranting and rumbling in the background.

The next day, my father went out to turn on the manure pump. He pushed the switch. The latch fell open. The elbow lifted off. I heard a choked cry and a torrent of profane exclamations from that corner of the farm.

He came squishing into the kitchen where I was sipping coffee. I didn't say a word. "Disgusting business," he muttered under his breath as the manure dripped.

Don and Mary Wheeler standing on the concrete slab above underground manure tank. Photo by Bob Coe

We Host Barack Obama (the Elder)

Slightly altered from story printed in the *Sequim Gazette* (Story first appeared in *The Ditchwalker,* newsletter of the Sequim High School Alumni Association) August 3, 2014

SEQUIM, WASHINGTON—I had gone back to the University of Washington in the spring of 1961. By then I was courting Joyce Provost who was to become my future wife.

I ran into Muga Ndenga hurrying across the Quad. He was the exchange student from Kenya who had suffered such grief from the eruptions of our infernal manure pump when he visited our farm a few weeks earlier. He was fully recovered from that tragedy.

"Tim," Muga exclaimed. "It's so good to see you. I enjoyed the visit to your farm soooo much! Is there any chance I can come back for a second visit?"

"Of course, Muga. You're welcome to come anytime you like."

"Is it O.K. if I bring my best friend? He too is an exchange student from Kenya. He has a big, fast car. I think it's a Buick. We could all ride up to your farm together."

"That's a great idea, Muga. What's his name?

"Barack Obama."

And indeed we did ride in Barack Obama's Buick. He was sitting in the front seat with his girlfriend and another woman classmate. Joyce, Muga and I sat in the back seat—frozen in white-knuckle terror.

Obama drove at eighty or ninety miles-an-hour on the twisting curves of Old Olympic Highway. We were convinced we all would die. We made it safely to our other handsome farmhouse, the Bell House up on Bell Hill.

Obama slept in one of the upstairs bedrooms. Next morning, we drove down to our new farm along the west bank of the Dungeness River. I took Muga, Obama, his girlfriend, the other young woman, and Joyce on the Cooke's Tour of our State-of-the-Art dairy farm. I sized Obama up: slim, dark-complexioned, strikingly handsome, courteous and soft-spoken. Like Muga, he spoke the "King's English."

He was dressed in a cashmere sweater, neatly creased chinos and a pair of Gucci loafers. He looked like he had just stepped out of the pages of one of those fashion magazines. I decided then to remove from the tour a demonstration of the wonders of our manure pump.

He died years later in a fiery auto accident in Kenya—but not before he fathered a son.

Over four decades later, I was sitting at our breakfast table in Baltimore reading the morning paper.

"Listen to this, Joyce," I said. "Some guy named Barack Obama is running for the U.S. Senate from Illinois. That can't be the Barack Obama we know can it? This guy is far too young."

Joyce and I mulled it over. Maybe Barack Obama was a commonplace name in Swahili, like Smith. A bit more research made it clear: The Barack Obama in Illinois was the son of the man we had hosted in Sequim. The son won a landslide victory in Illinois capturing seventy percent of the vote in winning a seat in the U.S. Senate in 2004.

Four year later, Senator Barack Obama was a candidate for President of the United States. Joyce and I worked hard in Maryland to help Obama carry that state. At the time, we were dividing our time between our home in Baltimore and our home in Sequim. I covered Obama's campaign writing many articles in the *PW* about his victories.

I remember with pride riding the Maryland Black Caucus bus down to Columbia, South Carolina to campaign for Obama in the spring of 2008. I also went door to door for him in Virginia, Pennsylvania, Ohio, Oregon, and Washington State.

Clallam County, Washington, where we now live, is a swing district. George W. Bush carried Clallam County, narrowly, in 2000 and 2004. Obama carried the county narrowly in both 2008 and 2012. We think our diligent work was a factor in his victory.

We organized street corner "waves" in Sequim and Port Angeles in 2008. Four years later, I marched with the Democrats in the Irrigation Festival Parade in Sequim and the

Fourth of July parades in Forks and Port Angeles holding up a giant sign that I had lettered, "OBAMA: FOUR MORE YEARS!" We got resounding applause and cheers in all these parades from the crowds that lined the parade routes.

The last weekend of the 2012 election, about thirty of us met at Democratic Party headquarters in Port Angeles. A gifted Obama campaign organizer told the meeting, "Let's set ourselves a goal: We will knock on 1,000 doors for Obama this weekend."

Joyce was there even though she was badly crippled with pain in both knees. She was scheduled to have both knees replaced.

I was working with another woman and we finished up our list as the sun was setting that Sunday evening. I called Joyce on her cell.

"I have about fifty names on my list," she told me. "My partner has to leave. Can you come and help me?"

I drove immediately to pick her up. Then together we drove from one farm house to another in the pitch dark. She had a flashlight and climbed painfully out of the car and limped up to each door, knocked, and spoke to the voters. We completed the list. That weekend, our valiant team achieved our goal, knocking on 1,000 doors, talking with hundreds of voters on why it was so urgent to defeat Mitt Romney and reelect Obama.

Washington State has an all-mail ballot so on election day, Joyce was scheduled for her knee replacement surgery at Olympic Medical Center in Port Angeles. When the votes were counted, Obama carried our country by a margin of fewer than 100 votes. We celebrated in Joyce's hospital room, both the success of Joyce's surgery the day before and Obama's reelection victory. Sylvia Hancock, a wonderful grassroots leader of the Democratic Party came to visit Joyce and thank her for her heroic effort. She gave Joyce a comical figurine of a snowman. We treasure it still.

Joyce's "bum-knee-be-damned" attitude is one reason Obama won. We were part of the vast majority movement that elected—and reelected—our nation's first Black president, a victory over racism.

Plotting to Defend Free Speech at the "Blue Moon"
People's World April 26, 2016

Gus Hall was coming to the Pacific Northwest in February 1962. Members of the Communist Party of Washington State were elated. Party organizer, Milford Sutherland, had worked hard setting up speaking engagements for Hall to speak at campuses all across the state from Spokane to Bellingham to Ellensburg to Seattle and Tacoma.

Clip from "The Worker" of Gus Hall with his photograph courtesy of *People's World*

Hall had recently been released from Leavenworth Penitentiary where he had been railroaded to prison for over six and a half years falsely charged under the Smith Act of "conspiring to teach or advocate the overthrow of the government by force and violence."

Hall and the twelve others jailed under this infamous witchhunt law were not accused of a single act of violence. They had not stockpiled arms or trained in the woods for terrorism or guerrilla warfare. No, Hall was imprisoned for his ideas, for upholding the notion that at some time in the future, the majority of the people of the United States might decide to "alter or abolish" the government and replace it with another government. In Hall's words, he was jailed for "the crime of thinking."

Hall's life was an open book. He had been a steelworker, a founder of the United Steelworkers, one of several Communist Party union activists recruited by United Mine

Worker President, John L. Lewis, to help organize the Congress of Industrial Organizations (CIO). He had served in the U.S. Navy during the war against fascism.

Now he was on a nationwide speaking tour telling the crowds that the Smith Act was an assault on the Constitution and the Bill of Rights aimed at smashing the labor movement and all other movements seeking progressive change.

He was scheduled to speak at the University of Washington.

Members of my youth club at the University were mobilizing to hear Hall speak.

Then, one by one, the colleges and universities where Hall was scheduled to speak started canceling the speaking engagements. Virtually every day, another cancellation was announced in the media. A day or so later, the University of Washington cancelled Hall's appearance on campus.

I had stopped with a friend, Tim Lynch, at the Blue Moon saloon on 45th Street to quaff a pint of ale. We sat at a booth, a large crowd of other students sitting nearby. Tim started ranting angrily about the cancellation of Hall's visit.

"We ought to do something about it," Tim said.

"I agree. It is really outrageous. You know Boeing and other corporations are threatening to cut off funding to intimidate people. Why don't we try to think of somewhere Hall could speak where the sponsors won't cave in to the fearmongers?"

I thought of Eagleson Hall at the YMCA-YWCA right in the University District. It was located off-campus at the corner of 15th and 42nd.

"We should start at petition right now," Tim said. "We don't even have time to get it printed."

I pulled out a yellow legal pad from my book-bag and handwrote across the top: "We, the students of the University of Washington, who uphold freedom of speech and assembly, appeal to the UW YMCA-YWCA to open the doors of Eagleson Hall for Gus Hall to speak."

Tim Lynch signed on the first line. I signed on the second. It turned out that many at the tables and booths around us had heard Tim and me ranting and raving about the vile crime of barring Gus Hall from speaking. We passed the petition around in the dimly lit bar room. Virtually everyone signed. We had to handwrite the petition on another sheet and it too was filled. Others in the bar took out notepads and wrote out the petition text and promised to circulate it among their fellow students.

The next day, Tim and I were racing around campus gathering signatures on sheets of notebook paper. My Party club meeting at the home of Kae and Ted Norton was that evening. Tim and I went to the meeting in their cramped street level apartment and reported on the petition we had launched at the Blue Moon Tavern.

Every member of the club agreed to circulate the petitions. Within seventy-eight hours we had collected well over 500 signatures. Tim and I went to the YMCA-YWCA. Luckily, Frank H. Mark, Executive Director of the UW YMCA and Elizabeth Jackson, Executive Director of the UW YWCA were there. We met with them and presented the handwritten petitions. We already knew them as friends of the Student Peace Union, the civil rights movement, and other progressive causes.

They studied the petitions and told us they would get back to us soon—within hours—because they knew, as well as we knew---that time was of the essence. Sure enough, within a few hours, when Tim and I returned to the "Y," these two courageous leaders gave us the nod. Yes. They would provide a meeting place for Gus Hall to speak. We settled on a date: February 10, 1962. Tim and I would contact Hall immediately to give him the news.

We were—no pun intended—over the moon!

Yet as we walked down the steps of the "Y," I told Tim. "This is just the beginning of the fight. You know the FBI, Boeing, the rightwing extremists, are going to descend on the UW 'Y' with a vengeance. We have to launch a counter attack right now!"

We telephoned Milford Sutherland, our own club chair, Kae Halonen, to ask them to start mobilizing in support of Frank Mark and Elizabeth Jackson immediately.

Within hours, the phone began to ring at the "Y" with people calling to thank them for taking a stand for freedom of speech. Bouquets were delivered so that the reception room of the "Y" was filled with flowers.

And sure enough, the FBI and other anti-communist witch-hunters were busy. The whole story is contained in a report posted online at the Washington State HistoryLink.org. The YMCA officials said the scheduled Hall appearance "has brought the wrath of the town down on us."

The web site adds that "An executive with the United Good Neighbors (predecessor to the United Way and a major source of funding for the Seattle YMCA) said contributors were 'raising hell with us.' Representatives of the Boeing Company asked that United Good Neighbors cut allocations for the YMCA."

This crude, strong-arm intimidation was aimed at the UW "Y" officials even though they were not the sponsors of the event. As the story in the HistoryLink.org put it, "His (Hall's) appearance at Eagleson Hall . . . was sponsored by a group of UW students, faculty, and staff rather than by the UW YMCA itself."

I had an idea. My mother's first cousin, Herb Robinson, was the news anchor of *KOMO TV*. He was a widely respected journalist, chief editorial writer for the *Seattle Times*. I telephoned *KOMO* and asked for Herb Robinson. He came on the line. I told him that "Y" officials, Frank Mark and Elizabeth Jackson had taken a courageous stand in defense of free speech in opening Eagleson Hall to a speech by a Communist Party leader. Could he arrange an interview? He said he would. "By the way," he asked, "We're cousins aren't we?"

"Yes we are."

"Give my fond regards to your mom," he said.

Herb Robinson, himself, came to conduct the interview with Mark and Jackson. These two "Y" officials stood their ground. And so did my cousin, Herb Robinson.

Gus Hall came to Seattle. Eagleson Hall was packed to overflowing. The windows were opened so the vast crowd of students and faculty that gathered outside could hear.

He blasted the Smith Act, J. Edgar Hoover and the other redbaiters. Hammering the air with his steelworker fist, he warned that the aim of this assault on democracy is not the Communist Party alone but all progressive forces seeking to change our nation for the better. Those who cave in to the hatemongering John Birch Society and Minute Men terrorists were placing all the rights of the people at risk. The crowd gave him a strong ovation.

Frank Mark and Elizabeth Jackson pushed ahead after that battle to establish an "open door" policy giving speakers a platform at Eagleson Hall to express divergent views on a wide range of issues. The UW "Y" became the recognized forum for free speech in the City of Seattle.

Doing research for this book a few weeks ago, I drove from the University of Washington Library up past the "Y" to 45th. I turned left and was inching my way toward I-5. There on my right was the Blue Moon Tavern, the saloon where Tim Lynch and I hatched a plot on behalf of Gus Hall and freedom of speech.

Seattle 1962: "Rising Hopes for Peace"
April 25, 2016

Ironworkers were putting the finishing touches on the Seattle Space Needle in January of 1962 and construction workers were laying tracks on the elevated Monorail. The entire Pacific Northwest was anticipating with great excitement the opening of the Seattle World's Fair, also known as "Century 21" in April of that year.

I was a student at the University of Washington active in the campus chapter of the Student Peace Union. At one of our meetings, a member raised the question of the World's Fair. Why not stage a march or rally of some kind to demonstrate that this event should be a celebration of world peace? Why not highlight the menace of the nuclear arms race and especially atmospheric nuclear testing that was poisoning the global atmosphere with strontium 90 and other deadly, radioactive toxins?

We all jumped at this idea. I suggested that we inflate a thousand balloons with helium the night before the scheduled opening ceremony April 22. I would draft a leaflet with drawings of the balloons and the headline, "Rising Hopes for Peace." We would march to the gates of the World's Fair carrying the multi-colored balloons and passing out the leaflets. At the signal that the fair was opening, we would release the balloons symbolizing those rising hopes.

Everyone was enthralled by this idea. We hoped that the rest of the anti-war movement in Seattle would join us making it a demonstration of many thousands. We were deeply disappointed that the American Friends Service Committee and other antiwar groups settled on a different plan. They decided to hold a similar march three or four days later on the weekend when far more people could participate.

Nevertheless, we forged ahead with our idea. I drafted the leaflet. Artist Ray Cooper designed the front. We mimeographed several thousand copies.

Seattle Women Act for Peace donated the use of their storefront office less than half a mile from the front gates of the World's Fair. The evening of April 21 before the fair was scheduled to open, twenty of us gathered at the WAC office around a big helium tank and began inflating the balloons. We had no idea how labor-intensive inflating 1,000 balloons would be. It takes nimble fingers to stretch the mouth of a balloon around the tip of one of those tanks, inflate the balloon, remove it, tie it in a knot, attach a string and let the balloon float up to the ceiling.

We worked into the wee hours of the morning and as we completed the task, the entire ceiling was covered with balloons four or five deep. Others were hand-painting placards with messages like "Stop Nuclear Testing NOW" and "Hands Off Cuba" reflecting the rising fear of a U.S. invasion to overthrow the socialist revolution in Cuba.

The next day, students, members of WAC, and many other peace activists gathered in front of the WAC office. The crowd swelled until several hundred were present.

As I recall, the World's Fair was scheduled to open at about noon that day. So at 11 a.m., bleary-eyed and yawning, we began our march to the gates of Century 21, singing peace songs and chanting, "Stop Testing NOW!"

The colorful balloons floated overhead as we marched through the immense crowds also headed to the fair.

We handed out our "Rising Hopes for Peace" leaflet explaining the meaning of the helium filled balloons, that we would release them at the World's Fair gates at the exact moment of the opening of the fair to symbolize our determination to stop nuclear testing and move the world away from nuclear terror toward peace.

We arrived at the gates of the fair and formed a picketline walking back and forth with our balloons and signs to educate the crowds on the need to speak out and act for peace.

A few minutes later, a cannon boomed inside the fair grounds and a flight of warplanes zoomed in tight formation overhead. The World's Fair had opened.

We released our balloons and they rose up above our heads. I said to myself, "I wish we had more, enough to blot out the clouds!"

Unbeknownst to us, Century 21 officials had the same idea! They too released balloons at that very moment, 2000 of them. So the sky was polka-dotted with three thousand multi-colored balloons and since many, though not all, those inside had seen our leaflet, they knew that all the balloons symbolized rising hopes for peace.

Century 21 was officially designated a World's Fair. Yet it fell short of a true World's Fair. The Soviet Union and China were not there. None of the eastern European countries had pavilions. Cuba was absent.

Yet in early May, Gherman Titov, a Soviet Cosmonaut and his wife came to visit the World's Fair drawing huge crowds wherever they went. Joyce had a job as a waitress at the World's Fair so I spent much of my spare time hanging around the restaurant where she worked. Often, I strolled around among the various pavilions.

One morning I visited the NASA Pavilion. I knew that Soviet Cosmonaut, Gherman Titov was in Seattle and was scheduled to visit the NASA pavilion. Maybe I would catch a glimpse of him. I heard a din of voices and footsteps of many people coming near. I looked down the corridor and there was Titov headed my way, led by NASA officials and followed by a hundred reporters and photographers and many autograph seekers.

I could see that Titov was a lively, gregarious man, laughing, exchanging witticisms with the people around him. He paused in front of a NASA space capsule. He listened gravely as a NASA official explained the inner-workings of the capsule to him.

I wanted to wade through that crowd, shake his hand, explain to Titov that we members of the Student Peace Union were working hard to prevent war, that his presence here in Seattle reflected our "rising hopes for peace."

Alas, instead of peace, our world lurched toward war, an epoch that would cost many millions of lives in the years that followed. I found a job working in the wholesale tobacco business owned by Anci Koppel, one of the staunchest leaders of Seattle Women Act for Peace.

Joyce continued her waitress job at the World's Fair all that summer and into the fall.

She was at work when the Columbus Day storm hit Seattle October 12. The sky turned an ominous deep dark gray. The wind screeched and howled. Trees were uprooted. Power lines came down. Sometime in the late afternoon, the power for the entire city went out. Joyce was trapped at work. She managed to make a brief phone call to tell me not to worry, that she would somehow make it home. She walked the entire way in the pitch dark city, arriving at her tiny apartment about two a.m.

As bad as that storm was, it was nothing compared to an evening ten days later when President John F. Kennedy went on the air.

Tim Lynch and I were walking home from downtown Seattle and stopped at the Red Rooster Inn for a beer (Honestly, I am not a heavy drinker!). Kennedy came on the television screen above us. We listened in appalled silence to his ultimatum: The Soviet Union must remove all nuclear missiles from Cuba NOW!

We left our beers on the bar untouched and hustled the rest of the way home. I was on the phone to J.C. Burdick to find out what the Student Peace Union was going to do. Already the organization was in motion. He told us a group, independently, was going to stage a peace march to the Federal Building immediately with the message: "No nuclear war! Hands off Cuba!"

And march we did. A menacing looking gang of toughs were already in front of the Federal Building, ready to attack and beat up any one like us protesting preparations for war. We picketed across the street. We had been on the picketline only about half an hour when the police who had been keeping the demonstrators separated, withdrew. The thugs starting taunting us, shaking their fists and screaming, "Go back to Russia."

One of the SPU leaders walking beside me said in a low, worried voice, "I think we had better leave. This is a very dangerous situation. They are about to come across the street and attack us."

I argued vehemently against it. "We just arrived. We are exercising our rights."

J.C. Burdick spoke up. "I think he is right. There could be violence."

So we terminated the picketline.

We did not know then that cooler heads were working to defuse this menacing confrontation. *ABC News* reporter, John Scali, was meeting over lunch with Soviet Embassy counselor, Alesandr Fomin, to exchange proposals aimed at de-escalation of the crisis.

Fomin told Scali that Soviet Premier Nikita Krushchev would withdraw all Soviet missiles from Cuba in exchange for Kennedy's promise never to invade Cuba. The deal also included U.S. agreement to remove missiles from Turkey aimed at the USSR. The U.S. and the Soviet Union both agreed to this solution.

It was a masterstroke that removed a nuclear danger to the U.S. and the USSR while also securing the Cuban revolution from U.S. intervention.

It was an agreement that averted war. It also enraged the most extreme warmongers in the U.S. including Kennedy's own appointee as head of the Joint Chiefs of Staff, Air Force General, Curtis Lemay. He had seen in this crisis an opportunity to invade Cuba and destroy the revolution. LeMay had the bombers on the runway, troops ready to board the invasion landing craft. Kennedy and Krushchev had jerked the rug from beneath them.

The warmongers never forgave JFK. They were ready to commit murder to avenge what they regarded as betrayal.

The years that followed were filled with tragedy: multiple assassinations, starting with the murder of President Kennedy, his brother Robert, Martin Luther King Jr., Medgar Evers, Malcolm X.

The war in Vietnam escalated, a conflict that cost the lives of millions of people in Vietnam and Cambodia, Laos, and nearly 60,000 U.S. G.I.s. I might have been one of them.

And all through those tragic years, Joyce and I and our comrades never wavered. We kept marching and held on tight to our "rising hopes for peace."

I Wed a Gal Who Dances the Hornpipe

During the following two years, I left the farm in Sequim, relieved from my "hired hand" duties helping my father with the endless farm chores. I enrolled at the University of Washington full time and loved it. I took courses in English Literature. I excelled in a creative writing course taught by Thomas Gaddis, author of *Birdman of Alcatraz*. I submitted a fictionalized short story about Leonard Wood, a Clallam Indian

I had known in my youth who had won a marathon race from Port Townsend to Sequim during the 1930s. By the time I knew him, Wood was a derelict alcoholic who panhandled on the streets of Sequim, drank himself into a blind stupor and slept it off wherever he passed out. Yet once he had been a lean, swift long distance runner.

I remember Gaddis reading my story aloud in that small class and telling me afterward, "Wheeler, you can WRITE." It was published in the UW creative writing journal under the title *Sparrow*. Later it was republished by *Masses & Mainstream*.

I joined the Student Peace Union. My first meeting was in the student union building called "The HUB." A crowd of thirty-five or forty students were there, including some I had known since childhood, including: Karolyn Hamerquist, daughter of Clallam County logger, Don Hamerquist, Sr. and his wife, Virginia. The chairman of SPU was a tall, lean, handsome guy named J.C. Burdick, from Spokane. Karolyn and J.C. would soon marry. Kae Halonen, daughter of Oiva and Taimi Halonen, also someone I had admired since my teenage years, was also there. She was married to a graduate student in history, Ted Norton. Joyce Provost, an undergraduate anthropology major was in the circle too. She had a clear, bell-like voice and spoke up in favor of militant, direct action to oppose war and militarism. She was a staunch opponent of the Cold War and the nuclear sword of Damocles that hung over the human race. She was lively, graceful, with a droll wit. I was to learn that she was also a gifted ballet and modern dancer who had studied dance since she was a little girl. I was attracted to her and looked for chances to see her.

One day at the Roosevelt St. Commune, I was strumming my autoharp and humming the *Sailor's Hornpipe*.

She stood and danced that charming folk-dance. She laughed gaily and told me her English ballet teacher in Caldwell Idaho taught her many folk dances. To prove it, she danced the "Irish Jig" followed by the "Highland Fling," spinning on her toes, her graceful arms akimbo.

Later, I witnessed her gifts as a dancer in a dramatic setting. One of her anthropology professors was a Japanese man who helped organize an October festival on campus called "Gujo Odori."

He invited his daughter, one of Japan's most celebrated dancers, to come to the University to lead the dancing. She did in an open air street festival with thousands of UW students turning out to watch her perform.

Dressed in a full length, pink silk geisha gown, she danced the dance with lovely restraint and understatement. Then the professor invited people in the crowd to join her. Joyce was the first to step forward. She stood beside the Japanese woman and within a few seconds was imitating her every move, flawlessly.

The crowd applauded and cheered. I was smitten! I moved in to her apartment. We went down to City Hall and obtained a marriage license. Anyone who could dance like that would make an excellent wife, I decided.

But we postponed marriage because she had romantic notions of the wedding. She wanted to weave her own wedding gown out of fine white wool. She wanted to get married in a clover pasture on our farm with hundreds of guests from the anthropology department Student Peace Union and of course our herd of Jerseys and Guernseys mooing in the background.

She was invited by Seattle Women Act for Peace to be one of the panelists on a radio program. The other panelists were Alice Franklin Bryant, the beloved peace advocate who had run repeatedly for office on a peace platform, Taimi Halonen, Anci Koppel, and Thorun Robel. I listened to the radio program. It

Marriage of Joyce Provost and Tim Wheeler at Justice of the Peace in Seattle. Photo courtesy of Karolyn Hamerquist Burdick

was excellent. As the only youth, Joyce was a hit, stating her views on ending nuclear testing clearly and persuasively.

After the radio program, Mrs. Bryant took Joyce by the hand and asked sweetly, "When are you and Tim going to get married?"

"Yes," interjected Anci Koppel. "When?"

Taimi and Thorun were waiting for Joyce's answer too.

Joyce came back to her apartment that afternoon. I was reading. She opened the door, stepped inside. "Tim. Get ready. We're going to get married."

"When?"

"NOW!"

I got on the phone and found a Justice of the Peace who said he could perform the ceremony that afternoon at four pm. I then called J.C. and Karolyn Burdick and asked them if he would be my best man and Karolyn would serve as Joyce's Matron of Honor. The word was spread as widely as we could spread it. Come to the wedding.

When we arrived at the JP's home, he invited us into his living room. A plastic model of the Space Needle was sitting on top of his table TV, illuminated and rotating. He leaned over and unplugged it. Several of our guests were hippies. One was barefoot. I had no wedding ring so Ray Cooper, who had recently married Margaret Arducci, lent me his, a lovely green jade wedding band.

We exchanged vows. I kissed Joyce and embraced her. The little crowd of twenty or twenty-five friends applauded.

J.C. & Karolyn were not fond of Mexican cuisine but they knew we loved it. So they took us to "Campos," a few blocks away, the best Mexican restaurant in Seattle.

Also, Joyce and I did not have a car. J.C. & Karolyn served as our chauffeurs and drove us in their car up to Vancouver, British Columbia for our honeymoon. We were threadbare students with only a couple of dimes to rub together. So we checked in to dormitories at the University of British Columbia. We stayed literally in a barracks with rows of bunks from one end to the other. J.C. and Karolyn slept at one end and Joyce & I slept at the other.

It was a wedding suite fit for a king and queen! Sitting on the top bunk, I pulled out my autoharp, tuned it up and sang a song or two.

We have been married now for fifty-four years, proud parents of three children, seven grandchildren and two great grandchildren, and a third great grandchild expected any day.

Pete Seeger: Standing Tall at 85
December 17, 2004

Pete Seeger turned eighty-five last May 3 and could be forgiven if he hung up his five-string banjo and relaxed with his wife Toshi at their home up the Hudson River in Beacon, New York. But that is not Pete Seeger's way.

During a fifty-minute interview by telephone with the *People's Weekly World*, the famed folksinger and fighter for peace and environmental justice enthused on his immersion in a half-dozen projects.

Seeger was on his way down to Texas for the National Assembly of the Unitarian Universalists. He is a man of restless energy and creativity.

He is completing a new edition of his songbook, *Where Have All the Flowers Gone?* A CD of the songs will accompany it. "People need to hear the songs so they can sing them," Seeger said. "You have to hear the syncopation of African songs to sing them right."

He has set up a foundation so that Third World nations will receive royalties from songs and folk tales he has popularized, such as the South African *Abiyoyo* and *Wimoweh.*

The last time this reporter spoke to Seeger in person was at the February 15, 2003 demonstration a few blocks from the United Nations, protesting George W. Bush's rush to war on Iraq. A biting wind tore up the avenues. Surly New York police were treating the freezing protesters like cattle to be herded and penned.

Pete Seeger led the crowd in *Somewhere over the Rainbow*. Over the decades he has become a familiar sight, singing and playing his banjo on behalf of every conceivable struggle for democracy and human rights. "I will come and sing again if I am asked even though my voice is ninety percent gone," he said. "The list of songs is down to about a dozen, *This Land is My Land, Over the Rainbow, Where Have All the Flowers Gone?*"

He relies now on a time-tested strategy. "I line-out the hymn," he said. "I recite the lines of songs everybody knows a few beats ahead of the crowd so that they can do the singing." Getting crowds to sing along with him is part of Pete Seeger's genius in enlisting grassroots people in the rebirth of folk music as a living art form.

He understood early the power of song as a force for social change. He said he was not surprised that singer Bruce Springsteen was a huge draw as he campaigned alongside Democrat John Kerry before the November 2 election. Kerry often thanked Springsteen for turning out more people than he himself could attract. "Many movements now realize that music can bring the crowds to listen to speeches," Seeger said.

Yet he was not surprised that George W. Bush captured a second term. "I kind of expected it, because the Bush gang had so much money they could pay for any kind of trick, big or small," Seeger said. "On the other hand, I'm more encouraged by this election than ever before. So many people voted and 56 million voted against Bush. We had more voters than in any election in thirty years. The very worst thing is for people to say: 'My vote doesn't count. So why bother to vote at all?' People rejected that and turned out. That gives us good reason for hope."

Seeger was not alone in the movement that succeeded in reclaiming folk music. There were singers like Huddie Ledbetter, better known as "Leadbelly," with his twelve-string guitar. From his experience as a prison inmate in the Jim-Crow South, Leadbelly immortalized African American work songs like *Take this Hammer* and *Midnight Special*. Seeger also spoke warmly of Woody Guthrie who joined Seeger, Lee Hays, and Millard Lampell in The Almanac Singers in 1941. They were favorites at rallies of the Congress of Industrial Organizations, singing *Talking Union, There Once Was a Union Maid,* and *We Shall Not Be Moved.* They also sang sea chanteys like the *Greenland Whale Fisher Song* and other work songs.

Woody was out in Oregon composing ballads for the Bonneville Power Administration such as *Roll on Columbia,* Seeger said. "I called him up and invited him to join The Almanac Singers. He hitchhiked across the country. Along the way, he went into a diner and heard on a jukebox Kate Smith singing *God Bless America.* He started right then to pen his answer; *This Land is Your Land.*

The song was never on the hit parade, Seeger said, but was spread as sheet music and 78 RPM records mainly through the nation's public schools. "Music teachers would hear it and say, 'That's a good song. Children can sing it.' Now it is so widely beloved that it has become a sort of unofficial national anthem."

"Woody showed up at Almanac House June 23, 1941, the day after Hitler invaded the Soviet Union," Seeger continued. "I opened the door and said, 'Woody! You got here!' And he replied, 'Well, we won't be singing those peace songs.' Three weeks later he wrote *The Good Reuben James* about the Nazi torpedoing of a Liberty Ship with all hands lost."

Seeger spoke of his ties to the *Daily Worker.* He remains today a reader of the *People's Weekly World.* His father, an ethno-musicologist at Juilliard and later at UCLA, wrote a

Pete Seeger reads the Daily World with a headline article by the author. Photo courtesy of the Tamiment Library, New York University

column for the *Daily Worker* under the byline Carl Sands. "Woody wrote a column called 'Woodie Sez' for the *Worker*," Seeger noted.

Seeger was summoned to appear before the House Un-American Activities Committee during the depths of Cold War McCarthyism to be questioned on his ties to the Communist Party USA. He cited the First Amendment in refusing to testify. He would not "name names." He was cited for contempt and sentenced to a year in prison. The sentence was overturned on appeal. But Seeger endured years of blacklist.

Bobbie Rabinowitz, founder of the New York City Labor Chorus and a longtime friend of Seeger's, spoke for many. "Pete was a major inspiration," she told the *World*. "He would come to our rehearsals and teach us songs." Now, she said, labor choruses have sprung up in Seattle, San Francisco, Washington, D.C., North Carolina and Brooklyn. "I first heard Pete sing as a teenager at Camp Kinder-land," she said. "He was on the stage with a log and an axe. As he sang a logger's song, he chopped and the chips flew. I caught one. I have it still. It's like one of those home-run balls that kids catch at a baseball game."

Joe McCarthy, Richard Nixon, and J. Edgar Hoover have been disgraced and thrown in the "dustbin of history." George W. Bush is likely to join them.

As for Seeger, he is a man beloved of the people and standing tall at eighty-five.

Not Merely a Teenage Crush
By Susan E. Wheeler

Portland, Oregon—When I was a fifteen-year-old girl with stars in her eyes I wrote a fan letter to Pete Seeger. My contemporaries were in love with Elvis Presley, but I fell in love with Pete.

Pete and my parents were fond acquaintances, sharing a history of struggle and resistance to political persecution. My father was subpoenaed numerous times. There was a strong connection between our families.

Pete had been blacklisted for years [due to his politics] and it was difficult to find a hall for him to perform in. He sang at venues like the Rotary Club in Grand Rapids, Mich.; Osteopathic Association in New Mexico; Ethical Culture Society in New York City; Home for the Aged, Portland; and at various universities. We organized a concert in Port Angeles, Washington, in 1957, which drew seventy-five people.

A year later that number was doubled for a concert he did with Sonny Terry and J.C. Burris, Sonny's nephew, who played the spoons. Pete sang two of local logger Russ Farrell's songs; *There Shall Be Peace* and *The Scaler had a Long Thumb*, which Pete got published in *Sing Out* magazine. I could not believe so few people turned out, but Pete said it was a good turnout for a town without a college.

I wrote in my diary, "I've met the man with the banjo the first time outside the Moore Theater in Seattle. I knew his music; I'd heard him sing and play, and I loved him for that, as did thousands of other people across the country. There, under the glaring lights of the ticket office, was the top-coated, striding Pete Seeger. I became suddenly timid, my voice failed and my knees knocked, my heart thudding uncontrollably in my throat."

My brother rescued me. I shook hands with him, the world's greatest banjo picker. His eyes were as warm as his handshake. He had a large nose and irregular teeth, and in one cheek was a ragged crease made because he sings with his head back and his mouth crooked to one side. He wore a red scarf about his neck, for it was November and hands-plunged-in-pockets cold."

I felt as if I were shaking hands with every person, great and humble, Black and white, who has ever had faith in the people and hope for the future. Here was Sean O'Casey, John Keats, John Brown, Thaddeus Stevens, Karl Marx, and a multitude, and I was face to face with them. "I'll never forget it, not in a thousand lifetimes. Tongue-tied, all I could manage was an intelligent, 'Golly.'"

133

Pete and Lee Hays organized The Weavers in 1950. They were an enormous success, selling over 4 million records. But the organized blacklist intervened. The House Un-American Activities Committee began an investigation into the entertainment industry. Pete's FBI file was leaked by J. Edgar Hoover to the *New York World Telegram.*

Radio stations stopped playing the Weavers' music, concerts were canceled, and the group was banned from television appearances. The Weavers were the first musicians in American history to be investigated for sedition.

Then Harvey Matusow named Pete as a member of the Communist Party. Pete was called before the committee, where he pled the First Amendment, not the Fifth. A photo with the caption, "Sings for people, not committees," appeared in the left-wing press.

On July 26, 1956, the House of Representatives voted 373-9 to cite Seeger for contempt of Congress. Pete was indicted along with playwright Arthur Miller and six others for contempt. After worldwide protests, an appeals court eventually ruled Seeger's indictment faulty and dismissed it.

But Pete was still blacklisted in many places until the late '60s. In September 1967, Pete appeared on the *Smothers Brothers* TV show, where he sang "Waist Deep in the Big Muddy," and the censors axed it. (He later appeared again and the song went on.)

Pete once said, "I'd sing for the John Birch Society or the American Legion if they asked. So far they haven't." But he was invited to the White House, and received the nation's highest artistic honors at the Kennedy Center in December 1994.

The album "Pete" won a Grammy in 1996. The album includes How *Can I Keep From Singing,* with the lyrics penned by Doris Plenn during the '50s Red Scare: "When tyrants tremble sick with fear/and hear their death knell ringing/when friends rejoice both far and near/how can I keep from singing."

Pete can't.

[4]

WHERE HAVE ALL THE FLOWERS GONE?

Corporal Francis Marion Wheeler, Company A, 141st New York Volunteers.
Photo by Matthew Brady studio, Washington, D.C

Great Grandfather Fought to End Slavery and Save a Nation

People's World May 7 2014; Revised 2015

An unpublished manuscript *The Diary of Francis Marion Wheeler 1842-1899* has been gathering dust, unread, on a bookshelf in our house for many years. It had a blue card-stock cover with a handwritten title. It was mimeographed, difficult to read because the print was blurred. While I was searching for something to read to put myself to sleep, I picked it up and began to read. I could not put it down.

On August 12, 1862, at age nineteen, Francis Marion Wheeler, my great grandfather, answered the call of President Abraham Lincoln and joined the Union Army.

He writes, "Mother's stories of the Revolutionary War, my admiration for the Revolutionary hero for whom I had been named, Francis Marion, greatly increased this feeling. I determined that my country should never in vain need my arm for assistance."

The Civil War had been raging for a year, he writes, with "numerous defeats and disasters" spreading "gloom and anxiety over the North."

It became apparent to him "that the whole military power of the Nation, or the loyal part of it, must be exerted or the enemy would . . . surely succeed in disrupting the Union and establishing their confederacy. President Lincoln issued a call for 300,000 more volunteers . . ."

My Great Grandfather joined an infantry regiment Company A, 141 New York Volunteers. While stationed in Washington, D.C., he had his picture taken in the uniform of a corporal at a Matthew Brady studio. That image has been part of my family as long as I can remember.

Great grandfather writes that he and his fellow soldiers marched in blistering heat, pouring rain, carrying a heavy musket, ammunition, and backpack. He describes marching south in Virginia to the Rappahannock River. They bivouacked overnight. Then they were ordered to turn around and march back north to Manassas, tramping all night and the next day.

A train sent south from Manassas to pick them up was empty on the way down and returned to Manassas empty. No one can explain the mix up that led to this debacle. The forced march fueled deep anger in the ranks when the soldiers learned that somehow they had missed the train when the empty train arrived in Manassas. They boarded it so exhausted that they collapsed in the box cars. My great grandfather describes stretching out in the box car and falling into a deep sleep.

The train sped through Maryland, West Virginia, Ohio, Indiana, Kentucky and Tennessee. This was the famed emergency transfer of 30,000 troops, cannons, etc. ordered by Secretary of War Edwin Stanton to reverse a defeat inflicted by the Confederates on Union General Rosecrans in the Battle of Chickamauga.

Great Grandfather describes the trip as if it were a festive excursion. In Ohio, "Troops of rosy, laughing girls were to be seen at the depots," he writes. "They frequently flung apples, flowers, and bits of folded paper containing mottoes among the boys. . . . The good-natured engine drivers would sound the whistle vigorously several times before starting at which the stragglers would scamper back with commendable alacrity."

Within hours of detraining in Chattanooga, they marched to the rear of Rosecrans' army, a vast reinforcement that halted the Confederate advance. Later, he fought in the *Battle of Lookout Mountain.* It ended in victory for the Union Army.

They marched on to Atlanta, repeatedly engaging the Confederates. In a typical entry July 20, 1864, he wrote: "We had a bloody and desperate battle. We were surprised and were not in line when the enemy was upon us. We had to form under fire. I shot a man close to me in the advancing line. . . . It was in the thick woods . . . smoke concealed the enemy from us and us from the enemy. At sundown they withdrew leaving their dead."

He was only a corporal, yet he was assigned to command Company A because he was the highest-ranking soldier still standing, he wrote.

After the capture of Atlanta, he marched with Sherman to the sea.

He wrote, "Parties of soldiers foraged for themselves and messmates . . . Quartermasters' men drove off cattle, horses and mules . . . plundered hen roosts, ransacked cellars, kitchens and pantries to the dismay and distress of the people who never thought of resistance as it would have been folly unspeakable to attempt it."

He added, "In short, the country through which we passed was exhausted and temporarily ruined. Railroads were torn up, piled and burned . . . bridges, depots and engine houses burned. Saw mills, tanneries, cotton gins, cotton presses, sugar mills. . . .

"It was awful. My heart ached for the miserable people and I reflected on the years of toil that would be required before this lost property could be recreated."

He continued, "One reflection however, showed me why all this evil had come on them. It was the remark of an old Negro (sic) with whom I was conversing. Said he, 'This property was not theirs. They never earned or cared for it. We earned it. It was ours.'"

He wrote, "This was true. The masters had acquired it unjustly and it perished with a sudden and irreparable destruction."

I found this passage remarkable. Here was an earnest young soldier, deeply religious, suffering pangs of conscience. And who gives him an insight into the meaning of that destruction? An African American, almost surely a slave who had freed himself and attached himself, like tens of thousands of other slaves, to the Union Army.

They captured Savannah, he continued, and then swung north marching into South Carolina. They crossed into North Carolina. On Mar. 24, 1865 he wrote:

We entered Goldsboro, N.C. and joined there Schofield's and Terry's forces which had come up the river, Cape Fear, from the capture of Fort Fisher and Wilmington.

Our appearance compared with that of the soldiers there encamped was striking. They were clean and but slightly sunburned, uniforms and equipment all new.

We were unwashed, tanned, and grimed, our clothing worn, tattered and faded out. We marched with a rapid step, with ranks and files loosely closed. We were carrying pieces of bacon or undressed pork, fowls in our hands or adjusted to our equipage in some way. Coffee pots, frying pans, hatchets were freely exhibited. . . .

Hence, our army entering Goldsboro was a singular spectacle. But it was formidable. They were all tried soldiers and were inured to tremendous exertions. At a word, they could bring their arms into position, dress the files, close their ranks and maintain every appearance of a disciplined army who knew their power and were proud of their record.

A few days later, Confederate Gen. Robert E. Lee surrendered at Appomattox, Virginia.

Great grandfather marched in the victory parade in Washington D.C. a few weeks after that. He wrote, ". . . we passed in Grand Review through the streets of Washington, passing from Capitol Hill down Pennsylvania Avenue by the Presidential Mansion . . . We filled the street from side to side . . . as many men in double rank marched abreast as would fill the street across and this occupied a vista of about three miles which could be seen looking up Pennsylvania Avenue like a vast and moving mass surmounted the while by the glittering sheen of arms."

He added, "The infantry were several hours in passing, then artillery, cavalry, hospital trains, pontoon trains and last of all, 'Sherman's Bummers' which created a great deal of merriment."

In her great book *Reveille in Washington*, Margaret Leech ends with a description of that victory parade with Sherman's army marching in the rearguard, blanket rolls across their shoulders, stepping with the easy slouch of soldiers who had marched thousands of miles, engaged in nonstop combat.

After the war, great grandfather became a Methodist preacher. He and his wife Esther Sackett went to India as missionaries and, while there, she gave birth to Faith and Rohilla. For Great grandfather, Esther and the children, it was an ordeal as difficult as the war. The adults suffered heat strokes that ultimately killed Esther. Great grandfather remarried Esther's sister, Adelaide. They moved to the Pacific Northwest with the children where he continued his ministry.

Medical research had not yet identified "Post Traumatic Stress Disorder" but great grandfather suffered a mental breakdown that surely reflected the trauma he had suffered both in combat and in later life. He died in a mental hospital in 1900 at age fifty-eight.

A monument still stands at 15th & Pennsylvania Avenue in Washington D.C. honoring Sherman and his army. Francis Marion Wheeler's scores of descendants should honor him as a hero. He fought to save our nation and end slavery.

A Marine on His Way to War

The war was raging in Korea, then called a "police action" by President Harry Truman. There was grave danger that the U.S. would escalate the conflict into World War III with U.S. troops deployed to crush the infant revolution in China. That, in turn, would escalate into war with the Soviet Union.

We could not escape the poison of that war. One frigid spring morning, a weird sight appeared at our front door, a barefoot U.S. Marine, dressed in his drab-olive semi-dress uniform, his tie pulled loose and hanging awry, his pant legs rolled up, carrying his dress shoes in one hand. He was shivering violently from the cold.

He and his buddies were on a drinking spree from the U.S. Navy base in Bremerton and had driven their car into the ditch up in Happy Valley. He decided to walk down through the woods hoping his drunkenness would wear off in the bitter cold as he fought his way through the underbrush.

We invited him in and sat him down with a hot cup of coffee. We were getting ready to eat a bacon and egg breakfast and invited him to join us. He became ever happier at this turn of events.

An hour later, life restored, he pulled himself together and got ready to leave. We had been good Samaritans and he fumbled for some way to express his gratitude. "When I get to Korea, I'll kill a couple of gooks for you," he exclaimed. We sat in stunned silence, horrified by his crude outburst so contrary to the altruism we had bestowed on him.

"No, don't do that," Daddy replied calmly. "The Korean people haven't done anything to harm us and we have no reason to harm them. We never should have meddled in that country and the sooner we end this war the better. We're very sorry they are sending you into harm's way."

The Marine, his face beet red, left us, trudging down the hill toward Sequim, on his way across the Pacific Ocean to a needless war.

Sergeant Provost Missed His Daughter

Daily Online, May 25 2009

Sergeant Roland Francis Provost with his daughter, Joyce Provost, at Hickam Field, Pearl Harbor, Hawaii. Photo by Leatha Provost

Just in time for memorial day, I took out the medals won by Roland Francis Provost for "combat valor" in World War II, pinned them to the flag draped over his casket and hung it up on our bedroom wall in Baltimore.

Those medals have been stored safely out of sight in a file cabinet for as long as Joyce and I have been married. He was the father she hardly knew. He died and was buried near the family home in Orlando, Florida, when she was just a little girl.

I did some research on the War in the Pacific, pinpointing where Provost was at various stages of the conflict. It is a story of a fiasco, a debacle, a huge human tragedy imposed on humanity by fascism and imperial ambitions.

That war has been called "The Good War." Whether "good" or "bad," World War II was a completely avoidable war. If the U.S., France and Britain had heeded the Soviet Union's call for "collective security" measures against Nazi Germany and the fascist axis, the war could have been prevented.

Provost was a U.S. Army Air Corps Master Sergeant, an aircraft engine mechanic, and a navigator stationed at Hickam Airfield, Hawaii, when Joyce was born January 26, 1941. He was a doting father.

But with ominous war clouds gathering, Provost was assigned to the 30th Bomber Squadron and flew September 20, 1941, in a flotilla of hundreds of B-17s and B-25s bombers to Clark Air Field in the Philippines leaving his wife, daughter, and stepson behind in Hawaii. A few weeks later, they survived the Japanese attack on Pearl Harbor.

One day later, December 8, 1941, the Japanese attacked Clark Air Field destroying all but fourteen of the planes on the ground, even though General Douglas MacArthur had been forewarned that the Philippines would be Japan's next target. Somehow, Provost escaped, flying with his comrades to an airbase outside Darwin, Australia.

A few days later, they flew back to Bandeong, Indonesia, joining in a futile attempt to block the Japanese invasion of Southeast Asia. Among Provost's papers is a yellow, mimeographed sheet dated February 12, 1942, and signed by Commanding General L.H. Brereton, citing Provost and his fellow airmen for "combat valor." They were awarded the Silver Star, the Purple Heart and the Distinguished Flying Cross even as the Japanese Imperial Army closed in for the final kill.

Outnumbered and outgunned, their defenses crumbling, Provost and his comrades scrambled their planes and fled back to Darwin, March 6, 1942.

Provost moved on a few months later to an airbase near Port Moresby, Papua, New Guinea and probably helped provide air cover for the U.S. Navy during the "Battle of the Coral Sea" May 3-7, 1942.

Retreat sometimes brings out acts of heroism, amid panic and confusion, even braver than offense when the attacker has the advantage of treachery and surprise.

I am reading, now, the memoirs of General Georgi Zhukov, who commanded the Soviet Army during World War II. He provides many examples of bravery among the Soviet people in the early weeks of the Nazi invasion of the Soviet Union in June 1941.

German General Hans Guderian, for example, was driving with an enormous force of Panzers and crack Wehrmacht infantry divisions to the southeast of Moscow. His aim was to capture the town of Tula, famed as the "Czar's armory," and swing around to encircle the Soviet capital. Fighting desperate defensive engagements, the Red Army was in retreat. Workers in the Tula plants left their lathes and drill presses, took up rifles and marched out to reinforce the Red Army. The Nazi advance was halted.

Workers in Moscow, Leningrad, Stalingrad and other cities carried out similar acts of mass heroism during the "Great Patriotic War," Zhukov writes. They were motivated by their hatred of fascism and fascist atrocities and their love of the socialist homeland.

The flower of Soviet society, those most loyal to the October Revolution of 1917, died, a blow that may have been a factor in the collapse of the USSR fifty years later.

So what if "collective action" had successfully blocked the fascist war?

Tens of millions of lives would have been saved. Joyce would have grown up with a father. This is not idle speculation about how we might have avoided a war fought sixty-seven years ago. Every war fought since then has been avoidable, a squandering of life, a waste of material resources needed to improve the living conditions of humanity.

On this Memorial Day, let's remember the words on those Quaker yard signs that went up five years ago and never came down: "War is not the answer."

The Soldier Who Fought with One Shoe On, One Shoe Off

June 12, 2015

Taimi Halonen approached me at the Communist Party's 21st Convention in Chicago in 1975. She was a convention delegate from Seattle and so was her husband, Oiva. "Will you interview Oiva and write up his story?" she asked me. "Every Lincoln Brigade vet I know has been written up, but not Oiva."

I told Taimi I would be honored.

Oiva Halonen was a hero of every progressive youth growing up in the Pacific Northwest in the 1950s.

Oiva Halonen, photo courtesy of Kathleen Robel

That included me. They were Finnish Americans who lived in Ballard, the Scandinavian neighborhood on the northwest side of Seattle. More than once, Oiva, Taimi, and their daughters, Kae, and ReeAnne, visited us on our farm near Sequim.

Oiva was a tall, lanky man, with a shock of gray hair, a wry grin and a twinkle in his eyes. He was deaf so it was hard to engage him in a casual conversation. Yet he was a lively, genial man. Despite his deafness, he played the piano and accompanied his family in singing.

We all knew that Oiva Halonen had been a machine gunner with the Abraham Lincoln Brigade in Spain, fighting to defend the duly elected Spanish Republican government from the Franco fascists. It was with some eagerness that I approached Oiva and asked him for the interview. We left the convention hall during a break and found a quiet corner in the lobby where we sat down for the interview.

I asked my questions loudly and often when I couldn't make myself understood, wrote out my questions on my notepad. He had that same mischievous twinkle in his eyes as I plied him with questions.

He told me his first major issue after arriving in Spain in 1937 was finding shoes big enough to fit his very large feet. He was six feet, one inch tall and was strong as a bull. "Finally, the quartermaster came out of the stock room with a pair of size sixteen shoes, about three sizes too big," Oiva said, chuckling at the memory. It was the best they could do. Oiva said he laced on the boots that made him look like Lil Abner and clomped out of the Quartermaster's supply store.

The boots tortured his every step, working loose while he carried the fifty pound machine gun on his shoulder and struggling to keep up with his comrades. The war was reaching fever pitch and came to a head in the famed "Battle of the Ebro."

They were face to face with Franco's fascist legions. Oiva's unit was ordered to advance into combat. Oiva told me he was racing forward with his machine gun when his right boot came loose, flopping as he attempted to run. He lost his temper. He laid the machine gun on the ground and pulled off the damnable boot and threw it into the brush. He picked up the machine gun and ran hard to catch up, fascist bullets zinging past his brow. "That's how I fought the battle," Oiva said. "One shoe on, one shoe off."

The battle raged all day and late into the night. Finally, long after darkness had fallen, the guns fell silent. It was a stalemate. His unit was ordered to hunker down, hold the ground. The exhausted soldiers fell into a deep sleep. Long after midnight, a sergeant crawled among the sleeping soldiers, shaking them awake. He whispered, "We've been ordered to pull back. Get your stuff together and move. Keep it quiet."

Somehow, the sergeant forgot Oiva who, in his deafness, was sleeping contentedly.

He awoke as dawn was breaking. He looked around and found he was by himself in no-man's land. The sun was rising. He would be totally isolated, the fascist lines only a few dozen yards away. Still missing one boot, he grabbed his machine gun and crawled away 100 yards then stood and ran for his life back to Loyalist lines. He made it successfully, his comrades pounding him on his back, congratulating him on his narrow escape.

A general retreat was then ordered. The Brigade formed up and began its single file march along a road away from the front. They were weary but glad to be alive.

An open staff car rolled up alongside the column of marching soldiers. Sitting in the rear seat was Robert Merryman, Commander of the Abraham Lincoln Brigade. Merryman spotted Oiva and ordered the driver to stop. "Soldier, what happened to your boot?"

Oiva tried to explain the issue as simply and quickly as he could.

"Get in," Merryman ordered.

"So I rode along in high style in Commander Merryman's staff car," Oiva said, "Still one shoe on, one shoe off."

He laughed merrily at the memory.

Oiva told me more of his war stories, his being sent to a rest and recuperation encampment on the Mediterranean Sea after months in fierce combat.

He returned to the U.S. and to Seattle where he became a machinist at Todd Shipyard. He and his best friend, Gene Robel, were among the staunchest members of the International Association of Machinists during World War II, producing ships for the U.S. Navy and the Merchant Marine in the struggle to defeat fascism.

When World War II ended, the Cold Warriors launched their anti-communist witch-hunt. Oiva Halonen and Gene Robel were subpoenaed to appear before the House UnAmerican Activities Committee. Both were expelled from the Machinists union.

Gene Robel's appeal against that expulsion went all the way to the U.S. Supreme Court which ruled in his favor in 1967.

Oiva and Taimi were mainstays of the Party and the progressive movement in Seattle. Taimi was a founding member and sparkplug of Seattle Women Act for Peace.

Oiva was a quiet man. But when he did speak in meetings everyone listened. He was an especially clear thinker and always steered us away from narrow or adventurist actions that would divide us and open us up for attack from the right. He was a unifier.

I must say I was taken aback when I interviewed Oiva in 1975. What he told me about his war experience was so much at odds with what I had expected. I revered Oiva Halonen. I had expected heroics. What he told me was anti-heroic. His story was about the absurdity of war, even a war waged for a noble cause.

That was the meaning of the twinkle in his eyes, the faint smile as he spoke. He was not going to give me any phony heroics, no glorification, no flag-waving.

He went into combat only because fascism was the greatest evil facing humanity. He picked up that machine gun because he had no other choice. He was a Cincinnatus, a citizen soldier.

148

[5]

BACK IN MY HOMETOWN, STILL COVERING THE NEWS

Asian American Worker Struggles (for Asian-American Workers, There are No Borders)

People's Weekly World, October 26, 2007

SEATTLE—A traveling exhibit, "Journey for Justice: 223 Years of Asian Pacific American History in the Puget Sound," opened at the Wing Luke Asian Museum here September 27 with its bold message that Asian Pacific American workers have won victories over racism and exploitation, yet continue to struggle for equality today.

Many of the workers whose photos and biographies are featured in the exhibit were present at the reception. Laurie Yamamura, a Japanese American postal worker, was there with her husband. She served as shop steward of her union local at the University of Washington post office before retiring in 2001. "This exhibit is fascinating," she told the World. "It is part of my history. Stand up for your rights. That's the lesson for me. That's why I joined the union. If you help yourself, then you can help your fellow workers as well."

Telling untold stories

Tracy Lai, president of the Seattle Chapter of the Asian Pacific American Labor Alliance (APALA), told the capacity crowd the exhibit has traveled widely since it was completed in 2004, displayed at the AFL-CIO headquarters in Washington, D.C., this summer, and [also] displayed in Vancouver, British Columbia, during the Labor Day weekend. It created such an impression, she said, that the Canadian labor movement "wants to form a Canadian version of APALA."

Ron Chew, director of the museum, said, "This exhibit . . . tells stories that have not been told, the struggle for justice. My father was a waiter paid $1 an hour, seven days a week, no vacation. My mother was a sweatshop worker. As a child, I watched people working literally until they died." He announced that the museum is near to completing its $23 million fund drive for a new, much larger building where this unsung history will be featured.

Peter Kardas, director of the Labor Center at Evergreen College in Olympia, which helped produce the exhibit, said, "It reminds people of the repression and the racism and the anti-immigrant hysteria that has gone on for so long."

The exhibit consists of photos of Asian American and Pacific Islander trade unionists active in the labor movement today with biographical sketches of their lives and struggles as union activists. The exhibit brings home just how rarely we see working people depicted as heroes in our mass culture, even though not a single wheel would turn without their work and every cupboard would be bare.

'Make the history'

One of those featured is Tracy Lai, herself, a social studies professor at Seattle Central Community College. Lai is the president of American Federation of Teachers Local 1789 on her campus. "I teach about history," she told an interviewer, "and one of the things that I emphasize with my students is when people are in those moments of making history, rarely do we know it. 'Make the history,' is what I say. Make the history."

The exhibit provides a timeline called "milestones" that begins in 1780 with the arrival of Hawaiians in the Pacific Northwest working as seamen and stevedores for the Hudson Bay Company.

The Chinese Exclusion Act of 1882 and the mass internment of Japanese Americans during World War II are highlighted in the exhibit, which features many archival photographs and drawings.

Another worker pictured in the exhibit is Richard Gurtiza, a Filipino American, director of Region 37 of the Inland Boatmen's Union in Seattle. An affiliate of the International Longshore and Warehouse Union (ILWU), Region 37 was once known as Local 37, representing the mostly Filipino cannery workers in Alaska and down the Pacific Coast.

"Sometimes even in the labor movement we are not recognized. We are not given a seat at the table," Gurtiza told the *World*. "It is important to raise the consciousness of the role of Asian American workers in the labor movement."

APALA and the exhibit, he said, can serve as a "bridge between the communities and the labor movement."

Defending immigrants, defending the union

One of the milestones featured in the exhibit is the struggle to defend Local 37 leaders Ernesto Mangaoang and Chris Mensalves, both based in Seattle during a Cold War drive to deport them back to the Philippines in the late 1940s and early 1950s. The timeline makes clear it is revenge for their militant role in defending the cannery workers using their left-wing political beliefs as a pretext.

Among the staunchest defenders of the two union leaders was B.J. Mangaoang, wife of Ernesto. B.J., as she was affectionately known to her friends and family, served for many years as chairperson of the Communist Party USA in Washington State. She died October 20 in Seattle at age 92.

The case, Mangaoang v. Boyd, went all the way to the U.S. Supreme Court, which ruled in 1953 that Mangaoang could not be deported under the Walter-McCarran Act.

"That was an era when everybody was being red-baited," Gurtiza said. "They were trying to break the union. They tried to deport ILWU President Harry Bridges. They were not able to do it because the ILWU wielded such power on the docks." Both Mangaoang and Bridges were well-known Marxists.

Against 'race hatred'

The Bush administration is engaged in dragnet raids and mass deportations of immigrant workers today, Gurtiza added. "They are fanning the fires of fear and anxiety. They are using that fear as a means of control. All these immigrant workers want is to work, to get a fair wage so they can support their families."

The exhibit points out that backward sections of labor joined in anti-immigrant witch-hunts that benefited only the bosses. Many workers, however, "were keen to the ways employers used immigrant and minority laborers to break strikes and weaken the power of organized labor," the commentary explains.

The Industrial Workers of the World (IWW) and later the ILWU "vigilantly organized Asian workers into their ranks."

Another milestone cited in the exhibit was the Seattle general strike of 1919. "For five days in February, 65,000 workers participated in a general strike in support of the city's wartime shipyard workers," the timeline states. The Seattle IWW issued an "Appeal to Japanese Workers in America." One "Wobbly" wrote to a newspaper at the time, "Teaching race hatred has been the foundation rock on which the capitalists have been able to induce the workers to sanction and enlist in war. If we would allow every (Japanese worker) in our unions, that would solve the question." He signed the letter, "Yours for one big union, with nobody that works barred no matter what his or her color, race, or creed."

During the ensuing general strike, "the Japanese Labor Union formally endorsed and honored the strike" despite the continued exclusionary policies of many unions, the timeline reports.

Art Shields' memoir, *"On the Battle Lines,* 1919-1939," (published by International Publishers, New York) is quoted in the exhibit. Shields, later a staff writer for the *Daily Worker,* wrote, "The general strike was the first mass demonstration of interracial unity I had seen. The Black migration from the Deep South had not yet reached Seattle. But the Japanese colony went on strike with us. Seattle had 10,000 Japanese immigrants ... any restaurants and hotels depended on them. The strike would have been weakened without them."

Wartime internment

Another milestone is the unjust and shameful mass internment of Japanese Americans after Franklin Delano Roosevelt signed Executive Order 9066 in 1942. The timeline records that 120,000 Americans of Japanese descent were "forcibly removed from the Pacific Coast to inland 'internment camps' on the bogus claim that they were "agents of the Japanese Empire."

The exhibit features a photo of one of those detainees, Karl G. Yoneda, although he, his wife Elaine Black, and their son Tommy, were arrested in California. Yoneda, a leader of the Communist Party USA, was a legendary organizer of Asian American workers and a member of the ILWU.

Yoneda recorded his heroic exploits in his 1983 autobiography, *Ganbatte, Sixty-Year Struggle of a Kibei Worker*, published by the Asian American Studies Center at the University of California, Los Angeles. The AFT's Human Rights and Community Relations Department published a beautiful poster of Karl Yoneda as part of its Asian Pacific American Labor Pioneers series, hailing him as "A champion for world peace and socialism."

The APALA exhibit cites a major milestone in 1946 when Washington state citizens of Asian, African American and Hispanic ancestry began lobbying for the enactment of a Fair Employment Practices Act. "This is finally achieved in 1949," the exhibit reads.

Yesterday and today

Today, globalized transnational capital is wreaking havoc in most of the developing world. A vast reserve army of labor, many of them forced from the land by the crisis in agriculture, is desperately seeking jobs to support their families, crossing borders seeking work in a strange land.

The parallels between the repression directed against immigrants today and that heaped upon immigrants 50 or 100 years ago is striking. Invariably, the bosses seek to inflame fear and to split, divide and confuse. Frightened people are easy to manipulate, their minds clouded so that they don't see their common interest and their need for unity against a common foe.

The Japanese Labor Association summed it up in a letter to the Seattle General Strike Committee in February 1919, declaring that they had joined the strike. The letter deplored the AFL's exclusion of Asian workers, adding, "If we laborers throughout the world have a similar position against the capitalists, no matter what jobs we occupy and what our nationality is, then there can be no borders for the laborers and we should do our duty in helping to win this fight."

Nash Huber's Farm Store, Dungeness.
Photo by the author

Bumper Crops in a World Facing Famine

People's World Online, June 21, 2011

SEQUIM, WASHINGTON— The United Nations reported recently that global hunger has soared 11 percent from 915 million to 1.02 billion as consumption of staple crops— wheat, rice, soybeans and corn—outstrips production.

It reverses half a century in which the so-called "Green Revolution" led to a six-fold increase in food production gradually reducing food deficits around the world. Global climate change, the resulting droughts, floods, and other extreme weather, coupled with population growth, are blamed. There is also a rising demand for meat, poultry, and other high protein foods as living standards rise in developing nations.

The *New York Times*, in a June 5 report headlined "A Warming Planet Struggles to Feed Itself" warned that these food deficits will grow with the danger of famines that would take the lives of millions.

Living on a farm, watching a team of energetic young farmers tilling and planting crops on our land, makes me think long and deep about food deficits here at home and around the world, deficits far more menacing than the budget deficits that keep lawmakers awake at night.

The young farmers working our land were recruited by organic vegetable grower, Nash Huber, who has raised vegetables, eggs, hogs and now grain on 400 leased acres in this valley since 1979. The American Farmland Trust awarded Huber its annual "Steward of the Land" prize in 2008.

Surely, farmers like Nash Huber are part of the solution.

He planted wheat on our farm a couple of years ago and it grew into a bumper crop. He sent off a sample for analysis and it came back with a stunning result: 15.5 percent protein, so high he thought it was a mistake. It was not. Washington State University chose Nash Huber's operation as one of three organic farms for testing the growing of organic wheat in Western Washington last year.

A few years back, Huber made a trip to Europe obtaining seeds for varieties of cabbage and other vegetables long vanished from our monoculture grocery stores. These "heritage" varieties are now growing luxuriantly in this valley, shipped to farmers markets here and as far away as Seattle.

The newsletter of the Nebraska Sustainable Agriculture Society featured an article by Liz Sarno, who visited here to see Huber's operation for herself. She hailed the young farmers as "energetic, enthusiastic . . . passionate about what they are contributing . . . caretakers for this special piece of fertile soil." Huber's operation could be a model to "help revitalize and rejuvenate our dwindling rural communities," by attracting thousands of young people back into farming.

Nash Huber. Photo by the author

Yet Huber and his young followers face a daunting struggle. This valley, once a thriving dairy center, has lost 70 percent of farmland to real estate development. Many of the houses now stand vacant in the collapse of the housing bubble.

Corporate agribusiness is another ruthless foe. A couple of months ago, about forty people, many of them Huber's partners, stood on the main intersection in Sequim holding signs like "Stop Monsanto" and " No More Frankenfood." It was part of the "Millions Against Monsanto" campaign.

One protester held a sign blasting Monsanto for its role in driving 100,000 Indian farmers to suicide rather than submit to a modern form of peonage, forced to buy Monsanto's sterile seeds rather than setting aside next year's seed corn from their own crops.

The *New York Times* article also warned that budget cutbacks are crippling agricultural research. Funding for the network of worldwide agricultural research stations set up under the leadership of Dr. Norman E. Borlaug, have been slashed by half in the past twenty years with some of these centers "suffering mass layoffs." These are the research institutions that developed the grains that made the "green revolution

President Obama is given high marks for pledging $3.5 billion to support this research during international meeting in A'quila, Italy, two years ago. Other governments pledged $22 billion. So far, though, Congress has approved only $1.9 billion and the balance is in doubt given budget deficit hysteria. And much of the $22 billion was not new money but rather reiterating a pledge of funds already pledged earlier.

The Republican deficit hawks are slashing and burning research, except for crazy schemes like a new generation of nuclear weapons. Politicians who slash research aimed at averting famines "know the cost of everything and the value of nothing."

Over half a century ago my father planted fifty acres of oats on our farm one spring. It grew with remarkable vigor.

When the breeze picked up in the evening, it sent rippling waves across a vast, emerald sea.

The combine arrived in late August and I was assigned to ride in the big box on the bed of our ton-and-a-half Dodge shoveling the grain into the corners to even the load. The oats poured around my knees, 140 bushels per acre. We harvested 2.9 tons per acre, about 147 tons total.

That's a lot of oatmeal cereal to fill the stomachs of hungry people. My father was elated. We need farm policies that keep farmers on the land, producing enough nutritious food to feed the hungry and sustain our planet.

At the end of January 2017, the North Olympic Land Trust announced that sufficient funds had been raised to purchase the development rights to the "historic Ward Farm" insuring that the farm, our property, will remain farmland forever.

15,000 Cheer Bernie Sanders in Seattle
People's World, August 10, 2015

SEATTLE, WASHINGTON—As 12,000 supporters cheered, Bernie Sanders appealed for unity against the "billionaire class," arguing that jobs that pay living wages, racial and gender equality, health care and higher education for all "is not utopian dreaming."

Sanders added, "When Black and white stand together, Hispanics . . . women and men . . . gay and straight, there is nothing, nothing we can't accomplish."

Sanders echoed a warning by President Obama when he was on the campaign trail in 2008. "No President can do it alone; no individual in the White House can do it alone. We need to do it together. . . . We need an economy that works for workers and the middle class and not just for the billionaires."

Sanders hailed Seattle for enacting a $15 an hour minimum wage saying it should be a model for an increase in the $7.25 federal minimum wage which he denounced as a "starvation wage."

The crowd in the Hec Edmundson Pavilion, he said, is the largest yet in his campaign. Another 3,000 were outside because of space limitations. Sanders was scheduled to speak Sunday in Portland, Oregon to nearly 20,000, and in Los Angeles, Monday.

Yet an incident in downtown Seattle earlier in the day underlined the danger that racist division poses to his campaign. Members of Black Lives Matter seized the platform at a rally that Sanders was scheduled to address. The event was sponsored by Puget Sound Alliance of Retiree Advocates to celebrate the 50th Anniversary of Medicare and to demand that the cap on Social Security taxes be lifted so that wealthy taxpayers pay their fair share.

The Black Lives Matter members demanded that the rally join in commemorating the first anniversary of the slaying by a white police officer of Michael Brown, an unarmed Black youth in Ferguson Missouri August 9, 2015. Sanders was unable to speak and the rally was cancelled.

Yet Sanders did not let the issue die. "Too many young lives are being destroyed by the so-called 'War on Drugs,'" Sanders told the mostly white crowd at the rally that same evening.

"Too many lives are being destroyed by our system of incarceration," Sanders charged. "No President will fight harder to end the stain of racism and reform our criminal justice system. Period."

Announced at the rally was the appointment of Symone Sanders as Bernie Sanders national press secretary. The young African American woman is the chair of the National Coalition of Juvenile Justice. She is an active supporter of Black Lives Matter.

Bernie Sanders for President bumper sticker courtesy of Bernie Sanders campaign

Symone Sanders delivered a fiery speech introducing Bernie Sanders as a candidate who will "turn words into action" in the struggle against racism. "You know which President will shut down the private prison industry," she thundered. "You know which candidate will have the courage to fight unjust mandatory minimum sentences and the death penalty."

Waiting in line for Bernie Sanders rally in Seattle. Photo by the author

Earlier, Lynne Dodson, Secretary Treasurer of the Washington State Labor Council, pointed out that this is the "anniversary of the Ferguson, Missouri" police murder of Michael Brown. Yet the violence against young African American men, she added, is not limited to police shootings. "Violence takes the form of poverty, denial of health care, shipping of good jobs overseas, the exploitation of workers in other countries."

She cited the "war on women" unleashed by the Republican Party with too many Democrats silent at the attacks. "We have Bernie Sanders to create a better world for all of us," she said as the crowd cheered.

Pramila Jayapal, a member of the Washington State legislature and a founder of "One America," an immigrant rights organization, praised Sanders as a fighter for immigration reform that includes a "path to citizenship" for 11 million undocumented immigrants.

"He has stood up against racist oppression and believes that Black lives matter," she said.

Sanders delivered a wide-ranging speech hammering on the domination of the nation's economy and political system by the super wealthy.

"We are not living in a democracy when as a result of the disastrous Citizens United decision, billionaires like the Koch Brothers are spending hundreds of millions of dollars electing candidates who represent the wealthy, the powerful. That's called oligarchy, not democracy," he said.

"You cannot get huge tax breaks when millions of children go to bed hungry. You cannot hide your wealth in the Cayman Islands and Bermuda. You will pay your fair share." The crowd roared its agreement.

He called for strong measures to reverse climate change. "If we don't get our act together, world temperatures will rise five degrees," he said. "We must lead the world in moving away from fossil fuels."

He also called for passage of an infrastructure repair bill that will create 13 million good-paying jobs.

Some of his strongest applause came from the many youth and students in the audience. Sanders blasted a system that leaves millions of youth, especially Black and Hispanic youth unemployed or saddled with ruinous student loan debt. He called for tuition free education at all public colleges and universities. It is time, he said, to invest more tax revenues in jobs and education than in building prisons.

He announced that he met with President Obama on the agreement to block Iran from acquiring nuclear weapons and will vote for the agreement. Republicans who seek to wreck the Iran deal, he said, "have forgotten the lessons of Afghanistan and Iraq, forgotten that half a million soldiers came home with post-traumatic stress."

He called for a foreign policy that "resolves differences even with nations we have strong differences with rather than go to war. I want to give peace every chance, every opportunity. I'm going to work with the President to insure that Iran does not get nuclear weapons."

Port workers spend Labor Day on picket line
September 7 2011

LONGVIEW, WASHINGTON—Embattled dockworkers marched on their picket lines, Labor Day weekend, standing tall against EGT, the international grain consortium that seeks to break the union at their huge new grain terminal in the Port of Longview.

The struggle has been raging since early June when EGT first filed a lawsuit demanding nullification of a long-standing agreement that the International Longshore and Warehouse Union will handle every commodity that moves through this port on the Columbia River downstream from Portland, Oregon.

Many of the women and men picketed the EGT terminal in the morning and then went to the Labor Day picnic at a nearby RV Park.

"We had a good turnout for the picnic," said ILWU Local 21 President Dan Coffman in a phone interview with *PeoplesWorld.org*.

"It was just a social gathering, a day of rest," he added, but with a strong dose of "multi-union" solidarity fired up by the struggle with EGT.

"We have such great union and community support here. We have over 300 businesses in the Longview-Kelso area displaying our sign in their front window: 'We Support the ILWU.'"

He added, "The community knows who has been here for 80 years. We've provided so much charity, given so much. EGT rode into town on their white horse with all these promises. But they hired outside the community, hired outside the state, even hired outside the country to build this terminal. The local businesses got nothing."

That union-community solidarity was on full display last July 14, he said, when 700 ILWU members and their union allies sat down on the tracks of the Burlington Northern Santa Fe Railroad stopping a mile long train loaded with wheat and blocking delivery of the first load of grain for the EGT elevators.

"We stopped that train dead in its tracks," Coffman said. "We had hundreds standing with us, men, women and children."

The railroad has since suspended all deliveries and the grain elevators stand empty awaiting the outcome of the struggle.

"Since 1934, the ILWU has represented grain elevator workers at all the Pacific Northwest ports," Coffman said. EGT, a multi-billion dollar outfit that includes St. Louis-based, Bunge International, demanded the port allow them to subcontract with non-union General Construction, a Seattle-based company which in turn would employ members of Local 701 of the Operating Engineers based in Oregon to handle the grain.

"EGT wanted to bring Local 701 in through the back door," said Coffman. "It's one union raiding another and it is unacceptable."

Prominent among the picket signs blasting EGT union busting are placards that proclaim "701 Scabs."

He pointed out that Local 612 of the Operating Engineers in Tacoma and Local 302 in Seattle have sharply denounced Local 701. The president of the Tacoma local said, "Never would we think that members of the Operating Engineers would do another craft's work."

EGT went to the federal court in Tacoma requesting a restraining order prohibiting picketing of the grain terminal.

"They wanted all unions, all people, removed from the site," Coffman said. "The judge refused all of it. He did not remove us from the site. We've got a ton of people walking with us. Other locals of the ILWU, United Food and Commercial Workers, International Brotherhood of Electrical Workers, Plumbers and Pipefitters, the Machinists, the Washington State Employees Association. It's very diverse. We have retirees coming down to join us, great support from the ILWU locals in Vancouver, Washington and Portland."

A member of the ILWU since 1974, Coffman said his hero is ILWU founder Harry Bridges, whose portrait adorns the wall of the Local 21 hiring hall.

"I thank Harry Bridges every day when I walk in the hall for what he has given us," Coffman said. "Here is a man who faced deportation back to Australia. He was fighting deportation, and he succeeded because ILWU members gave him such strong support. We're facing the same thing today. Collective bargaining is under attack by corporate America and the rich. We have to stand together and fight back."

Kaiser Strikers: 'SAVE JOBS, ENVIRONMENT'; Spokane labor leader runs for Congress
May 22, 2000

SPOKANE—Rick Olson was ready with his bullhorn when a pickup with Idaho tags rolled out of Kaiser Aluminum's Mead plant here May 21.

"You miserable maggot! You deserve a $3-an-hour job," Olson, a thirty-three-year Kaiser veteran, bellowed as the strikebreaker sped off into the sunset.

About fifteen women and men, members of United Steelworkers Local 329, were picketing Kaiser as they have for the past twenty months in the withering heat and frigid cold of the prairie north of Spokane.

The picket shack was adorned with slogans denouncing Kaiser Aluminum's union-busting. Another proclaimed, "Not another term for Nethercutt." This referred to Spokane's ultra-right congressman, George Nethercutt, a Republican elected on a promise of "term limits." He has changed his mind and is seeking another congressional term in November's election.

"Tom Flynn, one of our own, a member of the Carpenters Union, is running against him," said Steven Peak, a twenty-two-year Kaiser veteran, as he gripped his picket sign. "Tom is also the president of the Spokane Central Labor Council. We've become very political," he added. "I'm the legislative representative of my union in Olympia."

One of the union's demands is that the Bonneville Power Administration add a "Good Corporate Citizenship Clause" to their contracts as a condition for receiving discounted hydroelectric power. "Kaiser and these other corporate consumers should be required to treat the environment and their workers fairly if they are going to enjoy lower power rates at taxpayer expense," Peak told the *World.*

Reducing bauxite to aluminum is an electrolytic process that consumes millions of kilowatts of electric power generated at federally-owned Grand Coulee Dam, evident in the power substation and high tension wires that stretch off toward the horizon.

Kaiser produced the highest quality aircraft aluminum in the nation "but most of the aluminum produced by these replacements is being rejected," Peak said. "The pilots union just informed Boeing they will not fly planes made with scab aluminum."

The scabs are so incompetent, he said, that they blew up the Kaiser plant in Gramercy, Louisiana last July 5, injuring twenty-one people, showering debris and breaking windows over a five-mile radius.

The 2,100 workers at the Mead and Trentwood plants here went on strike September 30, 1998 protesting Kaiser's plan to subcontract 950 jobs to a nonunion operator. They were joined by Kaiser workers at plants in Gramercy, Tacoma, Washington, and another in Ohio—more than 3,400 workers nationwide.

Four months later, on January 13, 1999, the strikers offered to return to work under the old contract. Kaiser refused and the strike became a lockout.

On April 26 of this year the National Labor Relations Board (NLRB) charged Kaiser with two unfair labor practices, making the company liable for $500,000 in fines for each day the lockout continues.

Peak introduced us to Robert Kenyon who has worked thirty-three years at Kaiser. "We're road warriors," Peak said.

"We were at the 'Battle in Seattle' that shut down the World Trade Organization last December. We had members who travelled to Washington for the Mobilization for Global Justice in April. We called it 'Seattle East.'"

Kenyon said the Kaiser workers have joined with environmentalists to form the Alliance for Sustainable Jobs and the Environment because they face a common enemy. Charles Hurwitz, owner of Maxxam Corporation of Houston, Texas, used junk bonds to buy both Kaiser Aluminum and Pacific Lumber, owner of 22,000 acres of old growth redwoods in Humboldt County, California.

Pacific Lumber had practiced selective logging but Hurwitz's junk bond deals required an immediate, maximum return to satisfy Wall Street's voracious appetite for quick profits. Hurwitz turned to clear-cutting to satisfy that greed.

"Hurwitz has destroyed stands of redwood that took 1,000 years to grow," said Kenyon. "He's destroyed two rivers where salmon spawned. The clear-cutting caused mudslides that destroyed seven homes in the town of Scotia in Humboldt County, California." While Hurwitz was clear-cutting redwoods, he planned to clear-cut the jobs of Kaiser Aluminum workers, Kenyon said.

The search for allies also led the Steelworkers to Seattle's Jewish community, which held a Seder last month, attended by 150 people, to express solidarity with the Kaiser workers.

Local 329 President Dan Russell took time May 22 for an interview with the *World* at the local's union office. The hall was crowded with steelworkers who had come to prepare for that day's picketing. A pot of spaghetti was warming to feed those on picket duty.

Adjacent to the office was the union's food bank that has provided tons of food to the strikers and their families.

The international union is providing strike benefits to save workers' homes and cars from foreclosure. The union staff is also helping the locked-out workers find temporary jobs. One of the wives even serves as a barber offering free haircuts every Sunday.

The workers have won widespread sympathy from the eastern Washington community. The main headline in the *Spokesman-Review* that morning was "Steelworkers live with sacrifices."

"Last Saturday night, our local staged a 'Women in Steel' picketline at the plant gates. These are the wives, mothers, grandmothers of the Kaiser workers. It was more lively than usual," he said.

The Kaiser Steelworkers gave up $4.50 in hourly wages and benefits in the early 1980s to rescue Kaiser when it pleaded it was going bankrupt. Understandably, the workers now feel betrayed at Kaiser's vengeful attitude.

On the wall at Local 329 was a photo of trailers lined up like military barracks inside Kaiser's chain link fence.

Busloads of scabs had arrived Sept. 30, 1998 and when the deadline passed, they were driven into the plant.

"Kaiser hired IMAC, a subcontractor from Ohio to carry out this operation," Russell said. "Kaiser came in and told us, 'This is our final offer. Take it or leave it.' The overall plan was to break us."

For the first three months of the strike, "IMAC kept these strikebreakers in lockdown. They were not permitted to leave the grounds of the Kaiser plant," Russell said. "IMAC provided the mobile housing, a mess hall, a laundry. The workers worked twelve-hour shifts."

Displayed on the wall is a photo of Robert Lee Yates, a scab arrested inside the Kaiser plant a few weeks ago on charges of murdering several women in the Spokane area.

"He's one of many 'sterling' characters who are working at Kaiser these days," said Tim Charbonneau, Local 329 vice president. "They have a bank robber, a drug trafficker and a child molester."

The workers in the union hall laughed appreciatively. "Who knows what goes on in corporate boardrooms?" Russell said. "They have targeted the steel union, Bridgestone-Firestone, Titan, AK Steel, Oregon Steel and Kaiser.

"Here we are, sitting in Spokane, a spot on the map. In the past, we would reach out for help and it was not there," he said.

"This time, we reached out, we sent our members across the country, and all across the country, people have responded. Together, we are going to win this fight."

Hero of Labor, Will Parry, Celebrates 90th Birthday

People's World (Online) April 27, 2010

SEATTLE—At his 90th birthday party, April 24, Will Parry picked up his guitar and led 400 union brothers and sisters, family, comrades, and friends in singing "Carry It On," ending, "No more tears, for we're still singing."

Sponsored by the Puget Sound Alliance of Retired Americans (PSARA,) the celebration resounded with songs,

Will Parry. Photo by Tim Wheeler

poetry, and heartfelt tributes. Parry together with his late wife, Louise, helped build the labor movement and the senior citizen movement in the Pacific Northwest. A Phi Beta Kappa graduate of Washington State University, he worked as a factory worker at Longview Fiber, a box factory organized by the Association of Western Pulp and Paper Workers.

Robby Stern, PSARA president, told the banquet crowd, "Will has had an inspiring presence in the lives of everyone who is here. I have had the responsibility of stepping into the incredible shoes of the incredible Will Parry."

Stern urged the crowd to help place on the ballot an initiative to establish a "a really progressive income tax in Washington State." The initiative would tax couples with $400,000 income while lowering property taxes twenty percent. Washington State's soak-the-poor eight percent sales tax has generated sharply lower revenues during this recession, forcing health care and public education cutbacks. "Sign up if you are prepared to go out and collect signatures," Stern said. "This is the opportunity of our lifetime and we have to win it."

Representative Jim McDermott's aide, David Loud, read a letter from the lawmaker hailing Parry as a leader of the fight for comprehensive, universal health care reform. "We are indebted to you for your years of service," McDermott wrote.

Ed Coyle, executive director of the Alliance of Retired Americans, brought greetings from ARA headquarters in Washington. He said the staff waits for the arrival of the PSARA's newsletter, the *Retiree Advocate*, edited by Parry. He praised Parry as a national leader of the senior citizen movement.

Parry's family was there, including his daughter Naomi, his son Jon and his brother Tom who told the crowd of their childhood and youth together, Will's years in the U.S. Coast Guard during World War II and his excellence as a high school and college scholar and athlete.

Jeff Johnson, assistant to the president of the Washington State Labor Council, spoke of Parry's affiliation with the Communist Party of Washington State, the Pension Union and the Washington Commonwealth Federation that "became so strong they elected a Communist to the legislature" during the 1940s.

Parry was targeted in the Red Scare of the 1950s, Johnson continued. "The Taft Hartley Act was passed and radicals were being purged from the labor movement. As Will said, 'They drove the radicals out and it took the starch out of the labor movement.'"

In recent years, the Washington Labor Council "honored him as a hero of the Washington State labor movement," Johnson concluded.

Bill Farris, president of AWPPW Local 817 at the corrugated box plant where Parry worked for many years, said, "He's an advocate for people who needed help; an advocate for the union. I've lost count of the number of picketlines I've walked with Will."

Lynn Domingo, an organizer with Legacy of Equality, Leadership, and Organizing, said she enrolled in a labor history course Parry was teaching at Shoreline Community College. "I was floundering, wondering where I was going," she said. "I have to thank you for the salvation you provided in that class."

Thurston Muskelly, board member of the Central Area Senior Center, praised Parry for his fightback against President Reagan's drive to "destroy public health." The center was facing bankruptcy and Parry spearheaded a fund drive that brought in $131,000.

Ron McGaha, a member of Machinists Local 751, recited a poem he wrote about Parry: "On his very first night, he rose up in bed and to his mother he said, 'I'll nurse from the left, not from the right' ... Will taught us all in ways great and small, that progress always comes from the left, not the right." The room erupted in laughter and cheers.

Rebel Voices sang their ballad, *Borderlines*: "I lose my job to El Salvador where for fifty cents a day a woman sweats her life away and now they tell me she's my enemy" and the last line, "Someday our day will come around and we will stand and face our common enemy."

With his guitar slung over his shoulder, Parry thanked the crowd and echoed the appeal to get enough signatures to put the State Income Tax initiative on the ballot.

"I'm glad my birthday served as an excuse to get us all together," he said. It's time, he said, to celebrate the unity and strength of the movement, "not the feeble strength of one."

Youth Organize March against Police Killings
August 21, 2014

PORT TOWNSEND, WASHINGTON—Protesters, their hands up, marched through this paper mill town August 20, chanting "No Justice, no peace" to show their anger at the police shooting in Ferguson, Missouri, of Michael Brown, an unarmed African-American teenager.

Brown, eighteen, was killed by Ferguson police officer, Darren Wilson. Eyewitnesses and forensic evidence indicate that young Brown had his hands up when the police officer fired, striking Brown at least six times.

Frances Sheldon-O'Neal, seventeen, who enters her senior year at Port Townsend High School this month, initiated the protest rally and march. Marching with her were her sister, mother, and grandmother -- three generations of a family speaking out against what they see as a racist killing. Others came from Sequim, Port Ludlow, and other towns on the Olympic Peninsula.

"I wanted to raise awareness about this issue and also to support the people of Ferguson, Missouri, to let them know there are people here on the west coast who care about them," Sheldon-O'Neal told the People's World.

Port Townsend "Black Lives Matter" demonstration against police murder of Michael Brown in Ferguson, Missouri. Photo courtesy of the author

"Mike Brown was killed. He was shot so many times. He will never come back. He had his whole life ahead of him."

She added, "I think this is a national issue. Everywhere, police are using excessive force. There is a heavy influence of the military. There was the shooting of Trayvon Martin, Oscar Grant, the woodcarver in Seattle (Native American Indian, John T. Williams,)" she added.

Penelope Grace, a Port Townsend resident wore a T-shirt stenciled with the words, "No Justice, No Peace." She said, "I was visiting Los Angeles when police beat Rodney King and L.A. erupted in violence. This is a problem that repeats over and over. It has not changed. Racism is a factor in this situation. I've seen it and lived it and we've got to end it."

Linda Brewster, a MoveOn organizer held a sign that read, "Stop the War on People." She was elated that a teenager initiated the action and that so many other young people joined the protest.

Police violence is an issue that is certain to continue burning fiercely, she said.

"A Grand Jury report in Missouri is not expected to be completed until October," Brewster added. She pointed out that calls are mounting for the removal of St. Louis County, Attorney General Bob McCulloch from the case. McCulloch's father was a policeman killed in the line of duty. He has such close ties to the police that civil rights and civil liberties organizations have warned that he is incapable of insuring an impartial investigation. President Obama sent U.S. Attorney General, Eric Holder, to Missouri to launch a Federal probe.

The protesters joined hands and sang, "We Shall Overcome."

Sheldon-O'Neal sent out a message, later, that another rally against police violence will be held at John Pope Marine Park in Port Townsend, Wednesday August 27 at 5:30 p.m.

Canadian Town Hosts Conference on Utopian Socialist Colonies
October 1, 2011

SOINTULA, British Columbia—This Canadian fishing village lived up to its name, which means "place of harmony" in Finnish, hosting more than 100 visitors September 20-22 for a conference on utopian socialist colonies in the Pacific Northwest.

Sointula itself was the center of attention for the conference titled *"Culture Shock: Utopian Dreams, Hard Realities."*

Attendance was standing room only in both plenary and breakout sessions.

Participants traveled from across British Columbia and from Washington State, Oregon and California. Several historians gave lectures including keynote speaker, Dr. Edward S. Dutton from Oulu University in Finland. Over two dozen members of the Masala Youth Theatre flew in from Finland to perform their original play, "Sointula" a three-hour production, all in Finnish. It was the premiere performance in North America of the play by Tuomo Aitta.

Anne Marie Koch, who presided over the conference, welcomed the crowd to Finnish Organization Hall, an old clapboard building extensively renovated in recent years. The people, she said, still live by the egalitarian principles of the original socialist colony established in 1901 and have not lost their never-give-up spirit expressed in the Finnish word, "sisu."

Koch told this reporter that 100 volunteers worked tirelessly, cooking delicious meals, providing housing, decorating, organizing the program. Saturday night, they grilled fresh sockeye salmon caught in Broughton Strait just offshore by Sointula fishermen.

In his keynote, Dutton told the crowd that the late Dr. Kalervo Oberg an eminent Canadian anthropologist born in Nanaimo was brought to Sointula as an infant by his parents, August and Hilma Oberg. The father was a Nanaimo coalminer so dedicated to the teachings of the socialist founder, Matti Kurikka, that he became the treasurer of the colony.

A disastrous fire in 1903 destroyed the community hall, killing eleven residents. August Oberg's two young daughters—Kalervo's sisters—were among the seven children who died.

Dutton argued that the tragedy, coupled with other traumas, was central to Kalervo Oberg's theory of "Culture Shock" now widely accepted in anthropology to explain the roller coaster emotions experienced by newcomers forced to adapt to a new culture.

Although Oberg never mentioned the personal basis of his theory, "we can understand why Kalervo Oberg chose to write his 1928 undergraduate dissertation at the University of

British Columbia about Sointula and we can see why culture shock might have fascinated him," Dutton said. "Sointula was culture shock."

He added, "Oberg's culture shock bears Kurikka's stamp. It implies that all cultures are equal—just another way of living . . . it implies that you can change how you feel just by thinking differently and Kurikka believed in the power of mind over matter."

"And it implies that we are free. We can overcome our culture shock just as Kurikka believed we could improve humanity. We are not limited by some inherited human nature."

Historian, Charles Pierce LeWarne, author of *Utopias on Puget Sound, 1885-1915*, spoke about several utopian colonies in Washington State including the Puget Sound Cooperative Colony in Port Angeles, Equality near Bellingham, and Home, on the Kitsap Peninsula. LeWarne challenged the idea that these utopian experiments can be dismissed since they died so quickly. "I think it's a mistake to judge them on how long they survived," he said, arguing that the colonies promoted concepts of equality and solidarity that led to victories long after they were gone.

"I would like to write another book about the children of the colonists," he said. "There was a woman born in the Home Colony who came close to winning a Nobel Prize for her medical research. I can't remember her name."

I was sitting at the other side of the room and said under my breath, "Violet Russell's sister."

LeWarne overheard me. "That's right! Russell was the name I was trying to remember."

Rose Payne, born Rose Russell, in the Home Colony, was a research biologist at Stanford University who broke new ground on tissue compatibility, knowledge vital to organ transplants. She died in 1999. Her sister, Violet Russell, also born in Home, was a lifelong member of the Communist Party of Washington State.

Sointula was founded by a band of Finnish coal miners from Nanaimo about 200 miles south. The miners were so desperate to escape the brutal exploitation of mine owner, Robert Dunsmuir, that they formed a collective, Kalevan Kansa, (Socialist Pioneers). They contacted Kurikka and convinced him to come and lead the colony.

The 200 men and women rowed to remote Malcolm Island. They cleared the forest, set up a sawmill, constructed the wooden town, built a fleet of fishing boats. The town stands today, dominated by the Sointula Coop, the first cooperative general store in western Canada, still providing groceries and other necessities.

Just before we boarded the ferry back to Port McNeill, we walked down Sointula's main street to the cemetery and found an old weather-worn marble headstone with the epitaph, "Maria Hantula and her children, Herman, Ilmari, Aili. Died in the Sointula fire Jan. 29, 1903."

Why So Little Reporting on Bomb Threat in Spokane?
February 7, 2011

SPOKANE—Fairness and Accuracy in Reporting (FAIR) recently posted a story on its web site headlined *Terrorism and Spokane* assailing the media for mostly ignoring the bomb placed along the route of the January 17 Martin Luther King Day march in Spokane.

Luckily, city workers discovered the backpack containing the shrapnel-filled explosive device and the march was rerouted by Spokane police. The FBI removed the bomb, sending it to the FBI lab at Quantico, Virginia for analysis. Forensic investigators say the bomb also was laced with a toxic chemical to make it even more lethal. FBI Special Agent, Frederick Gutt, a spokesman for the Seattle Field Office said, "The device appeared to be operational, it appeared to be deadly, and it was intended to inflict multiple casualties." Another police official said, it is the "worst device, and the most intentional device I have ever seen."

It was described as "highly sophisticated," rigged with a remote trigger.

Spokane is the largest city in a region with a concentration of white supremacist hate groups and armed militias. The Aryan Nations and its leader Richard Butler recruited racists and anti-Semites to an armed compound in nearby Hayden Lake, Idaho. A civil lawsuit won by opponents of the Aryan Nations bankrupted Butler. His compound was confiscated. He died in 2004.

FAIR points out that the media downplayed the Spokane bomb threat even though it took place just a few weeks after the tragedy in Tucson in which a deranged gunman shot Representative Gabrielle Giffords (D-AZ), killed a U.S. Judge, an eight year old girl and four other victims and wounded a dozen more.

FAIR quotes Will Bunch of the *Philadelphia Daily News* who protests the media putting this case of "domestic terrorism" on their back pages.

Bunch asks if the underreporting is the result of intimidation of the media by former Alaska Governor, Sarah Palin, the Tea Party, and other rightwing extremists when the Tucson sheriff and others blamed the right for a climate of hate that made the killer think he was licensed to kill. Bunch cites the "massive pushback from conservatives who accused the mainstream media of jumping to unfair conclusions."

Palin herself called it a "blood libel." The former GOP veep nominee was savaged for using that term, Bunch continued, "but you have to wonder, now if the pushback from Palin is actually a case of 'mission accomplished.' That's because with this new episode in Spokane, not only have the pillars of the mainstream media not raced to any conclusions, but they seem to be in a competition as to who can most ignore the story altogether."

Bunch points out that there is a well-documented history of the corporate media playing down domestic terrorism threats "that don't involve Arab or Muslim" alleged conspirators. When Timothy McVeigh and his accomplice bombed the Federal Building in Oklahoma City on April 19,

1995, for example, law enforcement and the media instantly concluded that Arabs or Muslims were the perpetrators.

"But there's no need to jump to unwarranted conclusions here," writes Bunch, "the actual facts have been laid out by the nation's preeminent law enforcement agency, the FBI— that we are dealing with a case of 'domestic terrorism,' that the sophisticated device along the King Day parade route was capable of causing mass casualties, and the target was American citizens celebrating an icon of the progressive movement, Dr. King."

Hometown to Glenn Beck: This is a Hate-free Zone

People's World September 29 2009

Fox News talk-show host, Glenn Beck, arrived in his hometown, Mount Vernon, Washington, September 26, to be greeted by hundreds of protesters with signs that read, "Hate is not a Mount Vernon value" and "Hate kills!"

There were also "tea-baggers" in the crowd who embraced Beck's hate but the voices of sanity and reason seemed to carry the day. Beck delivered an unusually, low-key, non-political speech urging people to stop "tearing each other apart."

Beck, who recently touched off a nationwide furor by branding President Obama a "racist" with a "deep hatred of America and white culture," returned to the town where he was born in 1964 at the invitation of the town's mayor, Bud Norris, who unilaterally proclaimed September 26 "Glenn Beck Day" and presented him with the keys to the city. More than 800 turned out to protest, many wearing tee-shirts with the slogan, "Hate is not a Mount Vernon value." Overhead, a plane circled pulling a banner that read, "Change the Locks."

The mayor's action ignited an angry firestorm. A grassroots coalition circulated a petition signed by 16,000 people demanding that the invitation be withdrawn. Phillip

Holder presented the petitions to a September 23 meeting of the City Council, with the Mayor presiding. Holder said the invitation to Beck "disgraces Mount Vernon."

The council then went on to approve unanimously a resolution stating that the "City Council is in no way sponsoring the Mayor's event . . . and is not connected to the Glenn Beck event in any manner."

Holder, a member of FUSE, the progressive group that circulated the petition, told the *World,* "I wonder if the fact that hundreds of people were in the streets with signs that said, 'hate is not a Mount Vernon value' had anything to do with his toned-down speech. I wasn't in the hall but news reports said he urged people to stop tearing each other apart. We can second the proposal."

Holder added, "The trend of vilifying one's political opponents does not contribute to the quality of the debate over policy issues that have to be decided . . . It leads to confusion and stops us from resolving the difficult issues that we face as a nation including health care reform, global climate change and our dependence on oil."

Beck, he said, should heed his own call "and stop thinking about 'killing' Michael Moore," he said, referring to the documentary film-maker. He referred to the Wikipedia biography of Beck documenting his incitement to murder against Moore. "Beck has not been making a positive contribution to a dialogue on solving the problems we face as a nation," said Holder.

Judith Shattuck, chair of the Progressive Caucus of Washington State, that helped mobilize the protest of Beck's appearance, told the *World* that humanity is going through transformative changes deeper than any experienced in the "past 1,000 years." She added, "It's like the old stuff we did and believed in is dying. And it's dying hard. The Glenn Becks of the world are resisting with every fiber of their being. We spend a lot of energy trying to hold on to what is dead, or dying. What I hope is that we can say: O.K., that's gone. Let's turn our energy to what we want to create."

Beck may also be chastened by the impact of the boycott organized by Oakland-based "ColorofChange" (CoC) in which sixty-two corporate sponsors have withdrawn their advertising from Fox News' *Glenn Beck Show*. Now CoC and its partner, the Free Press Action Fund (FPAF) are circulating an online letter "Glenn Beck Doesn't Speak for Me," already signed by tens of thousands. CoC director, James Rucker and FPAF director Josh Silver write, "Some say that we should just ignore Glenn Beck's media circus and it will go away. But Beck's attacks have actually harmed people. We need to tell Beck and his bosses that their efforts to stoke fear and prejudice come with consequences of their own."

Beck, they added, has the right of free speech. "But he doesn't have the right to a cable news show funded by millions in corporate ad dollars. News media that have no sense of responsibility to the truth need to be held accountable."

[6]

ONE TOUCH OF NATURE

Hazel (Leo) Wolf with her attorney, John Caughlan, preparing her appeal against deportation. Photo courtesy of Goldie Caughlan.

"Women of Courage" Honors Hazel Wolf, Hattie McDaniel, Everywoman

(A shortened version of this article was printed as a Letter to the Editor of the *Peninsula Daily News* March 26, 2013)

SEQUIM, WASHINGTON— Hazel Wolf, leader of the Seattle Audubon Society who died thirteen years ago at age 101 came back to life, March 17 at the Olympic Theatre Arts playhouse.

Four women actors read aloud excerpts from her pithy comments contained in Rebecca Redshaw's brilliant *Women of Courage*, three one-act plays. The production, sponsored by the Clallam County League of Women Voters in honor of Women's History Month, attracted a near-capacity crowd.

The other plays in Redshaw's production were *A Conversation with Hattie McDaniel*, honoring the first African American woman to win an Oscar for her role in *Gone with the Wind*, and *Lunchtime Temp*, an amusing piece that celebrates the contribution made by millions of poorly-paid temporary women workers, "everywoman."

But I must confess that *Hazel Speaks* is the play that won my heart. That is because I knew Hazel Wolf well. Born in 1899 in Victoria, British Columbia, she grew up poor. She emigrated to the U.S. in 1921 and worked her way through the University of Washington. She joined the Communist Party in the 1930s and was a grassroots activist fighting poverty and outright starvation. Her militant activism made her a target for deportation during the worst years of Cold War repression. She joined the Washington Committee for the Protection of the Foreign Born working closely with WCPFB leader, Marion Kinney   and with Louise Pettibone Smith, founder and national president of the American Committee for the Protection of the Foreign Born. Marion Kinney later became the Pacific Northwest correspondent of the *People's World.*

Wolf—who went by the name "Leo" in those days—drove up about once a month to visit her daughter and grandchildren in Port Angeles. On the way back to Seattle, she stopped in at our family farm near Sequim to keep us posted on the latest news in her struggle with the INS. She was a feisty, witty person, full of beans and vinegar and she always regaled us with amusing stories about her battles with the FBI and the Federal bureaucracy.

She worked for John Caughlan, the civil liberties attorney, who served as my father's lawyer when he was hauled before various witchhunt hearings. Caughlan—together with an aroused, militant, mass movement—helped keep my dad out of jail and also helped Hazel avoid deportation.

In later life, she joined the Audubon Society organizing many local chapters across the Evergreen State. She was a skilled coalition builder, leading the environmental movement into joint work with the labor movement and the Native American Indian tribes of the Pacific Northwest.

One of the four actors reads Wolf's bold assertion of her Communist affiliations: "One of the things I'm most proud of is the organizing I did with William Pennock for the Washington Old Age Pension Union," Wolf declares in the play. "We gathered all the signatures, carried on a campaign and passed this thing, and it was the first government-funded pension program in the United States, the first time the term 'senior citizen' was used. The Communists made that one happen. . . ."

Wolf later became president of the Western Outdoors Clubs. Redshaw includes a section of Wolf's memoirs in which she was was critical of herself for keeping silent before a crucial vote at a WOC meeting in 1978 when a speaker unleashes a racist harangue. The Quileutes, confined to La Push, a one-square mile reservation at the mouth of the Quileute River, were demanding the return of 400 acres on a plateau so they could move the village out of the path of floods and tsunamis. The WOC board member snarled against the "greedy and aggressive Quileute Indians."

At the next WOC meeting, Wolf apologized to her audience for her earlier silence. "We have taken the land away from the Indians at the point of a gun," she said. "And I don't care if they get back the whole damn park, let alone this miserable four hundred acres they were asking for. This has been gnawing at me ever since we took the vote last time. I want it known loud and clear how I feel about the opposition we've taken to the Quileute Indians who haven't anyplace to build their houses."

The crowd responded to this episode with a strong ovation. The issue could not be more timely. The Federal Government has just agreed to return 400 acres of parkland on the plateau, a victory that Hazel Wolf would be cheering if she were alive. The Quileutes are already moving their homes to higher ground.

I was on a speaking and fundraising trip for the *People's World* in 1991 against "Operation Desert Storm," the ill-fated first war in Iraq. Seattle was one of my stops. I was delivering a hard-hitting harangue against President George HW. Bush, the elder. When I finished, out of the crowd stepped a person with a very familiar face. "Leo Wolf!" I exclaimed, throwing my arms around her. She was laughing merrily. "Yes, the one and only but I go by Hazel now." She was devoting all her awesome energy to saving birds from extinction. But she also knew about canaries in the mines. That if they die, we will be next. So she was also outspoken against war, like the one then raging in the Persian Gulf.

Redshaw hopes her play is performed before a larger audience in Seattle or elsewhere in the Pacific Northwest. It should be seen by audiences everywhere.

Digging for Gold in the Colorado Rockies

People's Weekly World, August 12, 2001

CENTRAL CITY, Colorado—Standing on the front porch of the Nicholas House high on a hillside of this once roaring gold mining camp a few days ago, I looked out across the valley toward the heaps of mine tailings that loomed nearly as high as the real mountains behind. They were a monument to the miners' backbreaking toil digging for those elusive flakes of gold.

Once a Cornish gold miner named John Nicholas lived in

Main Street, Central City, Colorado. From an original pastel sketch by the author

this modest frame house. According to a plaque attached to the siding, he died at the age of forty, his premature death hastened by twelve hours of daily pick-and-shovel work in one of the mines now idle and rusting up and down the valley—the Bobtail Mine, the Coeur d'Alene, the Boodle Mill, the Glory Hole.

Gold was discovered here in 1859 touching off a gold rush that swelled the city at one point larger than Denver. Cornish, Welsh, and later Tyrolean miners made Central City and neighboring Black Hawk "the richest square mile on earth." They were workers who lived by the sweat of their brow.

The city of wooden buildings burned to the ground in 1874 but was quickly rebuilt with brick in the crowded downtown. Ornate cast iron facades were brought in from Chicago for the rebuilt city that retains much of its Victorian charm today.

One of the handsomest buildings has the letters "AOUW" carved into its pediment. "What do you think those letters stand for?" asked my wife, Joyce.

I guessed, "American Organization of United Workers."

"Pretty close," she said, consulting a tourist brochure, "Ancient Order of United Workmen."

Central City is wedged down into a canyon and the houses cling to the steep surrounding hills. I wondered, looking down the hill, how a miner found the strength to climb that steep grade to his house after slaving for a twelve-hour shift underground. The town is at 8,500 feet elevation and I found myself huffing and puffing in the rarified atmosphere.

Our son Nick and his wife Maureen were living with two other ballet dancers in another of the miners' cottages, most of them donated by the miners' families to the renowned Central City Opera. They use the twenty or so cottages, many of them lovingly restored, to house the opera cast and musicians during the opera's annual summer festival.

That's why we had come: to see Nick and Maureen perform with the Opera Company, which also owes its existence to these very same Cornish and Welsh miners. Back in 1877, they launched the fund drive that raised the money to build the opera house.

It opened in 1878 and continued to stage world-class opera and theater productions starring some of the greatest operatic singers, actors and actresses until the gold ran out and the opera house closed in 1920. It was reopened again in 1932 with Lillian Gish starring as Camille. It has been operating ever since with packed houses.

In 1956, the Central City Opera staged the premiere production of *The Ballad of Baby Doe*, the true, scandalous story of Elizabeth McCourt's love affair with married

Nick Wheeler dances

187

silver magnate Horace Tabor, owner of the "Matchless Mine" in Leadville, Colorado. Tabor was ruined when silver prices crashed in 1893. He died of appendicitis in a Denver hotel. Elizabeth McCourt was left destitute with their two young girls. She froze to death in an unheated shack near the portal of the mine. This rags-to-riches-to-ruin opera has been a favorite in the company's repertoire.

But we had come to see the North American premiere of *Gloriana*, Benjamin Britten's 1953 opera commissioned in honor of the coronation of Elizabeth II. It, too, is a story of star-crossed lovers: Queen Elizabeth I and the dashing, hotheaded, Robert Devereux, Earl of Essex. Mezzo soprano Joyce Castle, as Elizabeth, sang majestically and the rest of the cast was superb. The Elizabethan costumes were sumptuous. It was awesome that they projected so much Elizabethan pomp, swordplay, romance and high Shakespearean drama from such a tiny stage.

Act Two featured the vivacious dancing of Kimberly Mackin, Gary-David Shaw, Sergei Vladimirov, Natasha Kiryanova, Julia Clime and our own Nick and Maureen Wheeler. The stage has a wicked rake, tilted so steeply that we feared the dancers, who leaped and pirouetted with abandon, would plunge into the orchestra pit or even into our laps!

Our favorite was the Renaissance court dancing, although the dancers protested that it was so simple a child could perform these stately, charming circle dances.

After the performance, we walked down to the Teller House, a handsome hotel, restaurant and bar with British Union Jacks fluttering in a row across the facade in honor of *Gloriana*. Protected by a brass railing and illuminated by footlights on the floor inside is the "face on the barroom floor," the mysterious portrait of a child painted a century ago. It is the subject of a famous poem and a one-act cabaret opera that premiered at the Central City Opera.

We were treated at the Teller House to an impromptu concert by aspiring young singers. Accompanied by a pianist, they stepped forward, one after another, to sing popular arias.

The crowd responded with stormy applause and shouts of "bravo!"

I asked Gran Wilson, the fine young tenor who sang the Earl of Essex, if the high altitude was a problem. "Yes, I had a panic attack or two until I got my breathing under control," he replied.

Central City has a permanent population of about 300 and would be nearly as deserted as the other ghost towns scattered up and down the Rocky Mountains without the opera festival. In an attempt to stimulate economic growth, the Colorado legislature approved the Limited Gaming Act of 1991, permitting slot machines in three gold mining towns, Central City, Black Hawk, and Cripple Creek.

A blackjack dealer on lunch break in front of the Dostal Alley Casino told us, "We started with eighteen casinos and now it is down to four." The others are dark and vacant. Gaming was a will–o-the-wisp that vanished quicker than the gold, although there is more business at the huge corporate casinos like "Isle of Capri" and "Riviera" down the hill in Black Hawk.

Vern Terpenning, a half-century resident, operates the Long Branch Trading Post in the old Wells Fargo stage coach station on Eureka Street in Central City. When Ulysses S. Grant came to Central City, "he stepped out of the stagecoach right here at the Wells Fargo station," Terpenning told me. "The street was paved with silver bricks for Grant to walk over to the Teller House. And Horace Greeley delivered his famous, 'Go West, Young Man,' speech over there, as well," he said.

The next day, many of the dancers crammed into Nick and Maureen's four-wheel drive Blazer with us and we toiled in low gear up the James Mountain Jeep Road, a boulder-strewn rut carved into the side of an 11,000 foot mountain in the Arapaho National Forest. Even here, on this windswept mountainside, we came upon the ruins of tiny log hovels and piles of dirt where fortune seekers a century ago broke their backs digging for gold.

We reached an alpine meadow carpeted with Indian paintbrush, bluebells, columbine, buttercups, and wild yellow

189

roses. The meadow was sheltered on one side by a grove of quaking aspen and on the other by gnarled bristlecone pines. In the distance loomed James Mountain, a black storm cloud rolling across its summit. While the rest of the gang hiked on to Paradise Valley, I sat and started a pastel sketch. Suddenly a strong wind arose and the aspen leaves quaked. Drops of cold rain blinded me. And then I saw falling on my pastel, flakes of snow.

Mountain-scape from Hurricane Ridge, Olympic National Park. From an original watercolor by the author

Wilderness Lovers Ask: Why Bring a Gun to a National Park?
June 14, 2008

OLYMPIC NATIONAL PARK, Washington—Nathan Goff, a house painter in Olympia, Washington, drove his wife, Missy, and nineteen-month-old daughter up to Hurricane Ridge here June 8. The ridge, just a few feet shy of one mile above sea level, is the crown jewel of Olympic National Park. It commands a stunning view of Mt. Olympus to the south and a breathtaking view of the Strait of Juan de Fuca and British Columbia to the north.

It was a chill spring day and the alpine meadows were still blanketed with snow. The young couple stood gazing down into the deep valley of the Elwha River. Directly across loomed the snowy crags of Bailey's Range. It was so silent and peaceful you could almost hear your heartbeat.

"I'm trying to figure out why anyone would want to carry handguns in a national park," Goff told a reporter. "To ward off cougar attacks? They are so rare.

"Allowing people to carry guns in the parks just adds another element of danger. It's so totally unnecessary."

To bring home his point he introduced his little girl. "This is Lily Grace," he said. "She is not at all armed."

He was commenting on a change in federal firearms regulations proposed by the Bush administration that would lift a ban on carrying loaded, concealed weapons in all national parks. Instead, the rule would conform to the state firearm law in the state where the park is located. Several states including Florida, Texas and Wyoming now permit carrying handguns either openly or concealed. The Interior Department, which oversees the National Park Service, is in the midst of a sixty-day comment period on the proposal to lift the general ban on carrying operable firearms in the parks that has been in effect since President Reagan signed it in 1982.

Bill and Nanette Londeree of Navato, California, echoed Goff's view. "This is a solution searching for a problem," Bill Londeree told the *World*. "There just isn't any big problem of crime in the national parks."

Standing nearby was retiree, Al Phillips of nearby Sequim. "What I'm afraid of is if somebody had a gun, they'd start firing away. I'd rather keep firearms out of the parks," he said. He glanced toward the mountain range in the distance. "It seems strange to have a natural setting like this and then introduce firearms into it. If we had guns in the parks we would have more problems. These parks are places where people are free to relax and not worry about guns and people who carry them."

Wendy Goldberg, a resident of Sequim, visible from a viewpoint half way up the road to Hurricane Ridge, was stirred to write a letter to the *Peninsula Daily News* arguing, "A gun-free park enhances public safety and helps prevent poaching." She urged readers to send comments on the rule-change to the Interior Department by going to regulations.gov and locating Docket FWS-R9-NSR-2008-0062-0001. Goldberg said in a phone interview that she and her husband—a board member of Friends of Olympic National Park—are strongly opposed to the rule change. "When we read the Second Amendment, we read a 'well-regulated militia' has the right to bear arms," not individuals spending recreation time in our nation's parks, she said.

Doug Pennington, spokesperson for the Brady Campaign to Prevent Gun Violence, told the *World*, "There is negligible crime in the national parks." The National Rifle Association, he added, "is trying to gin up as much fear as possible to push this rule through." He cited a flurry of statements by U.S. park rangers, both active and retired, arguing strongly against lifting the arms ban.

The Coalition of National Park Service Retirees blasted Senator Tom Coburn (R-Okla.) for his amendment authorizing the rule change. "It is a hoax to suggest that there is some big demand for people to be able to tote semi-automatic weapons on the trails of Yellowstone or 9-millimeter pistols on the steps of the Lincoln Memorial," they wrote. A member of the group's executive council, Doug Morris, called Coburn's bill "an appalling pander to a powerful special interest group," the NRA.

Some see an ulterior motive in this "states' rights" gun campaign. Since he took office, George W. Bush has been determined to open the 636 million acres of federal lands to oil, gas, mining and timber exploitation. Mobilizing the ultra-right gun lobby in opposition to the federal ban on firearms in the national parks fits in with the corporate drive to privatize the federal lands. The Natural Resources Defense Council warns that with the Bush-Cheney tenure nearing its end, "federal officials across the West are redoubling their efforts to lease these areas for oil and gas development and to approve permits to drill them, virtually guaranteeing the industrialization of millions of acres of previously wild and open land. Already, almost 26 million acres of these lands have been leased."

It adds that corporate greed threatens even the most "iconic" wilderness areas. "The White House energy plan endangers the wildlife and resources of several of our nation's most celebrated wild regions including unspoiled stretches of the Greater Yellowstone ecosystem and Utah's Redrock Canyon country."

Tribe's Hopes Soar as Elwha Dams Come Down and Salmon Return

People's World Online, April 13, 2013

PORT ANGELES, WASHINGTON—For 100 years, two hydroelectric dams on the Elwha river blocked fish from their spawning grounds, destroying one of the world's most bountiful salmon fisheries.

Now construction workers have blasted the concrete dams, removed the rubble, and slowly drained the lakes. The river is once again running free, flowing from its headwaters high in the Olympic Mountains to the Strait of Juan de Fuca. Most thrilling of all is that the Chinook, Coho, Chum, Silver, and Sockeye salmon and the Steelhead trout have appeared above the Elwha dams for the first time in a century.

The two dams, the lower Elwha Dam and eight miles upstream, the Glines Canyon Dam, were built in 1910 to provide electricity for a paper mill. Surplus electricity was sold to the city of Port Angeles. No fish-ladder was built so 400,000 or more salmon and steelhead were confined to the short stretch of the stream below the dams. A deal to build a fish hatchery to replace the upstream spawning beds ended after nine years, when the private owners closed the hatchery down.

It was a disaster for the salmon and also for the Lower Elwha Klallam Tribe who make their home on the river banks, drawing their sustenance from the salmon and steelhead.

"It messed up our diet, our way of getting food," said Robert Elofson, Elwha River Restoration Director for the Lower Elwha Klallam Tribe. The tribe ate the salmon, he added, and sold the surplus in Port Angeles and other markets, a mainstay of their economy. Now that lifeline was gone.

"When we first made the motion for dam removal, we did not have the support of any federal agency," Elofson told the *World*. "We did have the support of many environmental groups."

Finally, in 1992, the Klallam Tribe won passage of a federal act to remove the dams. Yet it took until 2009, another seventeen years, for Congress to approve the money to move ahead. Now the dams are mostly gone, the last concrete remnants due to be removed by 2014.

Workers have cut a trail through the deeply forested slopes of the Elwha River canyon to a viewpoint where thousands of tourists can look down on the open, fast-flowing Elwha where the lower dam once stood. Much of the $325 million for the project came from President Obama's economic stimulus package, including the $16.4 million for a new fish hatchery that Elofson called "state of the art" probably, he said, "the best one in Washington State right now."

Elofson is a trained biologist who has devoted his life to the restoration of the river. While we were speaking, he received a call on his cellphone from his son who operates a fishing boat in the Strait of Juan de Fuca and the Pacific Ocean.

"Eighty-seven percent of the Elwha watershed is in the Olympic National Park," Elofson continued. "We own the first mile of the river and the near shore. We know it is one of the best protected streams in America. The sediment transport has followed the modeling very well. We already have adult salmon and steelhead swimming up above where the first dam used to stand. They are spawning in Little River, a tributary of the Elwha.

"The tribe also physically moved some adult Coho salmon into Little River and Indian Creek. We had 100 hatchlings from the redds (spawning nests)—sixty redds in Little River and thirty redds in Indian Creek. These fish have not been up there for 100 years yet they liked the river there and they spawned in those streams."

"We expect the restoration of the Elwha to be very successful. We're not sure about the length of time it will take. But all the signs are good."

It is the biggest dam removal project in U.S. history, he said, one of the biggest infrastructure projects in President Obama's economic stimulus program.

There is also a dam removal project on the Klamath River in southern Oregon, Elofson said. "And there is a proposal to remove two dams on the Penobscot River in Maine."

On the other hand, in Alaska, the Anglo-American Corporation plans to dig the Pebble Mine, an enormous open pit three and a half miles across and a mile deep, destroying spawning beds for the world's richest Sockeye salmon fishery. The pristine waters of the rivers that empty into Bristol Bay would run red with arsenic and other toxic chemicals in mining the gold and copper. Pitted against this ruthless corporate greed are the Native American Indians of Alaska, the fishermen, the environmentalists.

So far, said Elofson, the Elwha Restoration Project "has created some jobs in construction and will create more jobs in the future. We have tribal fishing rights to harvest the salmon. There are only about 5,000 salmon coming back now but we expect between 300,000 and 400,000 when the river is fully restored. Half of these runs will be harvestable." It will be a new day for the Klallam tribe and for the salmon.

Navy Jet Noise, Electronic Warfare Stir Outrage
People's World Online, September 18, 2015

SEQUIM, WASHINGTON—Residents of Whidbey Island and the Olympic Peninsula are mobilizing against the U.S. Navy's plan to turn this peaceful region into an Electronic Warfare Range (EWR) with deafening, low-level overflights by squadrons of Growler jets.

The jets stationed at the Naval Air Station on Whidbey Island will take off and fly west over the Olympic Peninsula and engage in target practice over National Forest Service lands in the west end of Clallam County. The Navy plans to schedule these flights as long as sixteen hours daily, 260 days annually. The will fly as low as 1,200 feet altitude.

The Navy plan is to shift this EWR training from Mountain Home Air Base in Idaho to the range in Clallam County. Some have noticed that the Pacific Northwest has topography similar to that of Russia, China, and Korea, nations the Navy may be preparing to wage war against.

Outrage has been stirred by disclosure that the Navy plans to invade the airspace above the Olympic National Park, a World Heritage Site and an International Biosphere Reserve. It is pristine wilderness home to wildlife that will be put at risk by the Navy's war preparations. Three million people visit Olympic National Park each year, seeking peace, quiet, and clean air of the alpine wilderness and the Pacific coast.

Also in the flightpath of the jets will be the reservations of the Quileutes, Hoh and Quinault Native American Indians.

A grassroots organization, Save the Olympic Peninsula, charges in a fact sheet, "Growlers are the noisiest jets ever made, up to 113 decibels at 1000 feet. Exposure to that noise, even for a short duration, can permanently damage human hearing. Children's ears are especially vulnerable."

People who live near the Naval Air Station on Whidbey Island are living now with the earsplitting noise. Residents staged a mass protest at the air station last May holding U.S. flags upside down. Michael Monson, president of Citizens of Ebey Reserve explained that, "We are in dire distress because our homes and communities are being saturated with hazardous levels of noise and our elected officials seem to be powerless or unwilling to act." Noise levels have been monitored in Whidbey Island homes at 101.8 decibels and outside those homes at 134.2 decibels "far above the 85 decibels at which hearing loss begins," Monson said.

Yet a federal judge refused to grant injunctive relief to these communities despite proof of the health hazard posed by this noise.

Doug Goldie, who lives with his wife east of Sequim, testified before the Sequim City Council, this week, that he believes the U.S. Navy is harassing him because he is protesting Navy jets flying low over his home.

"I am really concerned," he told the Councilmembers. "Over a twenty-five day period, we made thirty-three calls to the (Navy) noise complaint hotline (360-275-6665). After a few calls, we were then just blanketed with Growlers coming over, multiple Growlers some as late as 11:30 p.m."

Sequim Mayor, Candace Pratt, responded, "It is disturbing and I think there are some on Whidbey Island that also feel they have been targeted for complaining."

Councilmember, Ken Hays, a former Sequim mayor, interjected that Navy jets have been flying low over his home on Sequim's east side. "I think the Navy has been persistently dishonest with the public on this issue," Hays said. "They are not being honest with us about their flight patterns, their flyovers. . . . I think we need to continue to press them."

The Navy has requested permission from the U.S. Forest Service to place radar-emitting trucks on Forest Service roads beaming electromagnetic signals to the squadrons of warplanes. The pilots will train to home in on these targets and knock them out with highly focused electronic beams. Defenders of wildlife charge that the noise, air pollution from jet fuel and the electronic radiation, pose a dire threat to animals and plants that now thrive on the Peninsula. Already, the Navy's submarine sonar is blamed for threatening whales and other marine mammals and the EWR is expected to add to the risks for marine mammals.

"A Huge Environmental Mistake Coming to the Peninsula?" is the main headline in the spring edition of *Voice of the Wild Olympics*, the newsletter of the Olympic Park Associates (OPA). OPA President, Donna Osseward, writes, "The Olympics urgently need your help. We need to convince our Congressional representatives, Forest Service administrators, and the Navy, that the Navy's shocking plan to create a Permanent Electromagnetic Warfare Training Range on the Olympic Peninsula is ill-advised."

The grassroots movement urges an outpouring of letters, emails, and other protests addressed to Robert Bonnie who oversees the U.S. Forest Service urging him to deny the Navy permission. His address is Jamie L. Whitten Building, 1400 Independence Ave. SW, Suite 240 E, Washington, DC, 20250.

Email: robert.bonnie@osec.usda.gov.

Also, suggested in messages to U.S. Senators Maria Cantwell and Patty Murray, both Democrats of Washington, U.S. Representatives, and to members of the Washington State legislature.

Exxon Valdez: The Spill that Waited to Happen
People's Daily World, March 29, 1989

The worst oil spill ever in North America might have been prevented if Exxon Shipping Company had not aggressively reduced the number of seamen manning company tankers.

That charge was made Tuesday by John Hillman, a governor of the Exxon Seaman's Union in Bayonne, New Jersey.

"We've been faced with an all-out management attack on our agreement," Hillman told the PDW. "The company's influence on the Coast Guard is so overwhelming that they approve Exxon's requests for waivers from manning requirements."

Hillman said that the Coast Guard approved Exxon's request to sharply reduce the crew of the Exxon Valdez. It eliminated a radio operator and slashed the number of deckhands from six able-bodied seamen (Abs) and three ordinary seamen (OS) to four Abs and two Oss. This crew operates a supertanker that is 978 feet long—the length of more than three football fields.

Hillman said, "The Company is trying to save nickels and dimes but one more man on deck might have prevented this costly disaster. And Exxon "wants further reductions in crews."

Loaded with 1.26 million barrels of crude oil from the Trans-Alaska pipeline, the Exxon Valdez ran aground last Friday night as it was steaming out of Valdez into Prince William Sound. Several compartments ruptured and the tanker spilled 200,000 or more barrels into the Sound, a body of water noted for its rich aquatic life.

This is not the first Exxon tanker disaster. Hillman wrote a letter to members of the seaman's union on March 14, citing the March 3 grounding of the Exxon Houston in high seas off Hawaii. "This is an incident where our union can say 'We told you so.'" Hillman wrote, "We are fortunate or lucky that some of our union brothers and sisters were not killed in a most dangerous and needless operation."

Hillman's letter charged that Exxon "didn't have enough personnel to deal with this situation. We have seen too many multi-million dollar screw-ups by senior officers—managers—to not begin to wonder whether our company can survive these costs."

Hillman said the union is awaiting results of the Coast Guard investigation before it issues a full statement of the Exxon Valdez disaster.

A West Coast Exxon tanker crewmember Tuesday told the *PDW* that the company's cutbacks in wages, increases in overtime and sharp reductions in crew size have created deep problems of morale among Exxon seamen, including officers.

"There are severe problems," the source told the *PDW*. "They eliminated a four-day paid leave, cut overtime wage rates ten percent and cut our base pay six percent, for an overall twenty percent cut. Officers took a cut four years ago and their morale has been low ever since."

Exxon, which has the largest tanker fleet of any U.S. oil company, has made energetic efforts to increase safety using propaganda, the source said. "But they are not going to succeed" with the ships so drastically undermanned.

The source said tanker crews work under conditions of extreme tension, especially during loading and unloading when the Captain and Chief Mate are often on the bridge for twenty-four hours straight. Frank Iarossi, president of Exxon Shipping Company, admitted Monday that the pilot steering the Exxon Valdez was not certified for commanding tankers in these waters.

A third mate, Gregory Cousins, was in command at the time of the grounding while Captain Joseph J. Hazelwood was below decks. Hazelwood has been convicted twice of drunk driving and had his driver's license suspended. But an Exxon tanker crewmember warned against scapegoating the captain while ignoring the underlying conditions caused by Exxon's crew-cutting policies.

Kayakers Chant "Shell No!" Photo courtesy of the author

Kayakers Paddle in Seattle Port Chanting "Shell NO"

People's World, May 18, 2015

SEATTLE—Protesters paddled and rowed in a vast flotilla of tribal dugout canoes, kayaks, row boats, surf boards, rubber dinghies, and sailboats, Saturday May 16 to the Port of Seattle's Terminal 5 to confront Shell Oil's monstrous arctic ocean drilling rig tied up here.

"Shell NO" the protesters chanted, hammering on their kayaks with their paddles or fists. "Climate Justice NOW" they roared at the rig, which loomed like an evil, yellow Darth Vader at Terminal 5 along the mouth of the Duwamish River.

The protesters came from the Seattle and Tacoma area but also from throughout Puget Sound and the San Juan Islands and the North Olympic Peninsula. This reporter came with Brian Grad, a fellow member of both Clallam MoveOn and Olympic Climate Action that mobilized protests against the

Shell drilling rig when it was moored in Port Angeles harbor for two weeks hoping the storm of protest would die down. Instead, it has grown steadily louder and more angry. Brian rowed and I served as coxswain giving orders from the stern of his rowboat as we joined the flotilla.

Sitting on a flat-topped buoy floating nearby was a family of harbor seals who barked joyously at all the excitement. One little wide-eyed fellow swam up and crawled on to the aft deck of a kayak, hitching a ride to the waterborne rally.

Alan Rosada, paddling his kayak from the boat launch at Seacrest Park on Alki Point told this reporter he lives on Orcas Island. "To be going down this path, more offshore drilling after the catastrophes we've suffered, it's just insane," he said. "We must push for alternative energy like solar."

Annie Leonard, Executive Director of Greenpeace U.S. one of a coalition of groups that organized the "Shell NO Flotilla" surveyed the hundreds of kayaks, the chanting protesters and told the *People's World*, "When I look at this, I see democracy in action. People have come together to raise their voices not our sea levels."

She said the protesters understand the science. "Drilling for oil in the Arctic is incompatible with a sustainable future. We are out here because we want a sustainable future and we know it is possible."

She pointed out that Royal Dutch Shell defied the opposition of Seattle Mayor Ed Murray and a unanimous vote of the Seattle City Council in towing the oil rig here from Port Angeles. The company claims a lease agreement was approved by the Seattle Port Commissioners. But the deal was reached in deep secrecy with no input from the people of Seattle or the rest of the Puget Sound community. Shell thumbed its nose at a request by the Port Commissioners that they delay the arrival of the rig until differences with the Mayor and City Council could be ironed out.

"What is on the line here is not just the future of our planet but democracy," Leonard added. "Who is in charge here? Is it the people and our elected officials? Or is it a multinational oil company with a horrific environmental and human rights record?"

Seeking to avoid paying Alaska state taxes, Shell hastily removed an offshore rig, Kulluk, in late December 2012, towing it with cables through a storm raging at seventy miles per hour. The cables snapped and on January 1, 2013, the rig ran ashore on an island near Kodiak. The rig had 150,000 gallons of diesel onboard. Environmentalists warned that this reckless operation proves that Shell Oil puts profits first, the environment and worker safety be damned.

Annette Klapstein, a member of Seattle Raging Grannies, told the *World* her organization joined the "Shell No Flotilla" to add their voice of outrage. The Polar Pioneer rig is "a horror! A monster," she charged. "I am also horrified that our elected Port Commissioners ignored the people's wishes. They knew we didn't like it. That's the reason they approved this lease behind closed doors. The Mayor and the City Council came out against it. The Port Commissioners and Shell Oil basically thumbed their noses at the people and the city government."

Shell drilling in the arctic "will guarantee that we will have catastrophic climate change," she said. Asked what alternative she seeks, Klapstein said, "First, corporations no longer rule the world. Second, we have a real democracy that invests in green energy, well-paid family wage jobs for everyone."

Hundreds of Native Americans joined the protest, including members of the Duwamish and Snohomish tribes who led the flotilla paddling their handsome dugout canoes. Among them was Faith Gemmill, who lives in Arctic Village, Alaska. She is a member of the Athabaskan tribe.

"We are the ones who live closest to where Shell Oil wants to drill for oil," she told the *People's World*. "We will be the ones most directly impacted. Studies show that there is a seventy-five percent chance of an oil spill. These oil companies have no consciousness of what it is like to live in the arctic. They already have access to ninety-five percent of our shoreline. They have no respect for the people, for the wildlife, for the oceans. I say 'Shell No!'"

[7]

BRING DOWN THAT WALL!

Town Asks Obama to Halt Border Patrol Raids

People's World Online, June 10, 2009

PORT TOWNSEND, WASHINGTON—The Port Townsend City Council voted 6-1 June 2 to send a resolution to President Obama, and leaders of the U.S. Senate and House asking for a halt to Border Patrol enforcement including checkpoint stops on U.S. Highway 101 with overnight deportation of undocumented people.

Before the vote, Carl Nomura, a highly respected community leader told the Council the checkpoints and raids on the North Olympic Peninsula remind him of the mass roundup and incarceration of Japanese Americans during World War II. Nomura said he himself was a victim, imprisoned in one of the Japanese Relocation Centers. "The law of the land is supposed to be innocent until proven guilty," he said.

Councilman Mark Welch said he was reluctant to get involved with federal policy but quoted Benjamin Franklin's warning, "They who give up essential liberty to obtain a little temporary safety deserve neither liberty nor safety."

Liz Rivera Goldstein, a veteran peace activist in the Port Townsend area hailed the near unanimous adoption of the resolution. "I'm thrilled about it," she told the *World*. "I think it is so important. So much money has been wasted in this misguided policy of harassment of citizen and non-citizen alike."

She said co-workers on her job have arrived late at work because they were held up at the ICE-Border Patrol checkpoints. "I know what this is like. I too am of Mexican descent," she said. "I have a great aunt who was in the U.S. legally. Yet she was arrested and deported back to Mexico. We live in America. We are supposed to have rights."

Many towns and cities across the country have enacted council ordinances declaring themselves "sanctuary" cities and proclaiming that their law enforcement officers will not assist the Border Patrol and ICE agents in enforcement of the dragnet raids and mass arrests of undocumented people.

That defiant attitude has enraged the ultra-right immigrant-bashers. An outfit calling itself Respect Washington is scrambling to collect 241,153 signatures by the July 3 deadline of registered voters in Washington State to place I-1043 on the ballot in the election next November 3. Petitions in support of I-1043 were inserted in local newspapers across the state under a lurid headline, *Stop State Funding of Illegal Aliens, Theft of Jobs, and Social Security Numbers.*

I-1043 would require state and local law enforcement to assist federal agents in the enforcement of immigration law. It would require employers, both private and public, to verify any employee's legal status through the federal government's "E-Verify." It would require the Department of Motor Vehicles to also verify the legal status of anyone applying for a driver's license. And it would also require state and local officials to verify a person's eligibility for social services and benefits including attendance at schools. medical care, food stamps, or unemployment compensation.

Goldstein denounced the ballot initiative as an attempt "to codify ignorance and hatred into law." She charged that the rightwing is trying to whip up "a backlash against the attempt in our country to reflect a more diverse and accepting community . . . the fact that our country was ready to elect Barack Obama, a real step in the right direction."

Among groups that have thrown full support to the immigrant-bashing ballot effort is Stormfront.org, web site of the Ku Klux Klan that features the "White Pride" ravings of Klansmen David Duke and Don Black. The Klan posted on their site Respect Washington's appeal for cash donations to hire contractors to collect signatures for I-1043.

The Washington State Hispanic/Latino Legislative Organization is working hard to expose I-1043 and an earlier version I-409, charging that they "would result in the growth of prejudice and discrimination against Washington's Hispanic/Latino and immigrant communities." It adds, "Hate groups are using numbers and figures accusing undocumented immigrants of adding to the economic crisis in our country. This is a campaign of misinformation to scare people."

*Editor's note: I-1043 backers failed to collect enough signatures to put the measure on the ballot in 2009.

Border Patrol Roadblocks Spread Fear on U.S. 101

People's World, September 10, 2008

PORT ANGELES, WASHINGTON—Edgar Ayala, who graduated with honors from Forks High School last June was arrested at a Border Patrol checkpoint on Highway 101 August 20 just a mile or so from the place that has been his home since he was an infant.

That made no difference to the enforcers of George W. Bush's draconian crackdown on undocumented immigrants across the U.S. Ayala, eighteen, was hustled off to a detention center in Seattle and deported post-haste to Mexico. Similarly, sixteen-year-old Carlos Bernabe was arrested at that same checkpoint and taken to a Seattle jail where he is awaiting deportation to Mexico.

These arrests are spreading a climate of fear in the mostly Latino immigrant communities here on the North Olympic Peninsula. ICE (Immigration and Customs Enforcement) and the Border Patrol, with forty-five officers, have clamped three checkpoints on the Peninsula, an isolated region where U.S. 101 is the only through highway.

The arrest of Ayala and Bernabe stirred such outrage that ninety

residents of Forks, a tiny logging town in the West End of Clallam County, joined a picketline in the center of downtown protesting the deportations. They held signs that read, "Border Patrol Terrorize Children," "Justice for All" and "Edgar Lost His Chance." Forks was the scene of a march by 700 people May 1, 2006, a day when more than one million demonstrated for immigrant rights across the U.S.

Nenita Bocanegra, who helped organize the picketline told the *Peninsula Daily News* (*PDN*), she opposes the targeting of immigrant workers, mostly employed as salal pickers, tree planters, and other forest industry workers in the West End. This community of immigrant workers has added riches to the local culture including the cuisine. Mexican restaurants abound and Spanish is the second language. "I don't think it's right for them to be taken out of their homes when their children are here and they're not doing anything wrong," Bocanegra said.

Tanya Ward, a leader of the Hoh Tribe, who also helped organize the protest, said she hopes Forks becomes a "sanctuary city" that refuses to help enforce repressive immigration laws.

The stepped up enforcement has stirred a flood of letters to the editor of the *PDN* with some likening the ICE-Border Patrol crackdown to a "police state" and even "fascism" that targets the Hispanic community citizen and non-citizen alike but also infringes on the democratic rights of everyone. Scores of concerned residents turned out for a protest meeting at the Port Angeles Public Library September 6. The group formed a new "Stop the Checkpoints" grassroots committee and voted to hold a mass protest rally or picketline Saturday September 20 in Port Angeles where the regional Ice-Border Patrol is headquartered.

One young woman who lives near Forks was at the meeting with her little girl. She is four months pregnant with her second child. She asked this reporter not to use her name but told a story of being victimized by the Border Patrol. Her husband, an undocumented immigrant, was on his way to his job as a tree planter one winter day when his pickup spun out of control on icy Highway 101. He ended up in the ditch and left the vehicle to go for help. A patrol car stopped and the officer hailed him by name. He was arrested and deported, leaving her with one child and another on the way.

"He was arrested on charges of 'leaving the scene of an accident' even though no other vehicle was involved," she said. "He was working every day to support us. Now I am the sole support for the family. I work here in Port Angeles. We live with this fear every day."

Another woman said her husband, too, is undocumented. They live in constant fear that he will be caught in the Ice-Border Patrol dragnet and deported to Honduras. They have a small business that had prospered until the current crackdown. Now Latinos who had been their main clientele are afraid to shop in her store. "I'm being forced out of business," she told the *World*. "We live under this cloud of fear all the time. I'm an American citizen but I live like he lives. I don't want them to take my husband."

Protests Force End to ICE-Border Patrol Checkpoints

People's World, May 14, 2009

FORKS, WASHINGTON—In the face of rising public anger, the U.S. Border Patrol and Immigration and Customs Enforcement (ICE) have ended their practice of stopping traffic at checkpoints on U.S. Highway 101 arresting undocumented immigrants, many deported to Mexico overnight.

The change was unannounced but residents here on the north Olympic Peninsula took notice that the last roadblock was taken down last September 9 in the face of marches, vigils, and mass demonstrations initiated by the Stop The Checkpoints Committee (SCPC).

Anger was stirred by the arrest at a checkpoint last summer of Edgar Ayala, eighteen, a mile or so from the home where he had lived since infancy. A star on the wrestling team, he had just graduated with honors from Forks High School. He was deported immediately to Mexico.

Nearly 100 protesters, the majority Mexican immigrants employed in the forest industry, marched through this logging town May 2 to celebrate May Day and Cinco de Mayo. They carried banners and placards that proclaimed, "Todos Somos Emigrantes" (We Are All Immigrants) and "Speak Out for Human Rights, Civil Liberties, Immigrant Workers . . . Stop the Checkpoints!"

At a rain-drenched rally in the town park, a Mexican American woman (she asked that her name not be used) told the crowd, "The checkpoints have stopped. Our voices are being heard and that's great. They are trying to be little more humane, letting women go when they have children. But now they are being more sneaky. They are still coming to the small towns, still doing racial profiling, still arresting and deporting people."

She added, "We need to make these immigrants legal so they can pay taxes and not be abused. I've been here thirty years. I'm very attached to the family-values workforce. With Obama in the White House, I'm very hopeful." Her comments came just days after Homeland Security Secretary, Janet Napolitano, announced a shift in emphasis from targeting immigrants to targeting employers raising hopes that ICE and the Border Patrol will end their workplace raids, mass arrests and deportations that have torn immigrant families apart.

SCPC Coordinator, Lois Danks, assailed the ultra-right Minutemen, who staged a "drive-by" counter-demonstration near the Sequim Wal-Mart a few months ago and then fled. "They are out there to terrorize immigrants," she said. "They use racism to set us against each other. They blame immigrants for the economic crisis when in fact immigrant workers are a vital part of our community. Who is taking away the jobs? The capitalists on Wall Street. We need to organize together, native born and immigrants, all races together."

Danks, a leader of Radical Women, urged a fight to stop the planned construction of a new Homeland Security Detention Center near Port Angeles and the scheme to arm

Coast Guard cutters and search and rescue helicopters with fifty-caliber machine guns. "Stop militarizing our borders. Normalize our borders," she said as the crowd applauded. The SCPC delivered 518 petitions to Representative Norm Dicks (D-WA) field office in Port Angeles, recently, asking him to oppose funding for the new detention center. The Border Patrol now has twenty-five agents on the Peninsula, up from only four agents two years ago. Dicks, who sits on the House Homeland Security Committee, released a statement that it is "not clear" to him the "security value" of inconveniencing thousands of travelers at roadblocks in his district.

Danks told the *World* SCPC is still celebrating a partial victory in winning release from detention of Tony Hernandez and stopping the instant deportation of his fellow worker Daniel Rodriguez. The two workers, employed by a landscaping company were driving in a truck to work when they were arrested last January 30. Hernandez is a legal resident who lives with his wife and two children in Sequim. But he had left his "green card" at home. The agents, Danks said, refused to listen to Hernandez' pleas and immediately detained him. Rodriguez is not documented but has lived and worked in the U.S. for many years. The SCPC organized a picketline at Sequim's main intersection the next day demanding release of the two men. "Tony was released and has returned to his family in Sequim," Danks said. Rodriguez is now awaiting a hearing on his appeal against deportation.

[8]

FIGHTING FOR JOBS, UNION RIGHTS

Depression Era Jobs Program is Model for Today

August 13, 2008

Bronze statue of CCC worker at Deception Pass State Park, Washington. Photo by author.

DECEPTION PASS STATE PARK, WASHINGTON—The Civilian Conservation Corps (CCC) put millions of jobless youth to work planting trees, fighting forest fires, building parks, roads and trails during the Great Depression. CCC alumni are now observing the 75th anniversary of the program founded by President Franklin Delano Roosevelt. Many say the CCC should be brought back to provide jobs and educational opportunities for millions of unemployed youth today.

Roosevelt signed the bill creating the program seventeen days after taking office in 1933. Within a month 300,000 jobless young men had enrolled. By the time the CCC was terminated in 1942 over 3 million men between the ages of seventeen and twenty-three had served. They were housed in hundreds of CCC camps across the nation. It included 250,000 African American men.

Some of the camps were integrated but racists demanded segregation and in 1935, Black enrollees were housed in 150 all-Black camps. The NAACP and other anti-racist groups protested this racist discrimination.

The young workers were assigned to a multitude of tasks mostly in the forests of the west. The U.S. Army requisitioned

217

trains that brought hundreds of thousands of CCC enrollees west. The CCC workers planted two billion trees on land decimated by timber company clear-cutting. The CCC earned the nickname "Roosevelt's Tree Army."

They also fought forest fires, erected thousands of fire lookout towers, built thousands of miles of roads and bridges and helped in soil conservation and reclamation. The CCC workers cleared hiking trails and built state parks like the dramatic Deception Pass State Park on Whidbey Island, still enjoyed by thousands of campers, picnickers, and sightseers today.

The park here hosts a CCC Interpretive Center established by CCC Alumni Chapter 78 in Everett, Washington. The centerpiece is a heroic bronze statue of a bare-chested youth, "The CCC Worker." An exhibit of photos, tools, mess kit, uniform, documents, and other memorabilia of the CCC is in a stone and timber bathhouse built by CCC workers. It features a video titled *The Best Time of My Life* in which CCC alumni recount the profound influence the CCC exerted on their lives.

Visitors are invited to write their comments in a log book as they leave the center. "Let's bring back the CCC," wrote a couple from Seabeck, Washington. It is one of many entries with that same message.

Duane Fuehr of Centralia, Washington, volunteer host at the park told this reporter that both his father and uncle were CCC workers. His father was a skilled logger and was placed in charge of a CCC crew at a camp near Centralia, he said.

"It would be good to bring back the CCC," Fuehr told the *World*. "Some of the young people who graduate from high school are going on to college. Others will join the military like I did. But a lot of these kids don't know what they are going to do with their lives. It would be good for them to give a year for the country."

A spokesman for the CCC Alumni Association in St. Louis, Missouri confirmed that "a lot of the alumni feel that way. They know what the CCC did for them. Many learned the trade that carried them through the rest of their lives in the CCC. It definitely worked back then. A lot of people have contacted Congress urging that the CCC be reestablished. But the lawmakers have rejected the idea."

Many local chapters of the CCC Alumni Association have already held events celebrating the 75th Anniversary and more celebrations will take place at the association's annual convention September 25-28 at Prince William Forest Park where Camp Roosevelt, the first CCC camp was established in 1933. The convention will recess and visit the Franklin Delano Roosevelt memorial in Washington, D.C.

The Interpretive Center records the memories of many of the CCC workers. "Food for the many hungry men was measured by the train-load," reads the explanatory text on one exhibit. One enrollee, Ed Devine, wrote, "Half of what we ate came from nearby suppliers. These large purchases helped the local economy. Plentiful food helped the young enrollees too. I went from 128 pounds up to 155 in nothing flat and none of it was fat."

John Tursi writes, "We came from very poverty-ridden circumstances. For many, many days, maybe a little bowl of soup a day would be it. We just didn't eat. But the food out here was just fantastic. To wake up and go into all the hotcakes you could eat and all the butter you wanted and milk and eggs!" An estimated fifty percent of CCC enrollees were high school dropouts, and an estimated three percent were illiterate. The CCC established an educational program, providing classes in a wide range of academic subjects as well as vocational training. Some even learned to read and write in the CCC or earned their high school diplomas.

I ran into a CCC veteran, Jim Cassidy of Puyallup, Washington, at a *PWW* picnic in Seattle. He told me he joined the CCC in 1933 in Bucoda, a tiny sawmill town in Thurston, County, Washington. "My dad hadn't worked for two years," Cassidy explained. "CCC workers were paid thirty dollars a month. Five dollars was pocket money for us, the rest was sent home. When my twenty-five dollar a month started coming home, it was a lifeline for the family."

He was sent to Leavenworth, Washington, a town on the eastern slopes of the Cascade Mountains, he said. His first job was helping build a road up the Icicle River to Lake Wenatchee. It is still in use today.

"That meant cutting down some trees," Cassidy said. "In some stretches, we had to blast our way through solid granite. The road was for fire protection. During the same year, there was a big forest fire over in Skykomish on the Beckler River. We went over there and put it out."

Being a CCC worker was not the only benefit Cassidy won from Roosevelt's New Deal. The Wagner Act was passed and signed by Roosevelt recognizing workers' right to join a union, bargain collectively, and go on strike to win higher wages and benefits.

"I had heard my dad talking about the Wobblies (The Industrial Workers of the World) and their idea of 'One Big Union.' My dad would go to union meetings. We were trying to organize the loggers and sawmill workers. It started out as the Carpenters & Joiners but they were like all the other craft unions. So we started to organize the Congress of Industrial Organizations and the International Woodworkers of America, one union for all the mill workers and loggers."

Cassidy said the nation needs a program like the CCC, today, to provide jobs and training for millions of jobless youth. "We need the camps but we don't need the military to run it," he said. "They put military officers in charge." The result was strict military discipline. The CCC workers were awakened by a bugle playing reveille in the morning and went to sleep with taps at night. There were regular military-style inspections of the barracks.

But a program that restores the CCC with an accent on "civilian," that abolishes the CCC's racially segregated camps, and opens it, this time, to young women as well as men, is an idea that should be "high on the agenda" of a new administration in Washington, Cassidy said.

Back in 1996, James C. Ronning, then president of the National Association of CCC Alumni pledged to fight to "bring back the CCC." He called the CCC "the greatest national youth program ever seen in the United States" arguing that the CCC's goals are still as urgent as ever. "The final one, to bring together people from all backgrounds teaches people to tolerate, and even appreciate each other and work together in a spirit of cooperation," he wrote. "This is one goal that, if anything, seems even more relevant as we face new divisiveness in our country today."

2,000 Rally for Union Rights US Canada Border
Special to the *People's World* April 4, 2011

BLAINE, WASHINGTON—Union members from Canada and the United States rallied at Peace Arch Park on the U.S.-Canada border, April 2, cheering calls to defend collective bargaining rights and booing every mention of union busters like Wisconsin Governor Scott Walker and Canada's Tory Prime Minister Stephen Harper.

The crowd held small placards emblazoned with U.S. and Canadian flags and the words, "Working Families Standing Together. We are ONE!"

Jeff Johnson, President of the Washington State Labor Council told the crowd, "Corporate America has declared war on the labor movement all across the United States."

Wall Street banks sit on $7 trillion in deposits, refusing to invest in job creation while whining that the nation is "broke" and must accept cutbacks, layoffs and austerity, he charged. General Electric reported $15 billion in profits and did not pay a dime in federal taxes, he said, even as Washington State and every other state in the nation slashes vital services and lays off public workers.

Dr. Martin Luther King Jr. died in Memphis, Tennessee, April 4, 1968, leading the sanitation workers' strike to win collective bargaining rights, Johnson said. He quoted King's last speech, "The arc of the moral universe is long but it bends toward justice."

Jabbing his fist in the air, Johnson added, "He was talking about union rights. We must torque on that arc! We've got to bend it down!"

221

He led the crowd in a chant: "We are union! We are one!"

Jim Sinclair, President of the B.C. Federation of Labor, said Canadian workers are facing a similar nightmare of union busting attacks by the B.C. provincial government and Harper. Canada is in the midst of a national election set for May 2 with Harper, now heading a minority government seeking to win majority control of parliament. "Stephen Harper with a majority is our Scott Walker," Sinclair said, as the crowd erupted in boos. "We can't let it happen!"

The Tories say there is no money, he continued, even as they rubberstamp billions in tax breaks for banks and corporations. "We can't fund our schools and hospitals. That's upside down. You've got to increase taxes on corporations. No one gave us anything we didn't fight for. Not one thing! Are you ready to fight?"

The crowd roared, "Yes!"

Susan Lambert, President of the British Columbia Federation of Teachers said organized labor is "building a movement that is global in scope." Nations like Honduras and Colombia have a "veneer of democracy" yet beat, torture, and murder trade unionists including schoolteachers. "We stand here in solidarity with the people of Wisconsin," she said. "Governor Walker is targeting teachers. Why? Because they know an educated population will not tolerate these huge disparities in income." She concluded, "Democracy! If you don't use it, you lose it."

Dale Anderson, a member of the Amalgamated Transit Workers, Local 519 in Wisconsin, said, "Scott Walker awoke a sleeping giant. Hundreds of thousands of union members and their supporters have joined the fight. We will not be denied victory."

He announced that the grassroots movement just filed 21,700 signatures to force a recall election of his state senator, Republican Dan Kapanke, a supporter of Walker's union busting law now blocked by a judge's restraining order. "He's the first to go!" Anderson shouted.

Reyna Lopez, a young Latina woman from Portland, Oregon, told the crowd she is the first in her family to graduate from college. Yet even as her generation goes in debt to finance college, many still cannot find a job. "Meanwhile corporations are making record profits. Corporations should pay their fair share in taxes," she said, adding, students and youth "stand with labor."

Barbara Byrd, Secretary-Treasurer of the Oregon AFL-CIO came with forty other union members on a bus from Portland. "This is a pivotal time when we have the opportunity to seize the initiative," she told the *World*. "Scott Walker could be a great gift in terms of our political effort if we can harness the anger of our members" in the 2012 elections.

A brief hailstorm gave way to bright sunshine. The cherry trees bloomed near the Peace Arch where the great African American baritone and freedom fighter Paul Robeson sang to 35,000 U.S. and Canadian trade unionists in 1952 and again in 1953. He had been invited to sing by the Mine, Mill and Smelter Workers who were meeting in convention in Vancouver, B.C. Robeson had been stripped of his passport and could not attend so they recessed the convention and came down to hear Robeson sing and speak here. This reporter, then twelve-years-old, was in the crowd cheering.

Will Parry, ninety-two, stood in the crowd, Saturday, holding the banner of the Puget Sound Alliance for Retired Americans. He too remembered the Robeson concert here fifty-eight years ago. "I was assigned to security and rode up in the car with Robeson from Seattle," Parry said. "It is not a concert I am likely to forget."

Stephen Von Sychowski, a member of the Young Communist League of Canada said he learned in his childhood of Robeson singing at the Peace Arch. "It showed that for the working class there are no borders," he told the *World*. "They attack workers on both sides of the border so we must stand together."

How a Small Town Council Routed the Union Busters

September 9 2014

SEQUIM, WASHINGTON—The Sequim City Council voted unanimously September 8 to kill two pending "Right to Work" (for less) ballot propositions, condemning them as "grossly invalid" and a flagrant violation of state law.

The action came during a regular meeting of the council in the Clallam Transit Center packed with union members and other foes of union busting.

A handful of sponsors of the two anti-union measures were also present. Proposition 1 would have explicitly terminated the right to strike and make union membership and payment of union dues "voluntary." (Union membership is already voluntary.) Proposition 2 would require that union negotiations with the city be conducted in public. Of Sequim's seventy-three employees, fifty are union members represented mostly by the Teamsters Union.

Sequim City Attorney Craig Ritchie told the council, "Nothing has changed my mind. These proposed initiatives do not meet the requirements . . . of state statutes. They put the city at some risk of unfair labor practices. . . ."

Freedom Foundation agents, most of them from Olympia, had collected a few hundred signatures on Proposition 1 and Proposition 2. A representative of the Olympia-based Initiative and Referendum Institute (IRI) told the council that it had only two choices, either approve the measures themselves or put them on the November 4 ballot.

To intimidate the council, IRI Washington State Director Shawn Newman announced two days before the meeting that their institute will sue the city of Sequim to force the measures onto the ballot.

Newman and IRI are close allies of the Freedom Foundation and of Tim Eyman, the ultra-right hustler who has become a millionaire by running professional signature gathering efforts to place rightwing extremist initiatives on the Washington State ballot.

But Ritchie told the council they could "opt for the third alternative"—rejecting the two measures themselves and also excluding them from the ballot.

Councilman Ted Miller then offered a motion to kill the propositions, telling his colleagues, "It's hard to come up with an initiative that violates more statutes . . . They are grossly invalid."

The mayor called the vote. It was unanimous. Even the lone rightwing member of the council cast his vote to kill the measures.

Before the City Council meeting, more than fifty foes of Proposition 1 and Proposition 2 stood outside the Transit Center adjacent to the construction site where union workers are constructing the new City Hall.

Many in the picket line were linemen of the Public Utility District (PUD), the publicly owned electric utility that supplies power to Clallam County. The workers are represented by the International Brotherhood of Electrical Workers Local 997 that negotiated for sixteen months before finally winning a modest pay raise. Others in the crowd were members of Clallam County MoveOn, and other union supporters.

They held signs that proclaimed "No Union busting in Sequim" and "Koch Brothers Go Home." They chanted, "Union busting is disgusting."

During the public comment period, Sam Woods, co-chair of Clallam County MoveOn, himself a disabled member of IBEW, told the council, "For outside groups to come in here and try to subjugate the citizens of this city to the billionaires back in Wichita, Kansas or in Olympia, it offends me."

Karen Parker, a hospice nurse and a Sequim resident, said, "These measures are a power grab by a rightwing outfit not based in Sequim. . . . I do not want to be used as a political pawn."

Proponents of the two union busting propositions denounced "union bosses" who, they claimed, are driving towns like Sequim into bankruptcy with exorbitant wages, and defined pensions. One speaker branded opponents of the anti-union measures as "communist sympathizers" and slammed "unemployment checks" as "nothing more than taking from one group and giving to another."

But Rex Habner, a working lineman for PUD who is paid $277 monthly for leading his union local, told the council, "I am the President and Business Manager of IBEW Local 997. I negotiate contracts. I'm a full time lineman. I'm the 'Big Boss' you just heard about."

The aim of these union-busting measures, he said, "is to gain a greater chokehold on the people who work in the city, to lower their standard of living."

The Olympia-based Freedom Foundation is linked to the extremist American Legislative Exchange Council (ALEC) bankrolled by the oil billionaire Koch Brothers. At its secretive annual meeting in Dallas, last month, ALEC launched a spinoff, the American City-County Exchange (ACCE) that seeks to railroad through towns and counties union busting measures and other profit-driven measures like those in Sequim. Similar measures are pending in the towns of Shelton and Lake Chelan.

Habner told the *World* the Sequim council vote is a "win." He warned, however, that Sequim still has a union-busting lawsuit hanging over its head.

"They'll be back. We have to be ready." He added, "It goes back to the Koch Brothers. . . . The more little cities they can get to approve these anti-union measures, the more pressure they can put on Olympia (the State capital) to enact Right to Work (for less) for the entire State of Washington."

September 11 update: Tim Wheeler writes, "The city commissioners of the town of Shelton also voted unanimously to kill two anti-union propositions identical to the ones rejected by the Sequim City Council. And in the town of Chelan, east of the Cascades, dominated by the Republicans, the Freedom Foundation linked to the Koch Brothers could not collect enough signatures to put the 'Right to Work (for less)' propositions on the ballot. Three strikes and you're OUT!"

Paperworkers End Strike, Resume Talks with Nippon

People's World, March 26 2013

PORT ANGELES, WASHINGTON—Union paperworkers walked their picket line round-the-clock in chill spring weather here last week demanding that Nippon Paper resume "good faith" contract talks. They ended the walkout March 25 when the company came back to the bargaining table.

The 130 workers at the mill voted unanimously to strike Wednesday, March 20 when the company attempted to impose, unilaterally, their "best and final offer," a take-away scheme. It was the first work stoppage at the mill since 1984. The walkout was greeted with strong support in this union-conscious mill town with residents delivering food, doughnuts, coffee, and leaning on their horns as they drove by.

The owners plead that they have lost market share and the workers must sacrifice to keep the mill profitable. Picketers marching near the mill entrance last Friday debunked the company's pleas of poverty.

"They are building that biomass plant at a cost of over $71 million," said Rod Weekes, a spokesman for the strikers pointing to a big plant under construction just inside the mill entrance.

The biomass plant is scheduled to begin operations this September despite strong protests by the environmental movement. "That plant will run a generator and provide power for the mill and generate surplus electricity that the company can sell," Weekes said.

Nippon pleas of poverty, he added, ring hollow in the face of this major upgrade in the mill's efficiency.

"Right now we are engaged in an unfair labor practices strike. We feel that we have been bargaining in good faith," Weekes continued. "We'd like the company to come back to the bargaining table. It's just a 'take it or leave' package they have offered. That's no way to reach an agreement."

The mill at the base of Ediz Hook, a sand pit that stretches out into the Strait of Juan de Fuca has been a landmark of the Port Angeles skyline since Crown Zellerbach opened it in December 1920. Crown-Z sold the mill to Nippon Corporation in 2003. It produces newsprint used in the production of the *Peninsula Daily News* and other newspapers in the U.S. The mill also produces paper for advertising flyers and other light-duty paper products. Much of the paper produced at the mill is exported to Asia and Australia.

Nippon placed quarter-page ads in the Sunday edition of the *Peninsula Daily News* that read, "Now Hiring: Nippon Paper Industries USA is accepting qualified applicants for all positions. . . . Successful applicants are intended to be hired as permanent replacement workers." The jobless rate on the North Olympic Peninsula is above eleven percent and Nippon is resorting to the dirtiest of dirty tricks to break the strike.

Greg Pallesen, the International Vice President of the AWPPW drove up from Portland, Oregon, to assist the workers. "We want the company back at the bargaining table to bargain in good faith. Good faith bargaining is required by law," Pallesen told the *People's World.* "We've been bargaining with them for two years. We believe their goal is implementation of their final offer. We are still bargaining. We believe their attempt to implement their final offer unilaterally is illegal."

Represented by the Association of Western Pulp and Paper Workers (AWPPW), Local 155, the workers earlier filed an "unfair labor practices" complaint with the National Labor Relations Board charging that the Japanese-owned company has engaged in stalling tactics for nearly two years. That complaint is expected to be heard in April.

Pallesen said there are many unresolved issues on the table. "Nippon is a multinational corporation making a lot of money in the world. They have been given a lot of tax breaks."

AWPPW Local 155 "testified in Olympia in support of the biomass facility," he added. "As soon as the biomass plant is near completion, this is the thanks the workers get. Nippon wants to operate that plant on the backs of the workers. They ought to be ashamed of themselves."

Pallesen pointed out that the stock market is soaring with corporations reporting record high profits. "We have the right to be bargaining and getting the best pensions ever, the best medical benefits, and the best wages." Instead, the corporations demand outrageous takeaways in wages and benefits.

"International Paper got more than three billion dollars in tax breaks over two years. What did they do with those tax breaks? They invested in paper mills all over the world, in Indonesia, China. The Koch Brothers own Georgia Pacific. I don't even know how much they got in tax concessions. They get these tax breaks with no strings attached and then export the jobs overseas."

Weekes said he has been employed at the paper mill for 17 years and before that worked at the Rayonier mill for twenty-three years until that plant closed down permanently. "The way the economy is going, right now, the tax dollars we generate with our labor and the revenue we earn, we are a vital part of the local economy," Weekes added. "We spend our wages locally. There are more than 200 employee at this mill—130 hourly employees and seventy salaried. We create maybe another 1,000 jobs."

The mill, he said, is in the "top ten" employers on the North Olympic. The jobs and income generated by these millworkers, Weekes concluded "are the lifeblood of our community."

Walmart Workers Strike on Black Friday
November 26 2012

PORT ANGELES, WASHINGTON—Nearly 100 supporters joined Walmart workers who walked out on strike, here November 23. They joined a picketline in front of the store chanting, "What do we want? Respect!" and "Walmart,

Walmart, you're no good! Treat your workers the way you should."

The walkout in this papermill town was one of dozens against the retail giant across the nation protesting Walmart's bully tactics aimed at silencing the "OUR Walmart" worker upsurge.

It was a dreary day after Thanksgiving with sullen clouds hanging over Mount Angeles. Yet the strikers' spirits were high. Many couples brought their young children who walked with the picketers carrying bright green helium balloons.

In the crowd were members of the United Food and Commercial Workers (UFCW), International Brotherhood of Teamsters, and other unions. MoveOn members from Clallam County and Jefferson County joined the march.

The strikers carried signs charging Walmart with unfair labor practices for firing or otherwise punishing workers who dared to speak out against the company's employment practices.

Edythe, a fifteen-year veteran worker at the Port Angeles Walmart store said, "This picket line is for the thousands of Walmart workers who are going out on strike and the thousands more who are afraid of losing their jobs if they speak out."

When she began working at Walmart, Sam Walton, then Walmart's CEO, paid time-and-a-half to any worker working on Sunday. After Walton died, "that was cut to a dollar-an-hour extra for Sunday work," Edythe said. "It's the same for

shift differential. Anybody hired after January 12 of this year does not get that fifty cents per hour shift differential."

Walmart claims the average pay for their employees is $12.85, she continued. But a recent analysis proved that the average Walmart worker is paid only $9.04 per hour—less than the minimum wage in Washington State. "That is not a living wage," Edythe charged. Walmart reported profits of $16 billion last year.

Elena Perez, a leader of the Making Change at Walmart Puget Sound Coalition told the *World*, "This is a national campaign. A coalition is building across the country to hold Walmart accountable. One of our main goals is to support the workers, to make sure that management knows that we will stand by the workers. These are our neighbors and retaliating against our neighbors will not be tolerated. We're not going away. As long as these workers stand up, we're going to stand up with them."

Dave Schmitz, President of United Food and Commercial Workers Local 21 in Seattle, came with a dozen other UFCW workers to show support for the Walmart workers in Port Angeles. "You think of everything that has happened over the years. These are some of the most courageous, the bravest workers I have ever known taking on this retail giant."

He pointed out that Walmart filed a lawsuit with the National Labor Relations Board against the UFCW. "They claim this is a 'union recognition' fight when in reality it is workers taking a stand against the company's retaliation" on workers exercising their freedom of speech."

Schmitz said it is a sign of Walmart's panic that in one store they expelled Walmart shoppers mistaking them for protesters. There were walkouts by Walmart workers in Mount Vernon, Renton, and Seattle as well as in California, Colorado, and in Florida where one protesting worker was arrested.

When Schmitz and other protesters arrived at the vast, half empty parking lot, the Walmart chief of security walked up and told them they were trespassing. "This is a strike and federal law allows pickets on company property during a strike," Schmitz replied. The Walmart security chief threatened to call the county sheriff. A half hour later, sheriff's deputies arrived. But they did not order the picketers to vacate the premises.

The picketline continued, loud and clear, in front of the Walmart store.

Woody Guthrie, songwriter and *People's World* columnist, sings again
February 2, 2017

SEATTLE—Cheers from a capacity crowd greeted *Woody Sez: The Words, Music and Spirit of Woody Guthrie*, during its final matinee at the Seattle Repertory Theatre January 29.

An ensemble of four singer-musicians from Edinburgh, Scotland brought Woody Guthrie's radical, pro-worker songs and commentary to life singing *This Train is Bound for Glory, Jackhammer John, So Long It's Been Good to Know Yuh, Oklahoma Hills, Pastures of Plenty, All They Will Call You is Deportee*, and many other immortal songs of the great troubadour. They drew big crowds during their gig here January 10-29.

David Lutken conceived the production and plays the role of Woody Guthrie. He has even mastered an Oklahoma nasal twang so his singing and speaking is a great impersonation of Woody Guthrie. He told the crowd they have performed *Woody Sez* in seventy-three countries since it premiered ten years ago at the Edinburgh Festival Fringe in 2007 in Scotland.

It follows the rambling of our nation's greatest folksong composer starting with his childhood and youth in Oklahoma. His affluent family is financially ruined by the Great Depression and the drought that brought on "Dust Bowl days."

The play-musical recounts touchingly Guthrie's affliction with Huntington's disease at the very time Cold War anti-communism was clamped on the nation, which saw an attempt to silence Woody Guthrie, his close friend Pete Seeger, Huddie Ledbetter, and other great folk singers.

Woody's lines in the spoken part of the musical includes a tribute to the role of the Communist Party USA in organizing the fightback against outright starvation in the 1930's. He mentions by name famous party leaders William Z. Foster, Elizabeth Gurley Flynn, and "Mother" Bloor.

Darcie Deaville and Helen Russell, with Lutken and Andy Teirstein as backup, brought the house down when they sang Woody's *Union Maid*, a song that more than any other expressed the fighting spirit of the Congress of Industrial Organizations (CIO), whose founding ushered in a time when millions of workers flooded into the labor movement. The two women in the cast belted out that song and the crowd erupted in cheers.

The four cast members sang Guthrie's *The Good Reuben James* about U.S. seamen who died when a Nazi U-boat torpedoed a Lend-Lease Liberty ship, the "Reuben James."

Then Lutken opens a newspaper clipping and reads Woody Guthrie's latest "Woody Sez" column against fascist-instigated wars. It was published in the 1930s in the West Coast paper *People's World* and on the East Coast in the *Daily Worker*, both forerunners of today's *PeoplesWorld.org*.

The score is so faithful to the life and spirit of Woody Guthrie that they sing *Riding in My Car*, one of Woody's gentle songs that also included *Don't You Push Me*, and other songs for children.

Many in the crowd had tears in their eyes as they stood and joined in the final song,

In the 1930s, Woody Guthrie's column, "Woody Sez," appeared regularly in the pages of the West Coast People's World and the East Coast Daily Worker, predecessors of today's PeoplesWorld.org. | People's World Archives, Tamiment Library

This Land is Your Land.

The crowd was so enthusiastic that the performers sang an encore with *Roll On Columbia*, a song Guthrie composed during a brief stint as an employee of the Bonneville Power Administration (BPA) in Portland, Oregon. The song celebrates the construction of the Grand Coulee Dam.

Lutken came out to the lobby to greet people after the performance. I introduced myself as a reporter who worked for fifty years on the *People's World*, the newspaper that printed "Woody Sez." He greeted me warmly and signed my compact disc: "For Tim Wheeler and the *People's World*." (If you want to order the CD, check out the play's website or send an email to woodysezNYC@aol.com)

I asked Lutken where they are headed next assuming that he would answer along the lines of Portland, Oregon, San Francisco, or L.A.

"We are headed back to Europe," he replied. "We perform widely in the U.K. and on the continent. Our next show is in Vienna."

What a shame, I thought to myself. Not perform in Portland where Woody composed *Roll on Columbia*, and *Pastures of Plenty* and twenty-four of his other greatest songs?

I Googled when we got home and found that over the past decade, Lutken and his fellow singers-musicians have performed *Woody Sez* in Cambridge, Massachusetts, as well as in Oklahoma.

But people all across the U.S. should be hearing *Woody Sez*, a musical that celebrates us and our struggles for equality, jobs, and peace.

It is as if the election of the billionaire, Trump, as president, last November, has brought Woody Guthrie back from the grave to lead us all in songs of mass fightback, like the slogan he had lettered on his well-worn guitar: "This Machine Kills Fascists."

A week before we attended "Woody Sez," a singer-musician, Randy Noojin, was performing *Hard Travelin' With Woody*, to appreciative crowds in Seattle. Last year, a book by Greg Vandy with Daniel Peron titled *22 Songs in 30*

Days recounted Woody Guthrie's outpouring of great songs while employed by the BPA. And Smithsonian Folkways has just released a two CD album *Roll Columbia: Woody Guthrie's 26 Northwest Songs.*

Some of the songs have never been heard and now we hear them for the first time sung by Woody Guthrie himself.

This was my first visit to the Seattle Repertory Theatre since 1947 when I went with my second grade class at Queen Anne Elementary School to a performance of *Heidi.* Soon after, the Canwell Committee, the local rendition of the House Un-American Activities Committee, launched a vile redbaiting attack on the Repertory Theatre branding it a "Communist front." The witch hunters forced that theatre to close in the University of Washington District.

But the Canwell Committee and HUAC are dead and gone. The Seattle Repertory Theatre is alive and well, drawing capacity crowds to cheer Woody Guthrie and other anti-fascists.

[9]

NATIVE AMERICANS
CELEBRATE THEIR CULTURE AND SOVEREIGNTY

Corporate Threat to the Quileute Indians

The Daily World, September 3, 1981

La Push, Washington—Summer afternoons, fog rolls in from the Pacific Ocean, blotting out the horizon and chilling this tiny Indian fishing village at the mouth of the Quileute River.

The mournful cry of the James Island foghorn and the boom of the surf warns homeward bound fishermen of the mist-shrouded rock monoliths just off shore. They idle their trawlers up river between the jetty and James Island to the La Push fish docks. In the air is the tang of salt spume and the

A fishing boat motors up the Quileute River to Lapush. In the background is James Island. From an original pastel by the author.

aroma of fresh fish. In the moorage, the masts and booms of the fishing fleet are a naked forest against the sky. The dusty summer streets of the village ring with the laughter and shouts of Quileute children playing.

For centuries, the Quileute Indians of La Push have harvested from the Quileute River and its tributaries—the Soleduck and the Bogachiel—a plentitude of salmon: silver, humpies, chinook. Yet the fish revered the most by the Quileutes is not a salmon at all but rather its cousin, the sea-going trout called the "steelhead." Of silver and rainbow hue, the fish is prized by game fishermen for its fighting spirit and its sweet, firm, pink meat.

In the winter months when the steelhead begin their annual run to the spawning grounds of the headwaters of the rivers, the Quileute fishermen take to the river in their dugout canoes still fashioned from cedar logs but now fitted with outboard motors. They string gill nets to harvest the steelhead and the salmon.

The fish is not only a staple of their diet; it is one of their few sources of cash income. Sold to one of the two Seattle based fish docks, the cleaned fish are packed on ice, trucked, and later flown to the gourmet restaurants of the world. Even as the wealthy  gourmands of New York and Washington D.C. feast on the delectable fish, the people of La Push, westernmost settlement in the lower forty-eight states, eke out a life of bare subsistence.

It is virtually unchanged from the days in the late 1950s when I came here as a youth with my cousins to go deep-sea fishing: the same jarring contradiction of heartbreaking poverty, unemployment and slum housing set down amid unsurpassed primeval beauty. The contradiction is without reason since the Olympic Peninsula is rich in timber and seafood resources and is a strong magnet for fishermen, hunters, hikers, mountain climbers, and sailors.

The Quileutes were forced off the land of Clallam County's West End by timber companies at the turn of the century, confined to their one-square-mile reservation at La Push. A treaty recognized their right to fish all the waters of the Quileute and its tributaries. But the Washington State and federal government moved quickly to abrogate the treaty.

Lillian Pullen, seventy, an elder of the Quileute tribe, recalled that her grandfather, Chief Thomas Paine, led the battle to force the government to restore their ancestral fishing rights. A genteel, beautiful, witty woman, mother of ten, grandmother of forty-six, Ms. Pullen has been fighting the oppression of her people for as long as she can remember.

Together with other women, she led the fight to compel the U.S. Bureau of Indian Affairs (BIA) to reopen the Tribal School in La Push, closed several decades ago. For many years, the children had to board buses to travel twenty-five miles to Forks, the nearest white town, to attend school leaving before dawn and returning home after dark. The dropout rate was high, she said, and the children were not instructed in the culture of their people.

Two years ago, she said, they won a victory with the opening of a federally funded tribal school in the handsome, recently vacated U.S. Coast Guard Station. Ms. Pullen is now a volunteer teacher of Quileute language and culture.

As I was ushered into her classroom, she was conducting a class in traditional basket weaving and leading the students in a song, "BIA ain't no friend of mine."

During her youth, she said, speaking to both me and her students, La Push was separated from Forks by miles of virgin timber. "There was no road. When people left here, they went by canoe," she said. Periodically, a coastal steamer called to pick up passengers and mail and to drop off supplies.

Tim Wheeler's catch of the day on the Quileute River.

"It used to be that the Quileutes could only fish on the south bank of the river in La Push. The hoquats (whites) fished the north bank," she said. "But in 1933, my grandfather, Chief Thomas Paine, Colonel Martin, Stanley Gray, Arthur Howeattle and other Indian leaders started the fight to win back our fishing rights. They went to court and won the case.

"In those days, the fishing was good. We put away all the salmon we needed and sold the rest to the barges that came in."

That court victory spurred the twenty tribes of the Pacific Northwest to launch a militant struggle during the 1960s with mass marches, rallies, and "fish-ins" to press for fishing rights. Washington State police and county sheriffs unleashed a brutal campaign of repression, clubbing many and shooting several Indian leaders.

In 1974, U.S. Judge George Boldt handed down a landmark ruling, later upheld by the U.S. Supreme Court, that the twenty tribes are entitled to half the annual salmon catch.

Russ Woodruff, Quileute tribal chairman told *World Magazine* the ink was still wet on the Boldt decision when the state and federal governments were moving to undermine it.

"The federal court clarified that the fish should be managed on a river-by-river, run-by-run basis. But the state doesn't want to abide by that," he said.

The result is deliberate manipulation in estimating the salmon runs to cheat the Indians of their fair share. Few of the Indians, furthermore, own the big ocean-going trawlers, gill or purse-seine netters needed to harvest their share of the fish.

A new federal program to provide $15 million worth of low interest loans so Indians can purchase modern fishing boats has been viciously cut to $2.5 million by President Reagan's Interior Secretary James Watt. Many fishing boats now cost as much as $250,000.

Woodruff confirmed that the Indian people have been among the hardest hit by Reagan's budget cuts. Many of the services in La Push were provided by men and women hired under CETA. All those jobs were eliminated by Reagan. BIA ordered the Tribal Council at La Push to slash a $28,000 grant under Title One of the Elementary and Secondary Education Act serving seventy children at the tribal school. The cut is so drastic it means that the one paraprofessional teacher's aide, one of a handful of Quileutes employed, must work for subminimum wages or be laid off.

Also endangered is the full-time doctor and clinic with offices in the beautiful new tribal headquarters designed in a style reminiscent of the magnificent cedar long-houses of the Pacific Northwest Indians.

I asked Woodruff if he foresees participation by Native American Indians in the September 19 Solidarity Day demonstration in Washington D.C. called by the AFL-CIO. He warmly endorsed such actions and said he, himself, had just returned from Washington D.C., where the Quileutes are demanding return of 200 acres of seashore adjacent to La Push, now a part of the Olympic National Park.

A centerpiece of the federal assault on Indian fishing rights is a bill in the U.S. Senate by Senator Slade Gorton (R-WA) to "decommercialize" steelhead fishing, outlawing the sale of the fish vital to the Quileutes during the winter months. Gorton, a member of the "Gorton Frozen Fish" family, stands to benefit personally from ruining both Indian and non-Indian commercial fishermen. La Push residents charge that the senator, a diehard Reaganite, is also a hardcore racist.

"At least half the people here depend on fishing for their livelihood," Woodruff said. "There's nothing left on the outside. Logging is down; the mills are down and unemployment is up over 50%."

Reactionary elements have used the Boldt decision to whip up a racist vendetta, seeking to pit white game and commercial fishermen against the Indians, who face brazen job discrimination off the reservation.

"The tribe and the (white) fishermen are fighting for their livelihood," he said. "They look at things the same way. It seems to me they are going to come together."

They face giant corporations like Crown-Zellerbach and ITT-Rayonier and their federal and state government agents. Crown Z has rapaciously clear-cut timber in the West End of Clallam County denuding the mountainsides in a region with the nation's heaviest rainfall—over 140 inches yearly.

"There is nothing on those mountains to slow the runoff. There is heavy silting of the spawning beds," Woodruff said.

The result is a drastic reduction in the salmon and steelhead population. Crown Z has also poured sulfite fumes and effluents into the air and water of the northwest for many decades killing millions of fry at the mouths of many rivers.

Washington State fishermen netted 86 million pounds of salmon in 1947 and averaged 60 to 70 million pounds throughout the 1950s. Last year they caught only 24 million pounds.

This month, Crown Z finished its war against the white and Indian people of Clallam County by closing down, permanently, their West End logging operation laying off hundreds of loggers.

"It was a cut and run operation from the beginning," said one life-long resident of Clallam Bay, daughter of a progressive logger who founded the International Woodworkers of America here. "They could have managed the timber so that it would last forever. But they preferred to clear cut and then abandon the people."

Vast miles of once magnificent forest just off the Quileute and Makah Indian Reservations are now wastelands of stumps, charred underbrush and churned up mud.

George Morford, a veteran of twenty-six years as a commercial fisherman, much of it out of La Push, is a lifelong friend of the Quileutes. He is also one of the growing corps of white fishermen who recognize the common corporate-state foe.

Having severely wounded many of the best steelhead and salmon rivers, the big pulp and paper and timber firms, he said, are moving in to grab the lucrative fish market for themselves. Already, in Oregon, he said, these firms are engaged in "Aquaculture," hatching fish in hatcheries, releasing them when they return to spawn.

As we sat in the foc'sle of his seventy-foot fishing boat he told us that fishing will be doomed for both the Indian and white fishermen if the monopoly takeover succeeds.

The shift to hatchery breeding of fish, he charged, has already decimated many races of salmon which once teemed Pacific Northwest rivers. Genetic manipulation has produced strains of smaller, weaker, and more disease prone fish. Recognizing this, the hatcheries constantly raid the wild river spawning grounds to collect the precious roe of wild fish to revive overly inbred hatchery strains.

If the monopolies succeed in their profit-crazed "Aquaculture" scheme, it could also mean the extinction for the steelhead and salmon, he warned.

Christian Penn Sr., an original plaintiff in the Boldt decision, a past Quileute tribal chairman, told *World Magazine* he has been fishing for steelhead and salmon "since I could walk."

"We have never been a threat to the survival of the fish," he said. "The fish are our life. Without them our people would die. We won a victory in the Boldt decision but the victory was always there. We shouldn't have had to go to court to win a right that was ours in the first place. Now they are trying to take it away from us again. I tell the (white) fishermen if they don't support our fishing rights, then they are going to be next. They will be in the same situation we are in."

American Indians Pull with Pride in Elwha
People's World, August 26 2005

PORT ANGELES, Washington—"Paddle to Elwha" brought thousands of Pacific Northwest Indians and their friends to the waterfront of this old Olympic Peninsula mill town August 1 to celebrate the arrival of seventy-six dugout canoes from as far north as Alaska and far south as Coos Bay, Oregon.

Voyaging hundreds of miles across the often windswept waters of the Pacific, the Strait of Juan de Fuca, the Inland Passage and Puget Sound, the "pullers," mostly youthful Indian men and women, were greeted as heroes as the canoes arrived one by one at Hollywood Beach in downtown Port Angeles.

The canoes are cedar dugouts like those that once plied these waters carrying trade goods or used in fishing and whaling. Makah whaling canoes, some eighty feet long, ventured into the Pacific on whale hunts. Today the canoes are carved and painted with dramatic images of ravens, eagles and whales as authentic as those of the past.

This year, fourteen Aleuts from the Pribilof Island in the Aleutians joined the paddle in their bidarkas, or kayaks, made of stitched seal skin.

'Now we are awakening'

David Hudson, hereditary chief of the Quileute Tribe of La Push, stood on the beach beaming with joy. "That's my son, my daughter, my nieces and nephews in the Quileute dugout there," he told the *World*, pointing toward a handsome canoe riding a few feet offshore. "They came all the way from La Push on the Pacific Ocean around Cape Flattery into the Strait. They camped at night, at Wyaatch, Neah Bay, Clallam Bay, Pillar Point. They carried no modern navigational equipment. No cell phones."

The idea of resurrecting their seafaring heritage began many years ago, he said. "We started back in 1976 when we paddled from La Push to Neah Bay. I participated in that paddle. Now we are one big canoe family from Alaska to Quinault. This is an alcohol-free and drug-free event."

The annual celebration, a combination of powwow and potlatch, combines cultural pride, good food, dancing and music as well as much athletic prowess. "It is pretty emotional for our elders seeing this comeback by our people," he said. "Some told us we had lost our culture. But our elders told us it was just sleeping. Now we are awakening."

The waterborne ingathering won national attention in 1989 when nine canoes joined the "Paddle to Seattle," a centerpiece of the centennial of the founding of Seattle. One of those canoes was skippered by Frank Brown of the Bella Bella tribe of British Columbia. He threw down a challenge to tribes in the U.S. to "Paddle to Bella Bella" in 1993. It was a triumphant success.

The Bella Bellas also took the lead in reviving the craft of canoe carving. Now Bella Bella carvers travel from tribe to tribe teaching them how to build canoes. Two Bella Bella canoes, again skippered by Brown, arrived from British Columbia, conspicuous

for their sweeping lines and magnificent painted prows.

Ten days to paddle 200 miles

Among the newest entrants were tribal members of the Nooksack tribe. The Nooksack pullers, young men and women, had just dragged their canoe up on Hollywood Beach when they spoke with this reporter.

"Our journey took ten days and over 200 miles," said Alex Cooper, who works fulltime at the Nooksack tribal casino. "We stopped at each village along the way. This was the first time the Nooksack joined. We didn't even have a canoe. Luckily, another tribe lent us one of theirs. We plan to carve our own canoe. This is the reunification of our native people. It is rejuvenating our spirit. Everyone is welcome."

Jeremiah Johnny, employed by the Department of Natural Resources at the Nooksack Tribal Center, said the many stops at villages along the shore "gives us an awareness of our gravesites and our sacred grounds. It is a good reason to bring so many of us together. This is our way of honoring the oldest ones, honoring our past and standing up for our future."

Remembering Tse-whit-zen Village
People's World, August 25, 2005

"Paddle to Elwha" was sponsored by the Lower Elwha S'Klallams for which Clallam County is named. In the 1930s the tribe was forced to leave their ancestral village site where Port Angeles now stands, as well as a site at the base of Ediz Hook across the bay. They had to purchase land to provide the site for the reservation that exists today at the mouth of the Elwha River eight miles west of Port Angeles.

They and all other Pacific Northwest Indians were even denied the right to fish, salmon being a staple of their diet, until 1974 when Federal Judge George Boldt handed down a landmark ruling that half the annual salmon catch belongs to the Indians. The Elwha River has been in the news in recent years because of a plan to remove a dam in hopes of reviving the salmon run that once spawned in the headwaters of the river.

The theme of this year's paddle was "Reflections on our past: Honoring Tse-whit-zen Village." The village, sheltered in the cove of Ediz Hook across the bay, is estimated to have been inhabited 2,700 years ago. The archeological site was discovered when the Washington State Department of Transportation began construction of the so-called graving site where giant pontoons were to be fabricated to replace aging pontoons on the Hood Canal floating bridge.

During excavation, intact remains of hundreds of ancestors of the S'Klallam people were unearthed, while the scattered bones of hundreds more were churned up during construction. It touched off an outcry from the tribe that their most sacred burial ground was being destroyed, a protest so strong that the state was forced to suspend construction on the twenty-two-acre site near the old Crown Zellerbach paper mill. The steel ribs of the graving yard now loom silent over the site.

A team of archaeologists, including more than 100 Klallam tribal members, established an archaeological sift for more intact graves and to preserve the human remains and artifacts. Tse-whit-zen is now recognized as the most important archaeological site in the Pacific Northwest since the discovery in 1970 of the Ozette landslide site on a remote stretch of the Pacific coast. (A Makah Indian village had been inundated, instantly, in a landslide 800 years ago, preserving everything so perfectly it was called the "Pompeii of North America." Artifacts from the Ozette site are now housed in a splendid museum in Neah Bay. The day after they arrived at Hollywood Beach, the canoes streamed across Port Angeles Bay to the site of Tse-whit-zen Village for a solemn memorial ceremony.

Tribes came in solidarity

As the canoes rode on the tide, Lower Elwha tribal chairwoman, Frances Charles, told the crowd, "We have 316 cedar boxes on our reservation that are waiting to be placed back into their resting place. We have the remains of thousands upon thousands who have died here. We are looking for healing here. We are asking for songs and prayers of healing here."

An elder stood at the stern of the Blue Heron canoe and replied, "We come here to show our strength when we are together, to show the strength of our solidarity."

A woman elder from the Muckleshoot tribe thanked the S'Klallams for the difficult struggle they have waged to defend Tse-whit-zen Village. The pontoon construction project had been greeted for the jobs it created in a region with chronic high unemployment and poverty.

"We are thankful to the Elwha people, thankful for the things you are doing to bring out who we are inside," the Muckleshoot leader said. "Our Indian-ness was almost taken away from us but now you are winning it back."

There have been Cold War-style attacks on their patriotism. Bangor on Hood Canal is the base for nuclear submarines deployed in the Pacific. The Hood Canal floating bridge is designed to draw back for passage of these menacing leviathans.

In an open letter headlined, "I Wish This on No Other Nation," Charles wrote, "They tell us that it's a safety factor that we are faced with—that there is a war out there, and that the submarines have to continue to pass through the Hood Canal Bridge, and that if the submarines can't get through . . . we will be to blame. . . .We are being threatened and threatened."

Of course, nothing the S'Klallam tribe has done is having any affect whatsoever on passage of the nuclear subs in and out of Hood Canal.

'We want our dead reburied with dignity'

Charles told the *World*, "Paddle to Elwha was important for our community in terms of our theme, 'Reflections on the Past of Tse-whit-zen Village.' This is a unique situation here, but all the other Native American people across the nation have similar stories of their ancestral gravesites being destroyed. It has given our community the strength and unity to carry on."

The entire project for constructing the floating bridge pontoons at the Ediz Hook location has been halted since last December, she said. Yet the final outcome remains in limbo. "The goal of the Lower Elwha community is we would like to see the reburial of these remains on that site if possible."

Asked about discussion of a Tse-whit-zen museum like the Ozette museum in Neah Bay, Charles replied, "What we would like to see in the future is for our people to have a curation facility. It is really important for the Elwha community. We want to maintain and have ownership of the artifacts. We don't want to be going to any of the other museums to be viewing them. We have over 13,000 artifacts. There are many, many unique arrows, harpoons, etched stones. There are Chinese coins. We have unearthed 800 etched rocks. We found beautiful combs."

This archaeological dig has also unearthed the foundations of six cedar longhouses. The team is trying to figure out how to preserve the remains of cedar planks on the longhouses, which crumble apart when exposed to the air.

"This village was standing there 2,700 years ago," she said. "It is reviving me personally, reviving our culture and our heritage. We were in danger of losing it. But now we have our heads held high."

She voiced frustration at the deadlock. "We are continuing the negotiations with all the key players to move forward with the reburial process," she said. "We feel we've been talking about this for the last seven months, yet we are moving backward."

The discovery of Tse-whit-zen Village and the struggle now to prevent it being covered over with concrete, she said, brings into sharp focus a centuries-long struggle. Our people were punished for speaking their own language, our children were taken away from their families, and we were forced to leave our ancestral villages. Now it is emotionally, physically and spiritually hard to see how these remains are being treated," she said.

"Every day is a funeral. We want them reburied with dignity."

(Washington Gov., Christine Gregoire later met with the Tribe and resolved the dispute by accepting their demands).

Makah Defend Treaty Rights
June 3, 2000

NEAH BAY, Washington—The Makah Indian Reservation is located at Cape Flattery, the northwestern-most point of land in the lower forty-eight states. Look due west from the deeply forested bluff at the cape and you will see the surf pounding the rocks of Tatoosh Island with its lighthouse and mournful fog horn. Beyond is nothing but the Pacific Ocean and a procession of ships arriving from the Far East.

To get here, you drive seventy-seven miles west from Port Angeles on Route 112, a twisting road with steep bluffs to the left and the Strait of Juan de Fuca to the right. Eighteen miles north, across the strait, loom the mountains of Vancouver Island, British Columbia. Neah Bay is as near the edge of the world as one can get.

Yet Ben Johnson Jr., chairman of the Makah Tribal Council, says his people have never been more engaged with the "outer world," both of American Indian affairs and the affairs of the U.S. as a whole.

The Makah burst into the headlines last year when they asserted their rights, inscribed in the 1855 Treaty of Neah Bay, to hunt for whales as they have for thousands of years.

Animal rights groups attempted to block the Makahs as they paddled into the Pacific in dugout canoes at Cape Alava. With the protection of the U.S. Coast Guard, the Makahs succeeded in harpooning one gray whale.

In an interview with the *World* in his office at tribal headquarters, Johnson said most of the hysteria over the whale hunt has dissipated. The Makah, he pointed out, had voluntarily suspended whaling when gray whales were listed as an endangered species. Recently, the gray whale was removed from that list. Harpooning one whale in the past seventy-three years will not drive the gray whale to extinction, Johnson said.

"I think there were many positive lessons to be learned and the main one is that we did not sell our treaty rights," he said. "All Indians, throughout Indian country got a message from our stand: We defended our treaty rights and they can defend their treaty rights as well."

Taking that stand has thrown the Makah, and all other tribes, into a bitter confrontation with two Washington state Republican lawmakers: Representative Jack Metcalf, who filed a lawsuit to block the whale hunt, and Senator Slade Gorton. Metcalf, an ultra-rightist elected on a pledge of "term limits," has announced he will not run in this November's election.

As for Gorton, he is very much a candidate and Indians all across the country are mobilizing to defeat him. It signals a new level of unity and political independence for the American Indian peoples. They are making common cause with the labor movement, environmentalists and other groups seeking to oust Gorton. "We call Gorton an Indian fighter," Johnson said. "He is always trying to abolish the treaties between the government and the tribes."

Back in 1974, he explained, Judge George Boldt ruled that the Pacific Northwest Indians are entitled by treaty to half the salmon and steelhead returning to rivers in the Puget Sound area. Gorton was then the attorney general of Washington State and appealed the case all the way to the U.S. Supreme Court. He lost when the high court upheld Boldt's ruling in 1979.

Ever since, Gorton has nursed a grudge, waging a fanatical war against the American Indian people. In 1981, Gorton introduced legislation to outlaw commercial steelhead fishing by Indians in Washington.

In 1991, Gorton denounced a Smithsonian Institution exhibit in Washington that dealt extensively with the genocide treatment of American Indians in the western expansion of the U.S. Gorton said the exhibit "depicts a terribly distorted, negative, and untrue statement about the settlement of the west."

Gorton asked Attorney General Janet Reno to shut down slot machines at the Two Rivers Casino operated by the Spokane Indians of eastern Washington. She refused.

In 1998, Gorton launched the biggest offensive of all introducing legislation to strip American Indians of sovereign immunity, making tribal governments subject to lawsuits. Gorton also proposed to slash federal funding for tribes that have established casinos on their lands.

"Gorton has always been against the Indian tribes," Johnson said. "Now he has turned it into a racial issue. Indians across the country are pooling their money together to defeat Gorton. We have a big push here in Washington State to register people because we have so many people who have not voted in the past. Now they plan to vote."

The Makah leader's words were confirmed by Ron Allen, tribal chairman of the Jamestown S'Klallam tribe, for which Clallam County is named. Allen served for several years as chairman of the National Congress of American Indians (NCAI) and is now the first vice president of the NCAI. He spoke with the World by telephone from New Orleans where he was attending a conference.

"We have set up an organization, which we call the `First American Education Project' (FAEP) that is being funded by tribes all across the county and by tribal sympathizers," he said.

"It's a non-profit organization so it can't campaign for or against a candidate. But it can educate voters on a candidate's record. Our agenda is to refresh people's memories on what Slade Gorton has done in the past eleven years."

Gorton, Allen continued, "has introduced riders on bills for wealthy corporations that would be detrimental to the interests of Indians. He has also slipped in riders that tried to redefine the political and legal standing of tribal governments," he continued.

"We were successful in challenging them and our friends in the House and Senate were able to fend these bills off," Allen said.

If they had passed, "this legislation would have undermined tribal governments and the sovereignty of the American Indian people. It would have subjected the tribes to an incredible barrage of lawsuits."

So far, the FAEP has raised between $125,000 and $150,000 to broadcast television ads exposing Gorton's record of hostility not only to the tribes but also his attack on the environment and health care issues. Gorton, long known as "slippery Slade" gained a new nickname, "Cyanide Slade" for attempting to slip through an amendment that would permit the Texas-based Battle Mountain Gold Company to build a gold processing plant in the Okanogan region of the state.

It would use lethal cyanide to extract gold from ore. The Okanogan's Colville Indian Nation is fighting the gold mine proposal as a deadly threat to the environment of the fragile and beautiful high plateau. The FAEP has not endorsed either of the democratic candidates running against Gorton. They are Deborah Senn, Washington State insurance commissioner who has won strong backing from organized labor and other progressive groups for her courageous stands against the giant insurance monopolies and Maria Cantwell who entered the race late. Cantwell served one term in the House and spent most of her time ingratiating herself with the Republicans. Many view her as a spoiler.

Keith Hunter, who is of Choctaw-Muskogee and Scottish-Irish background, has recently moved with his wife to Neah Bay. Over lunch at the Makah Maiden restaurant, he told us he has been researching Gorton's links with "Wise Use," a right-wing extremist outfit based in Bellevue Washington and its political arm, the Center for the Defense of Free Enterprise headed by two extremists, Alan S. Gottlieb and Ron Arnold. "Wise Use" is closely tied to the armed militias and is in the service of the giant mining, timber and oil corporations.

"Nothing will bring the people closer together more quickly than a common enemy," Hunter said. "Slade Gorton is that common enemy."

American Indians demonstrated their political clout when they mobilized and won voter approval of a ballot measure in California that gives Native Americans exclusive rights to operate casinos in the state. Johnson chuckled when I asked him if a casino is in the cards for Neah Bay. "We're too far out here on the Olympic Peninsula to build a casino," he said.

Neah Bay suffers a fifty-five percent unemployment rate and is struggling to secure funding for projects that will generate jobs. Fishing is one of the mainstays of the economy, he said, with many Indians owning trawlers moored in the little fishing port. The fresh fish are iced at the fish dock, loaded on eighteen-wheeler semis and rushed to Seattle. Depletion of the fish has hit the fishing industry hard.

There is also selective logging on the Makah's thirty-seven-square mile reservation. But with the closing a decade ago of Crown Zellerbach's mill in the west end of Clallam County hundreds of union-wage jobs were lost. Now, the tribe is struggling to create jobs from tourism and from a landfill dump that will create eighty or more jobs.

Johnson does not regret that a casino is unrealistic. "I like our community the way it is. We are one of the richest of all in terms of culture," he said. The Makah Cultural and Research Center with its magnificent museum of Makah art and artifacts in Neah Bay proves his point. The museum opened in 1979 based largely on artifacts recovered from the Ozette archaeological site excavated between 1970 and 1981. This was a Makah village inundated by a mudslide somewhere between 300 and 500 years-ago. The people in the village were buried instantly. It has yielded such a detailed picture of ancient Makah life that the site is referred to as the "Pompei of North America."

Janine Bowechop, a graduate of Dartmouth College with a degree in anthropology, is the director of the center. "I remember as a child going to Ozette at least once a year," she said in an interview in her office. "I don't think I realized until I was older just how unique our situation is. The Ozette site provides evidence that the Makah have lived here for 4,000 or more years. The Makahs have a very strong oral tradition and the artifacts have essentially verified the legends and stories of this oral tradition."

It is important because the Indians are now citing these oral traditions in court and in legislatures to bolster their treaty claims,, she said.

"Go through the museum and one of the cases explains the whale hunt. It was a very central aspect of Makah culture. I just presented a paper in London on the images of whales in Makah art made centuries ago. You see in this art reverence and respect for whales."

Hunting the whale, she said, "went beyond courage. It was spiritual. It was a symbol of strength and physical preparation. It took a lot of training to go in a dugout canoe into the Pacific Ocean to hunt for whales."

American Indians, she said, have not driven a single species of animal to extinction. "On the contrary, we have responsibly managed the environment for hundreds, even thousands of years. There is no compelling argument for denying the Makahs their ancestral whaling rights."

We stopped at Washburn's General Store on the way out of town. Makah children had organized a car wash in the parking lot to raise money for a school field trip to Seattle.

What will they do in Seattle, I asked. "We'll go to the science center and the aquarium," said April Thompson.

"We're going to have fun and to learn."

I asked them if they liked living in an isolated place like Neah Bay. "It is so beautiful here," said Daleena Lyons.

"We go swimming, fishing, hunting. We know everybody. We love it."

[10]

COMING FULL CIRCLE

Storyteller to Share Tales of Dungeness Valley During Tuesday's Story Swap in Port Angeles

Peninsula Daily News, February 15. 2015

PORT ANGELES—Journalist Tim Wheeler of Sequim is the featured storyteller at this month's Story Swap, a gathering in the Raymond Carver Room at the Port Angeles Library this Tuesday night. Admission is free to the 7 p.m. swap at the library, 2210 S. Peabody St.

Wheeler spent his formative years on his family's farm, living in the old Bell Hill farmhouse built by pioneer John Bell.

After graduating from Sequim High School in 1958 and attending Amherst College in Massachusetts and the University of Washington, he began a 40-year career writing mostly for *The Daily World,* now the online site *The People's World* and a direct descendant of *The Daily Worker,* a Communist Party-associated newspaper.

After Wheeler retired in 2006, he and his wife, Joyce, returned to Sequim, where he is working on his memoirs—stories of growing up beneath the Olympic Mountains with the women and men who toiled to make ends meet in the Dungeness Valley.

Wheeler's set will run until 8 p.m.; then comes a refreshment break. At 8:15 p.m., the open-mic section will start, and storytellers are invited up to share a tale. The swap will wrap up by 9 p.m.

For more information, see the Story People of Clallam County website.

164 Honeybee Lane
Sequim, WA. 98382
February 21, 2015

Mr. Barack Obama
President, U.S.A.
1600 Pennsylvania Ave. NW
Washington, D.C. 20500

Dear Mr. President,
Please find enclosed an article I wrote a few months ago that was featured in the Sequim Gazette last August. It is about the visit of your father to our farm in Sequim in 1961. You wrote a book about your father so I thought my account of hosting him on our farm in Sequim might interest you. I have read or told this story at public events in Sequim and Port Angeles now three times and it has appeared twice in print. Each time I tell it, it stirs interest.

I told it the other night at a gathering of the "Story People of Clallam County." Sterling Epps, a retired police officer in Port Angeles, told me he enjoyed the story much. He said he served for six years at the White House and suggested that I send the story to you. So I am.

Part of the story is the doorbelling my wife, Joyce, and I did urging our neighbors to vote for you in 2008 and 2012. You carried Clallam County both elections. Clallam County is a swing district that went narrowly for George W. Bush in 2000 and 2004.

We are proud of the job you have done as President, performing with so much dignity, intelligence, and wit in a political climate poisoned by rightwing extremism.
Sincerely,

Tim Wheeler

Tim Wheeler

Verbatim: Tim Wheeler

Tim Wheeler is a Sequim High School graduate from the Class of 1958. In the July edition of the The Ditchwalker, the Sequim Alumni Association's newsletter, Wheeler recounts a chance encounter with a man whose son would become President of the United States.

That article, "An Unforgettable Sequim Visitor," is reprinted here with permission from the alumni association.

(To subscribe to The Ditchwalker, send $10 to: Sequim Alumni Association, PO Box 1758, Sequim, WA, 98382.)

"In 1961, I was working on our Sequim dairy farm and taking classes at the University of Washington. I met my future wife, Joyce, at the UW and made many friends. Some visited our farm, including Muga Ndega, an exchange student from Kenya.

Later I ran into Muga on the UW campus. He asked if he might visit again and could he bring a friend? Muga said his friend, a fellow Kenyan, had a big car and we could all ride together.

Barack Obama, Sr.

So we did, with Muga and Joyce and I in the back seat, and his friend driving with two young women with him in the front. He was a slim, handsome man with an unusual and unforgettable name. I will never forget the white-knuckle terror as the Buick careened around the curves of Old Olympic Highway at breakneck speed to our home, the old Bell House that still stands up on Bell Hill. Muga's friend was gracious and polite. I remember little more about his visit.

However, 40 years later at breakfast, I read Joyce an item in the newspaper that featured that unforgettable name. I said, "Somebody named Barack Obama is running for the U.S. Senate in Illinois. That can't be the Barack Obama we know, can it? This guy running in Illinois is far too young."

We realized that our visitor in 1961 was Barack Obama Sr., father of our 44th president.

He survived two serious car crashes in his life before dying in a crash outside Nairobi in 1982.

Joyce and I worked to help elect his son as president. Obama carried Clallam County in both elections.

Whenever I hear President Obama describe his journey as 'improbable,' I nod my head and say, 'Only in America!'"

Everyone has a story and now they have a place to tell it. Verbatim is a first-person column that introduces you to your neighbors as they relate in their own words some of the difficult, humorous, moving or just plain fun moments in their lives. It's all part of the Gazette's commitment as your community newspaper. If you have a story for Verbatim, contact editor Michael Dashiell at editor@sequimgazette.com.

Sequim Gazette
Aug. 4, 2012

THE WHITE HOUSE

WASHINGTON

October 9, 2015

Mr. Tim Wheeler
Sequim, Washington

Dear Tim:

This is just a quick note to thank you for writing to share the
story you've told so many times over the years. Your letter reached
my desk, and I appreciate it. Hearing from people like you reminds
me who I'm here to serve, and it keeps me going as I continue working
to make America's promise real for all our people.

Thank you, again, for your thoughtful message. I'm deeply
grateful for everything you and Joyce have put into reaching for our
shared vision for the future, and I wish you both the very best.

Sincerely,

The Obama Coalition: the Winning Majority

Until President Obama had won reelection to a second term, I told only close friends the story of his father's visit to our farm. I didn't want to throw any raw meat to the ravenous beasts of the far right. They would seize on any tidbit no matter how irrelevant in their fanatic zeal to block the reelection of our first African American president.

Yet over the years, I have won acceptance as a consistent contributor to the ideological debate that pits the Tea Party Republicans against moderate and progressive thinkers here in Clallam County, Washington. My letters to the editor, 250 words each, are printed by the *Peninsula Daily News* about once each month, usually hitting hard at Republican extremism. I also send in contributions to the *Sequim Gazette*.

I began several years ago to read aloud excerpts from my writings at Ruth Marcus' creative writing workshop that at that time drew overflow crowds to the Rain Shadow Café in downtown Sequim. Some of those stories are included in this book.

One evening in 2014, I read aloud my story, *The Green Geyser of Clallam County*, the tale of our errant liquid manure pump. It was greeted with much laughter and applause.

Someone in the crowd invited me to read it again at a presentation at Olympic Theater Arts. I added in the story of Barack Obama, Senior, visiting our farm just a few weeks after our manure pump erupted. When I got to that part of the story I could hear gasps from the audience, a surprise ending to equal anything O'Henry ever wrote.

Doug McGinnes, a pioneer of the Sequim-Dungeness valley, was sharing the stage with me when I read the story that afternoon. He was then the editor of *The Ditchwalker*, quarterly newsletter of the Sequim High School Alumni Association. He asked me if he could print my story in the next edition of *The Ditchwalker*. I told him I would be proud to have the story in print.

He and his daughter insisted it had to be shortened down. It pained me, but I accepted the chopping. It too created a minor sensation. (Alas, Doug recently passed away). A week or so after it appeared the editor of the *Sequim Gazette* telephoned to ask me if I would object to reprinting the story in their "Verbatim" column on the editorial page. Again, I agreed.

Finally, a representative of a literary group called The Story People of Clallam County telephoned to ask if I would "tell, not read" my Barack Obama, Senior, story in the Raymond Carver Room at the Port Angeles Library.

I agreed. A near capacity crowd turned out that evening in February, 2015, including all the members of our family including my granddaughter, Erin, and her significant other, Darel Peyton.

This presentation was unique in that my sister and brother called out corrections to my story as I told it—the number of acres in our farm, for example. It was quite hilarious.

And again, when I came to the part about the visit to our farm of Barack Obama, father of our 44th President, there were gasps of surprise from the crowd.

Sterling Epps, a retired police officer, an African American man, came up and told me afterwards that he enjoyed the story immensely. He told me he worked with the U.S. Secret Service at the White House for six years.

"You should send your story to President Obama," Epps said. "I can assure you, he will see it."

So I wrote a letter to Obama, enclosed with it the newspaper clipping of the "Verbatim" column in the Sequim Gazette, and sent it off. That was back in February of 2015. I forgot about it.

Nine months later, a manila envelope arrived in our mailbox with the return address, "The White House, Washington." Inside was a note from President Obama thanking me for the letter and the newspaper clipping. He thanked Joyce, by name, and me for all our work in support of his efforts to turn the nation in a new direction.

I conclude this book with my letter to him and his reply.

Obama has won many victories in the face of fanatical rightwing opposition, so venomous in the case of Donald Trump and the so-called "Birther movement" that it exposes itself as the crudest racism.

Repeatedly when he ran for election and reelection, Obama warned us that "I cannot do it alone. . . .You, not I, are the change we are seeking." So if Obamacare is a long way short of Medicare for All, we need to look ourselves in the mirror. Where did we fall short as well as he? The list of his other victories is far too long to list here.

Obama created a powerful, majority, grassroots movement to win election, overcoming racism so deeply entrenched in American society that people believed the U.S. "will never elect an African American president."

The Obama majority pulled together all the main forces of what can be called, "The All-People's Front" against the corporate ultra-right. It included the labor movement, African Americans, Latinos, Asian Americans, Arab and Jewish Americans, women, youth, the environmental movement. He created for that moment in November 2008, a profound shift in the "relationship of forces." Alas, the relationship of forces shifted back quickly after the elections were over.

In our haste to criticize Obama, far too many forget or ignore the lessons to be learned by studying this Obama movement. Why weren't we able to hold it together after he was elected? Did the masses of voters cast their ballots, go home, and wait for Obama to deliver on his promises?

Obama won election by organizing a movement outside the Democratic Party although after he won the Democratic nomination, millions of grassroots Democrats worked hard to elect him. But winning election was only the first step. Any hope that Obama could break the corporate ultra-right's stranglehold on our country rested on the Obama movement continuing to organize and mobilize after he was in the White House—a permanent change in the relationship of forces in the people's favor. We needed a movement with staying power. The Democratic Party has not delivered.

Senator Bernie Sanders, the socialist from Vermont, ran for president and drew huge crowds with his grassroots appeals for a "democratic revolution." He garnered 13 million votes and won 22 state primary and caucus victories. He presented by far the clearest anti-corporate, "people and nature before profits" program. He made no secret of his belief in socialism and has gone a long way to making socialism a "household" word. As never before in recent history, millions of people are searching for deeper answers to the intractable crisis on monopoly capitalism and millions have concluded that socialism is superior to capitalism and the politics of greed.

Hillary Clinton ultimately won the Democratic presidential nomination but Bernie and his movement pushed Hillary to the left. Bernie Sanders has endorsed her and together they are campaigning hard to block Trump from winning the presidency. Many of the planks he campaigned on, like endorsement of a $15 minimum wage and opposition to the job-destroying Trans Pacific Partnership are written into the Democratic Party platform.

The Trump campaign has filled the air with the stench of racism, hatred of women, immigrants, Mexicans, Muslims, gay and Lesbian people, scientists who warn of climate change disaster. Trump rants and raves and his quest to become "Commander in Chief" sounds too much like Mussolini's March on Rome.

At this writing, we, the people, have no higher duty than to defeat Donald Trump, end the Republican stranglehold on the U.S. Senate and House of Representatives. This is a matter of fighting back against the fascist danger.

As Democratic Convention Opens, Thousands March for Clean Energy

This article is part of a series on the Democratic National Convention.
People's World, July 25, 2016
By Tim Wheeler and Patrick J. Foote; *Photo: Patrick J. Foote/PW*

PHILADELPHIA—With the sun blazing and temperatures soaring above ninety-three degrees, demonstrators marched to Independence Hall on the eve of the 2016 Democratic National Convention chanting "Hey, hey, ho, ho, fossil fuel has got to go" and "leave it in the ground."

The march was comprised of a vast coalition of organizations that are combating the devastating effects of climate change including *350.org* and Food and Water Watch.

Hundreds of nurses wearing red hospital smocks and red caps, members of the Oakland, California-based National Nurses Union, cheered as their Secretary-Treasurer, Martha Kuhl, told a pre-march news conference outside Philadelphia City Hall, "As nurses on the job we see the effects of the climate crisis, more cases of asthma and other respiratory illnesses, new rare forms of cancer. We declare the climate crisis is a public health emergency."

She added, "We believe our brothers and sisters in the energy industry should be retrained and there should be a just transition to a non-fossil fuel economy. It is really important that we not abandon these energy workers. They are not the cause of the problem. It is the greedy, big corporations that cause the problem."

The environmental movement must recognize that "people

of color and the poor suffer deeper impacts from the climate crisis" than white people, she added.

Kuhl told the *People's World* global climate change "is one of the top issues that we confront in this election. NNU has endorsed Bernie Sanders. The Republican convention? I can't say anything nice. The fact that Donald Trump could get elected is truly terrifying."

Robin Maguire, a leader of a grassroots movement in Lancaster County, Pennsylvania, was holding one end of a giant patchwork quilt that stretched from one curb of Market Street to the other. Overhead was a banner, "We Are Lancaster County: NO PIPELINE."

Said Maguire, "The Atlantic Sunrise Pipeline is being built by the Williams Corporation. It is a forty-two-inch diameter, high-pressure natural gas pipeline coming down from Marcellus Shale to an export terminal at Coke Point. It is destroying our way of life and crosses sacred Native American grounds. We think we have a good chance of stopping it."

The natural gas to be pumped through that pipeline is the product of "fracking" and many in the march carried signs and banners demanding that the federal government outlaw fracking.

John Bachtell, national chair of the Communist Party USA was leading a delegation of African American and white members of the CPUSA behind a banner that proclaimed, "People And Nature Before Profits...ONE PERSON, ONE VOTE."

Bachtell said, "There is a world of difference in the platforms of the Republicans and the Democrats on the environment. We face an existential environmental crisis. On the one hand, Hillary Clinton has vowed to continue and step up the policies of the Obama Administration to curb greenhouse gases and work with the world community of nations to reduce global warming. On the other hand, Donald Trump is a climate change denier. He vows to trash the Paris Accords and President Obama's agreement with China. The stakes could not be higher in the November election."

Mark Morris carried one end of the banner of "Save Porter Ranch," a movement that sprang up when a methane reservoir blew open near the community outside Los Angeles releasing a lethal cloud of methane that sickened thousands and forced the evacuation of 7,000 residents. It took until the end of February to seal the leak.

"It happened about the same time the Flint water crisis was in the headlines," Morris said. "It all points to the same thing: Decaying infrastructure owned by greedy corporations that don't care about the people. All they care about is profits. This is an ongoing disaster. There is dirty drinking water and leaking methane all over this country. Bernie Sanders was the one who came out to save us. He is the one who said global warming is the number one threat to national security."

As the march approached its terminus on the mall in front of Independence Hall, the thousands sought shade for the speakers program. In the shade, some remnants of the so-called "Bernie or Bust movement" held their own courts. Their numbers were small when compared to those seeking a clean energy future.

One of those seeking the clean energy future was Carl, twenty, a student from Green Mountain College and he spoke to *People's World* about Power Shift, the grassroots youth wing of *350.org*.

"We're trying to solve the problems affecting youth in the next generations," Carl said, "primarily the fact that we're stuck on fossil fuels as a society.

"Right now, the Democratic Convention is going on and it's a huge opportunity. We're not losing hope just because we have candidates in the race who aren't supporting clean energy as much as they should be. We need to fight harder than ever before."

Washington State Voters Approve Wage Hike, Send Jayapal to Congress
People's World, November 22, 2016

SEATTLE—The election to the U.S. House of Representatives November 8 of Indian American Pramila Jayapal was greeted with joy here in Seattle and across the

Evergreen State. She is a grassroots community activist in Seattle who spearheaded the defense of undocumented immigrants.

Endorsed by Sen. Bernie Sanders, of Vermont, Jayapal has denounced Trump's plan to deport 11 million immigrants. Currently a member of the Washington state legislature from Seattle, Jayapal also strongly supported Seattle's campaign to raise the city's minimum wage to $15. She is the first woman of Indian background elected to the U.S. House of Representatives.

Even before being sworn into office, Jayapal is already on the offensive against the Trump agenda with strong denunciations of his selections of Steve Bannon and Senator Jeff Sessions for key roles in his administration.

Voters in Washington State also cast their ballots November 8 to increase the state minimum wage to $13.50 an hour by the year 2020. Already, Washington has the nation's highest minimum wage at $9.47 per hour and voters in Seattle and SeaTac have approved measures to raise their minimum wage to $15 over the next few years. The Federal Minimum wage remains stuck at $7.25 per hour because the Republican majority House and Senate has blocked President Obama's measures to increase it.

Initiative 1433, the official name of Washington's ballot initiative, also indexes the minimum wage to inflation and requires employers to provide paid sick leave—all measures rejected by Donald Trump who claims that wages in the U.S. are "too high."

Voters also approved increases in the minimum wage in Arizona and Maine, underlining that issues of economic justice reach across the partisan divide. A weakness in the Democratic Party's strategy was its failure to campaign strongly enough in every state and region for an increase in the minimum wage and for other economic issues like affordable health care and tuition-free higher education at public universities.

Voters also approved in a seventy percent landslide Initiative 1491 that allows police and family members to take firearms away from an individual who may be suicidal or homicidal. The National Rifle Association attacked the measure even though Washington has suffered several tragic mass shootings in recent years by deranged individuals armed with assault rifles and handguns. Only seven of the state's thirty-nine counties voted down the gun control measure.

In another landslide, voters approved Initiative 735 instructing the state legislature to support a constitutional amendment to overturn the Supreme Court Citizens United ruling that "corporations are people and money is speech."

Initiative 735 passed in every region of Washington State with enormous landslide support in Western Washington and majority support as well in Republican dominated parts of the state like Spokane, Wenatchee, Yakima, the Tri-Cities (Richland, Pasco, and Kennewick). Only a handful of sparsely populated counties in Eastern Washington voted down I-735.

The infamous Citizens United ruling of 2010 swept aside all limits on how much money corporations can contribute to candidates and nullified requirements that these corporations and wealthy individuals publicly disclose their contributions.

A torrent of secret cash flooded into election campaigns, mostly to right-wing extremist Republicans—a corruption of the nation's political system which was on full display in this election cycle. Washington is the 18th state to approve a ballot initiative demanding a constitutional amendment to overturn the ruling. Similar measures to overturn Citizens United were also approved by landslide margins in Ohio, Wisconsin, and California on November 8th.

An army of volunteers collected many hundreds of thousands of signatures to put these initiatives on the ballot —WAmend for I-735, Raise Up Washington for I-1433, and the Alliance for Gun Responsibility for I-1491. Many of these volunteers put their personal lives on hold to get these measures on the ballot and push them to victory. They worked hard to collect signatures in "red" and "blue" counties in support of living wage jobs, an end to gun violence, and a political system that can't be bought by the billionaires.

271

Washington state voters also cast their ballots decisively against Trump for president. Clinton received 54.6 percent of the vote to Trump's thirty-eight percent.

It reflected a nationwide trend in which Hillary Clinton won a majority of the popular vote despite Trump winning the Electoral College vote. Clinton's lead nationwide as of this writing is more than 1.7 million votes, a number which continues to grow wider because as the uncounted votes are mostly in California, Oregon, and Washington—states that went heavily for Clinton.

When coupled with the fact that only about half the eligible voters cast ballots, it means that Trump will take office with only a quarter or less of the eligible vote, clearly no mandate for his vendetta against immigrants, unions, Muslims, women, African Americans, Latinos, and the LGBT community. Nor does a majority support his pro-billionaire, pro-Wall Street, trickle down economic policies.

Seattle Mayor Ed Murray convened a news conference hours after Trump's unexpected victory to announce that he will join in defense of Seattle's "Sanctuary City" program. He vowed to continue providing sanctuary for the city's tens of thousands of undocumented immigrants in the face of Trump threats to deport them.

As he spoke, thousands of demonstrators marched through Seattle, Tacoma, Olympia, Portland, Oregon, and other cities across the nation chanting "Not My President."

A Time to Stand and Fight!
December 20, 2016

I was waiting for the results of the 2016 presidential election to write this concluding entry for *News From Rain Shadow Country*. I worked hard for well over a year in that election cycle, with a lot of help from my wife Joyce, my sister Honeybee and other family members to defeat the ultra-right Republicans including Donald Trump.

We joined enthusiastically in the Bernie Sanders campaign. I served as co-chair of Clallam County for Bernie Sanders, attending a Seattle rally at Hec Edmondson Pavilion at the University of Washington in Seattle. The rally was jam-packed to the rafters with cheering Bernie fans and 2,000 more outside listening over a PA system. They were cheering too. Another high point was the labor march and rally for Bernie in Port Townsend, about forty miles from our home, addressed by Larry Cohen, former President of the Communications Workers of America. Cohen was serving as chair of Labor for Bernie Sanders. I wrote stories about this inspiring campaign, some of them reprinted in this book.

Bernie Sanders had the clearest message against the corporate forces that dominate every facet of our lives, the clearest program for ending that tyranny and putting in power a government that serves the needs and interests of the 99%.

I will never forget that day at Greywolf Elementary School in Carlsborg where we held our caucus meetings that turned into a Bernie landslide statewide. Washington State was one of twenty-three states he carried with 13.2 million votes for a self-avowed socialist, the most presidential votes for a socialist in U.S. history. By comparison, Eugene Victor Debs, leader of the Socialist Party, garnered one million votes from a prison cell in Georgia. He had been jailed for speaking out against the atrocious First World War.

Yet Bernie did not win the nomination at the Democratic National Convention in Philadelphia. I was in Philadelphia, writing stories about the events swirling around the DNC. Frankly, I did not expect that Bernie would win. Like a majority of those who had supported Bernie, including Bernie Sanders himself, I threw myself into the campaign to elect Hillary Clinton after she won the nomination.

Joyce and Honeybee and I went door to door in Port Angeles and Sequim working for her election. We could not muster the same enthusiasm for her that we had felt for Bernie. Yet Hillary was poised to become the first woman president of the United States. She was working to rally the same broad grassroots coalition that Barack Obama assembled in his victorious campaigns for president in 2008 and 2012.

I disagree with those who argue that Hillary Clinton was a "weak" candidate, that she "has nobody to blame but herself" for her loss of the Electoral College to Donald Trump. Incredibly, these people argued that there is "no difference" between Clinton and Trump. As my father often said, "There are none so blind as those who will not see."

The majority of Bernie Sanders fans followed his lead and worked hard to elect Hillary Clinton. The "Bernie or Bust" crowds were a minority, not nearly enough votes to have played a direct role in Clinton's defeat. But they did echo the Hillary-bashing by the ultra-right. They played a negative, de-mobilizing role that was one of many factors in her defeat. I find it hard to fathom some of these folks actually gloated at this disastrous defeat.

If Hillary Clinton was so weak, why did she win the popular vote with a 2.65 million vote margin, 64.6 million for her, 62 million for Trump? Anyone who watched the televised debates could see that Hillary Clinton was vastly superior to Trump. She stood up to his bully-boy behavior with poise and dignity. She waged a courageous struggle against deeply entrenched misogyny in American society, outright hatred of women who fight for gender equality.

The differences between Hillary Clinton and Donald Trump were stark. She is a progressive woman who stood for racial and gender equality, who embraced most of the platform that Bernie Sanders had championed including near doubling of the Federal minimum wage.

She refused to bow when FBI Director, James Comey, eleven days before the election, sent a letter to Republican leaders on Capitol Hill announcing that the FBI was investigating tens of thousands of emails in Clinton's inbox. They included messages from former Representative Anthony Weiner, estranged husband of Clinton's top aide, Huma Abedin. Weiner was forced to resign when his sexually explicit emails were exposed. How these emails ended up in Clinton's inbox remains a mystery. To her credit, Clinton did not fire Abedin.

Then two days before Election Day, the FBI announced it was all over. They had examined all the emails—which they had in their possession for many months—and found no incriminating evidence against Hillary Clinton. It was a perfectly timed dirty trick against Clinton by the FBI. It had instantly "changed the subject" from Trump's well publicized record as a sex predator. All those headlines quoting women who were victims of Trump sexual assault disappeared, replaced by phony stories about emails that Hillary Clinton had not written.

Trump is a vile racist, a sex predator, a union buster, who shouted his hatred of immigrants, Mexicans, Muslims. He proclaimed that "wages are too high." He refused to release his tax records. The *New York Times* revealed that Trump paid no Federal taxes on tens of millions of dollars in profits because he was able to game the system, a bankruptcy on one of his operations. Trump vows to impose more "trickle down" economics on us.

Those who joined in the movement to block Trump from the White House were acting on far deeper motives than loyalty to Hillary Clinton. We were joining forces with the powerful grassroots movement against the vast rightwing conspiracy that menaces our nation and the world.

At the head of that coalition is the labor movement, the strongest, multiracial, progressive force in our society. Its closest allies are the African American people, the Latinos, Asian American, Native American Indians—all the racially and nationally oppressed people in our society. The other key forces in that coalition are working women, youth, and the LGBT community. It is also a coalition that embraces key movements like the environmental movement, Black Lives Matter, Planned Parenthood, Moral Monday, and the Standing Rock Sioux struggle against the Dakota Access Pipeline. And yes, that majority coalition also included those who had campaigned so hard for Bernie Sanders.

I work with some folks who have told me we should not dwell on the past. We should focus on the future, unite to fight back against Trump and the racist, anti-labor onslaught he is already unleashing. Yes, I am in favor of unity. But it behooves us to try to understand what went wrong. Could we have done something different that would have succeeded in blocking Trump?

Is there something wrong with the "All People's Front" against the ultra-right? That strategy has guided my political activity for nearly thirty years. It was adopted at an "Extraordinary Conference" of the Communist Party USA in Milwaukee in 1981, following the election of Ronald Reagan in the 1980 election. It replaced an earlier strategy we called the "Anti-Monopoly Coalition." We decided that this anti-monopoly strategy was not sufficiently broad to encompass the class and social forces needed to defeat the rightwing extremist danger. It flowed from the "United Front Against Fascism," a conference of the Communist International convened in Moscow in 1937 to build a movement strong enough to defeat Hitler fascism.

On reflection, I think our "All People's Front" against the ultra-right is a correct strategy. Yet we are far short of the front broad enough and strong enough to defeat the ultra-right. This election debacle makes one point clear: We can never defeat the ultra-right danger without the white working class. Far too many white working class people, especially white men but even a majority of white women, voted for Trump. Clearly they were casting their ballots against their own self-interests and their class interests. They were committing an act of political suicide.

It shows that racism remains the nation's most dangerous pollutant. Too many white workers, especially those who are not unionized, were bamboozled by Trump. Even 37% of union members voted for Trump, surely the overwhelming majority white trade unionists. They fell for Trump's drumbeat of racism, misogyny, xenophobia, and homophobia.

We who were active in the campaign saw at close hand a profound weakness in the Democrat's strategy. When we went doorbelling, we worked from lists of voters carefully selected to be only registered Democrats. We did not knock on the doors and speak to the tens of thousands of voters who are independents or even Republicans. We were mostly preaching to the converted.

We speak with experience on this issue. No one in Clallam County has been more conscientious than my family in knocking on doors, speaking to hundreds of voters about the issues that face our country, state and nation. In 2015, the Democratic Party of Clallam County named the "Wheeler Clan" as Democrats of the Year. We were honored at the annual Franklin & Eleanor Roosevelt Dinner at the Seven Cedars Casino October 23, 2015.

Our experience taught us that we must reach across the divide. In doorbelling only Democratic homes we were not working to win over the majority of voters who are fed up and looking for real change. That is the secret of Bernie Sander's success: He was reaching across the divide, inspiring a vast, nationwide movement for progressive change.

The folks who were fooled by Donald Trump have seen their real income shrinking, the 99% getting steadily poorer while the 1% get ever more obscenely rich. No wonder these voters feel abandoned. They are vulnerable to the siren song of a loud mouthed demagogue like Trump who posed as an "outside the beltway" populist, an ultra-right caricature of Bernie Sanders. Trump tricked millions with his ranting attacks on Mexican immigrants accusing them of "stealing" jobs from white workers. He tricked more with his lying promises that he will scrap trade deals like NAFTA that cost millions of workers their jobs.

His sellout of the Carrier air conditioning workers in Indiana is an omen of more dirty tricks to

Clallam County Democrats announced the Wheeler Clan as the 2015 Democrats of the Year. From left to right: Steve Vause, his wife Carla Syvanen, Joyce and Tim Wheeler, and Marion Wheeler Burns (Honeybee.)

come. He is planning to give Carrier Corporation a huge, multi-million dollar tax break to keep a relative handful of the jobs in Indiana while allowing them to export the lion's share of the jobs to Mexico.

We had expected Hillary Clinton to win. We had high hopes that all the Democratic candidates for the U.S. Senate would win. We even hoped the Democrats would recapture the majority of the House of Representatives. If we had won the landslide victory we had hoped for, it would have been a turning point, a crushing defeat of the ultra-right. We knew the stakes were enormously high in this election because the Republicans had never before fielded a presidential candidate so openly fascistic in his behavior and his program. We knew that if Trump were to win and the Republicans were to succeed in retaining majority control of the Senate and House, we would be facing a nightmarish situation.

The nightmare is upon us. Trump won. The Republicans retained majority control of the House and Senate. Every gain we have wrested from stingy government and stingy employers in the past century is now in grave danger. House Speaker, Paul Ryan, had promised soon after Trump's upset victory that he will place at the top of the House agenda repeal of Obamacare. Gone will be the medical coverage for more than 20 million people won under Obamacare. Gone will be the coverage for children until they reach age 26. Gone will be the regulation that no insurance company can deny coverage because of "pre-existing conditions."

Ryan announced that he will attach as an amendment to that atrocious legislation, a bill to privatize Medicare, turning it into a voucher program. This will be a catastrophe for tens of millions of senior citizens including me, my wife, my entire family. There is not a single person among the 99% who will escape from the rightwing extremist juggernaut coming at us. That includes most of those who voted for Trump.

Trump named Steve Bannon, an open white supremacist, as his campaign manager. And now Trump has named Bannon as his chief media and political strategist. Once

Trump takes office, Bannon, a neo-Nazi, will be inside the White House, bending Trump's ear.

The specter of Nazis in the White House is so frightening that a movement has sprung up demanding that Trump fire Bannon. We are face-to-face with the reality that a man with close ties to Nazis and the KKK has been sworn in as President of the United States. As John Bachtell, chair of the Communist Party USA put it, "The wolf is not just at the door, he is inside the house."

Yet Trump has now been in office just over 100 days. Not one of his loudly proclaimd legislative goals has been approved by Congress, starting his scam to repeal Obamacare and foist Trumpcase on the people, stripping millions of desperately needed health insurance. The Republicans saw Trumpcare as so radioactive they did not even bring it to a vote. Trump has also pulled back from his vow to pull out of NAFTA. His wall along the Mexican border is stalled. The danger is that Trump and the other Republican demagogues will slip their agenda through piecemeal in hopes the people won't catch them in their dirty tricks.

We need courage equal to that of my parents, members of rthe "greatest generation," who pushed through the New Deal and went on to defeat fascism. Never before have we faced such a fascist-like danger as we do now with Donald Trump in the White House with cowardly sycophants like House Speaker Paul Ryan and Senate Majority Leader, Mitch McConnell in control of Capitol Hill.

I cheered when over one million people marched for women's equality and against Trump January 21 the day after his coronation. I have cheered at the outpouring of tens of millions here at home and around the world of people saying with one mighty voice: "Not My President!" I say to myself: We are the children of Paul Robeson!

NO FARMS, NO FOOD: Ward-Wheeler Farm Will Stay Farmland Forever!

Online *People's World* March 8, 2017

DUNGENESS, WASHINGTON—Steve Vause, President of New Farm Inc.—my brother—signed a contract with the North Olympic Land Trust (NOLT) last month, selling the development rights to the sixty acre "Historic Ward Farm" insuring that it will remain farmland forever. The deal was approved unanimously by the twelve shareholders of New Farm Inc.

Owned by my family since 1957, the farm lies along the west bank of the Dungeness River and has been leased for the past thirteen years to organic vegetable and grain grower, Nash Huber. He grows carrots, beets, kale, Swiss chard, cabbage, and many other root and leaf vegetables. He also grows wheat, barley, oats and other grains. He is growing crops of fava beans and quinoa, the protein-rich grain from the high Andes.

These crops luxuriate in the deep, alluvial soil called Dungeness loam, some of the most fertile soil in North America.

Situated right along the river, the water table for the farm is only twenty or thirty feet below the surface. The well on the farm produces so much water that Huber is always able to irrigate. Two years ago, Washington State was hit by a drought so severe the governor declared a statewide emergency. While crops shriveled on other farms in the valley, Nash Huber produced most of the vegetables he sold that year on our farm.

It was leased for over twenty years to mint growers and turf farmers who poured chemical fertilizers on it and over-cultivated it. Turfing is especially destructive because a sixteenth inch or so of the precious topsoil is stripped

Photo courtesy of the North Olympic Land Trust.

away with each layer of turf removed. The turfers also planted multiple times each year to carve as much turf as they could from the farm, a form of "mining" the land. When they moved on, the farm lay exhausted.

Nash Huber has worked strenuously for over a decade to repair and restore the land, plowing under nitrogen-fixing legume cover crops and spreading many tons of cow manure and compost that enrich the soil with organic nutrients. He allows parcels of the land to lie fallow for months so it has time to rest and recuperate before another planting. He has been a "husband" of the land and now it is blooming again.

According to a story by Alana Linderoth in the Sequim Gazette, William Ward arrived on the North Olympic Peninsula as a twelve-year-old cabin boy aboard a British windjammer that dropped anchor at Port Townsend in 1855. He must have been deeply unhappy—yet bold—because he jumped ship with no passport or other papers certifying his legal status, an early case of an undocumented immigrant who settled down to coexist with the Klallam Indians in the rain shadow of the Olympic Mountains. There was no Donald Trump to order his instant deportation.

If the history, *Sequim Pioneer Families from 1850-World War II* is accurate, he was only fifteen-years-old when he became a homesteader, digging a well within 200 feet of the Dungeness river, clearing the thick stands of cedar, hemlock and Douglas Fir, planting an orchard, and many acres of clover to feed his herd of dairy cows.

When we first bought the place, in my senior year at Sequim High School, a magnificent Victorian mansion with a mansard roof stood on the farm attesting to William Ward's tireless drive to succeed, a pioneer in the mold of Daniel Boone. I did a painting of that house on a piece of Masonite. The painting vanished long ago as did the mansion itself.

My father and my cousin, Dave Helms, then partners, milked more than 100 cows twice daily filling a 300 gallon refrigerated stainless steel milk tank—one ton of very rich milk. I too was a cow-milker on our farm rising at five each morning and finishing the evening milking at about 7 p.m.

The victory in preserving this farm is the latest triumph for NOLT and its affiliate, Friends of the Fields, which in the past twenty-five years saved 550 acres of farmland in Clallam County. It is one of the largest most popular organizations in the county and it has struggled heroically against the onslaught of real estate developers who have gobbled up most of the farmland. The developers have turned much of the valley into sites for luxury houses with breathtaking views of the snowcapped Olympics, and to the north, across the Strait of Juan de Fuca, the San Juan Islands and Victoria, British Columbia.

It is hard for farmers to compete with the real estate interests when land is so valuable for its views and its mild, sunny climate, such a tempting locale for a new suburbia. When I was growing up here, more than 200 dairy farms dotted the landscape. Now two dairy farms survive.

Yet an American Farmland Trust (AFT) bumper-sticker, to be seen on many cars and pickups in this valley proclaims, "No Farms, No Food." We had hoped that NOLT would obtain a grant from the federal government under the Agricultural Conservation Easement Program (ACEP) to help purchase the development rights and preserve our farm forever. But the Republicans in control of the House and Senate know the cost of everything and the value of nothing. Despite the appeals of President Obama, Senate Majority Leader, Mitch McConnell, and his cohorts in the House ramrodded a $6 billion cut to farmland conservation in the 2014 Farm Bill.

In testimony to the House Agriculture Subcommittee on Conservation and Forestry, February 28, AFT President John Piotti, pleaded that the Trump Administration and the Republican majority House and Senate act now to staunch the bleeding, the loss of forty acres every hour in precious farmland. Piotti pointed out that President Trump promised to push through Congress a $1 trillion infrastructure repair bill. Infrastructure repair, he told Congress, must include saving our nation's crumbling agricultural infrastructure that generates nearly $1 trillion annually for the nation's gross domestic product.

Instead, Trump has submitted a budget that adds $54 billion to the military budget and has vowed to slash vital domestic programs, including conservation, to pay for it.

The Republicans made sure that not a single penny of our tax dollars went to help conserve the "Historic Ward Farm."

State Representative, Kevin Van de Wege—now a State Senator—came to the rescue in 2015. Together with other Democratic legislators who reside in Clallam County, Van de Wege, pushed through a $344,000 grant to help fund the campaign to save the Ward-Wheeler farm. The grant fell short of the money needed to buy the development rights. But NOLT went into high gear and thanks to the skillful fund-raising of NOLT Executive Director, Tom Sanford, Conservation Director, Michele d'Hemecourt Canale, and the publicity efforts of Alana Linderoth, the matching funds were raised. The Wheeler family sold the development rights for $70,000 less than the appraised value so we too contributed to save our farm forever.

Our property line used to run down the middle of the Dungeness River. Years ago we donated our riverfront to Clallam County to create a lovely park named for my mother, "The Mary Lukes Wheeler Park." It is one of the few locations where people can get access to the Dungeness River and on hot summer days the air is filled with the shrieks of happy children wading in the river. Now, the farm across Ward Road with the stupendous mountain views will add to the serenity of this sublime place. Don and Mary Wheeler would be very, very happy.

—END

INDEX

ENJOY LIFE! KEEP ON READING!

If you enjoyed this book and want to read more of my writings, I invite you to read the stories I continue to write for the *People's World*. You won't find them in a print edition like ones in the bundle I have perched on top of my head in the photo below. The *People's World* can be found online at www.peoplesworld.org. And if you want more copies of *News From Rain Shadow Country*, you can order them from www.booklocker.com. Also distributing my book is International Publishers at service@intpubnyc.com. Watch for my next book *News for the 99%* soon to be published by International Publishers. That book, too, is a collection of stories I have written in the past half century about the endless struggle of working class people to make the world livable for themselves and their children.

—Tim Wheeler

A young Tim Wheeler just beginning his career.

CPSIA information can be obtained
at www.ICGtesting.com
Printed in the USA
FSOW02n0410250517
34429FS